Mr Hudson Explores

The Gay Man's Travel Companion

gestalten

TABLE OF CONTENTS

PREFACE

"The world makes way for the man
who knows where he is going."

Ralph Waldo Emerson

For as long as I can remember, I have enjoyed going places. The world offers so many worthwhile experiences that I'm in a near permanent state of worry about missing out and running out of time. Most of my happiest memories involve being on a trip of some sort—on my own or with the people I love. I fondly remember the summer holidays my family took in France during my childhood. We would stay in charming guesthouses in the smallest of towns, where my father would take us to buy fresh bread, fruits, and vegetables at the local farmers markets. From a young age, I was intrigued and strangely excited by how different things looked, sounded, and smelled in another country, not even far away. I like to think that these first steps abroad awakened my wanderlust. Later journeys took me further afield—to the Americas and Asia. I've trekked in the Himalayas in Nepal, swam with whale sharks in Mexico, gone on safari in Africa, got married in Ibiza, and the list goes on. When I feel

down or bored with my daily life, all I have to do is travel back to those experiences to feel grateful and alive, as well as excited about my next adventure. Where shall I go? What shall I do? Who will I meet? And what will I learn?

When I was younger, as a growing awareness of my sexuality began to unfold, I became interested in seeking out local gay people, experiences, and events on my travels—in addition to the other things that make exploring city destinations so enjoyable, such as the food scene, shopping, art, and culture. But things are not always simple for the gay traveler. When I started visiting countries with my husband, we became more conscious of the potential pitfalls associated with moving around as an openly gay couple, especially where public displays of affection are concerned—it pays to be conscious of local customs and values. Luckily, most countries have made significant progress in advancing LGBTQ rights, but we still have a long road ahead of us. As a new wave

of intolerance sweeps the globe—in which some Western nations seem to regress rather than move forward—we must continue to be visible, assert our claims, and celebrate who we are. And then there are the relatively harmless but still annoyingly heteronormative experiences like "I see we booked you into a double room. Would you like me to move you guys into a twin instead?" that every gay person on the road with a same-sex partner has probably encountered when checking into a hotel.

As someone who has worked in the tourism industry, and as a gay man who has traveled extensively, over the years I grew more and more frustrated by the lack of relevant content about up-and-coming destinations and the hidden gems of larger cities. Most LGBTQ travel sites and blogs only focus on the local gay scene, and generic publishers, online travel agents, and review sites don't necessarily understand our requirements or share our sense of style. My husband and I identified a gap in the market, and consequently, the inspiration for Mr Hudson was born. We created a site that is all about destinations for gays, but not necessarily about gay destinations. In other words, we don't assume that all gay men want a gay holiday. Of course, there's nothing wrong with partying and enjoying the local scene, but there are plenty of us who want to experience the very best a destination has to offer, in addition to those parts of cities reserved for the gay community. There are so many beautiful places on the planet to which everybody is invited. We want to make sure people know about them. Mr Hudson was inspired by a seventeenth-century British explorer of the same name whose pioneering travels encouraged the first settlers of the New World. It is wonderful that, since then, exploring has become decidedly more accessible for everyone, including for people who identify as LGBTQ. And while we don't have to let our sexuality define our journeys, we, as a community,

collectively share an appreciation of beauty, authenticity, and diversity, and a passion for meeting new, like-minded people. Many of us travel as couples; plenty of others go solo. But what we all have in common is the desire to seek out gorgeous destinations, unique experiences, and places for resting our heads in style. And it is with this in mind that we created the book you are about to read.

Our aim has been to curate a collection of places and events with character, that reflect the local perspective and way of life in 20 beloved city destinations in the Northern Hemisphere. To do this, we've highlighted organizations, businesses, and initiatives that get it right by being inclusive and relevant, and by delivering the goods in fresh and original ways. We take you off the beaten track to all of our favorite spots. We know who crafts the best cocktails, serves the tastiest food, showcases the most edgy creative talent, sells the most beautiful souvenirs and gifts, and throws the best parties. We have set out to

create the ideal travel companion for the discerning gay man, and for everyone else who is keen to ensure their trips are full of incredible experiences—for those who love to explore in style. Join us as we breach perennial big-hitters such as Paris, London, and New York City with a different perspective, and as we sample our way through less-charted territories such as Shanghai, Portland, and Tel Aviv. En route we'll introduce you to charismatic locals— each with a very personal take on their city and a compelling life story to tell. I hope you enjoy reading this book as much as we did creating it, and that it will inspire you to explore a new city, or pique your interest in taking another look at an old favorite with fresh eyes. Welcome to the world of Mr Hudson!

Bastiaan Ellen,
co-founder of *Mr Hudson* and co-editor of *Mr Hudson Explores*

Haarlemmerweg

Centrum

Weesperstraat

Linnaeusstraat

Wibautstraat

Overtoom

Stadhouderskade

Vondelpark

Ceintuurbaan

CLAIM IT

1. art'otel
2. Conservatorium Hotel
3. Hotel TwentySeven
4. Mr. Jordaan
5. QO Hotel
6. The Dylan

SAVOR IT

7. ANNA
8. Café George
9. De Kas
10. Envy
11. Georgette
12. Georgio's
13. IZAKAYA
14. Kaagman & Kortekaas

CELEBRATE IT

15. BAUT
16. Café 't Mandje
17. Club NL
18. De Hallen
19. De Trut
20. Door 74

OWN IT

21. Boerejongens
22. Concrete Matter
23. Hester van Eeghen
24. matter .of material
25. Misc Store
26. X BANK

EXPLORE IT

27. A'DAM Tower
28. Amsterdam City Archives
29. Eye Filmmuseum
30. Foam
31. The Pulitzer

AMSTERDAM

A Collection of Cultured Contradictions

If you were to ask any local, "What's so great about Amsterdam?," they would probably shrug and say, "Not the weather." But don't be fooled by this nonchalance—Amsterdamers might be modest, but they are proud of their city. A sober municipality traditionally run by the Protestant rulebook and yet associated with sexual freedom and equality, Amsterdam has cultivated its tolerance to a near-religious level. For centuries, a haven for people persecuted elsewhere because of their religious beliefs or way of life, this city is home to Cultuur en Ontspanningscentrum, which was founded shortly after the Second World War and is the world's oldest organization for the progression of gay rights; it saw the opening of its first gay club in the 1950s and its first gay bathhouse in the 1960s; it's also the capital of the first country to legalize same-sex marriages and to erect a monument for victims of LGBTQ persecution—all valid reasons it's considered by many to be the gay capital of the world.

Although its contradictions aren't always visible to the casual visitor, they form the fabric of the city's socially progressive character. Amsterdam is foremost a human capital, from its scale to its temperament; like a stern aunt who winks at you when she catches you with your hand in the cookie jar, it understands that having fun can sometimes challenge convention. Famously free-spirited, laid-back, and livable, its ancient canals lined with contemporary art galleries, cute cafes, and edgy restaurants, there's a good chance you may never want to leave.

As a charity venue for the old and poor ironically turned upmarket hotel, THE DYLAN is a one-stop, sumptuous, central hideaway. Although home to a more conservative, older crowd, everything spells sexy seclusion, from the quiet restaurant to the minimalist-styled rooms where you can focus on the one you're with. At the in-house Michelin-starred restaurant Vinkeles, the menu is a contrasting and nouveau blend of Eastern flavors and continental French dishes, while breakfast or brunch is served almost all day at brasserie Occo, which makes a killer brioche, poached egg, hollandaise, and crab dish they call Eggs Alaska—ask for it by name.

Culture goes contemporary at the CONSERVATORIUM HOTEL just off Museumplein, where Italian architect Piero Lissoni has installed a modern hotel in the former home of the Conservatorium van Amsterdam—now a favorite destination for design snobs as much as celebrity spotters. Its signature bar Tunes is a popular weekend haunt where guests dress the part and mingle around its central bar table or scan the crowd from a sumptuous booth. If iconic design is your thing, the ART'OTEL overlooking Centraal Station is an equally good fit. A large early-twentieth-century office block turned multipurpose hospitality venue, its art gallery, restaurant, bar, and library combine to create a buzzing of social interactivity. Although these spaces are designated, they remain connected through the clever use of semitransparent partitioning, which means you can have a drink at the 5 & 33 cocktail bar and still keep your eye on that guy at the gallery.

The noblest materials and swathes of luxury textiles in bronze, copper, and gold fill the suites at Hotel TwentySeven.

The kitchen's Mediterranean-inspired all-day dining maintains this super-smooth continuity down to the olive oil and the sassy Italian waiters.

Traditionally, Amsterdam isn't the royal seat of the Netherlands, but HOTEL TWENTYSEVEN, across from the Koninklijke Paleis on the Dam, probably could be. Situated in the old Koninklijke Industrieele Groote Club built in 1916, it's inherited all the smoky, plush ambiance of the era and then some.

Akasha Holistic Wellbeing, a luxury spa at the Conservatorium Hotel, with hamman and gym.

A glass-enclosed lobby at Conservatorium surpasses all others with its sleek styling.

With literally every surface covered, polished or gilded, the mise-en-scène is part Mata Hari, part King Midas—a level of ostentatious opulence that has not been seen in Amsterdam since the Golden Age. In contrast, the picturesque Jordaan area was a seventeenth-century response by the city to the influx of laborers and immigrants. Here, you'll find the industrial-nostalgic MR. JORDAAN, catering to urban explorers interested in an authentic insider experience and an unfussed style that's more hands-on than hip hotel.

Trends aside, hotels are becoming more conscious of their environmental impact, and Amsterdam's QO HOTEL is challenging it on another level—in fact, on an underground level with a thermal aquifer. Energy consumption and waste are the main concerns addressed by this venue, which succeeds in combining luxury accommodation with sustainability goals. Its gray-water system, which allows shower waste to be reused for flushing toilets, is just one example.

Famously free-spirited, laid-back, and livable, its ancient canals lined with art galleries, cafes, and edgy restaurants.

In a society that values its farmers as much as its merchants, it's no wonder DE KAS has become such a popular lunch destination for local business-men and foreign foodies alike. Located in an eight-meter-high glass greenhouse, it incorporates the main restaurant, a conservatory, garden room, and bar. Surrounded by the greenery of Frankendael park and the restaurant's own potager garden, it feels more like dining in the countryside. The food is exactly what you'd expect: fresh, homegrown ingredients served haute cuisine–style. At equally haut ENVY on Prinsengracht, the emphasis is on an ever-changing journey where small gourmet dishes are presented in succession or even simultaneously as part of an adventurous tasting tour. Whether you go paired or unpaired, the restaurant's long, high tables provide the ideal opportunity to dine alone or share alike.

Surrounded by its own garden, it feels more like dining in the countryside.

Tucked away on the narrow Sint Nicolaasstraat, you'll find KAAGMAN & KORTEKAAS. This table-d'hôte brasserie might be French inspired, but its dishes are guided by local produce—proof that the dynamic duo behind it are just as close to their humble homeland as to international culinary culture. Thanks to nearby ANNA, a visit to Amsterdam's sinful red-light district doesn't always have to include rent boys or bachelor parties. With an entrance on Warmoesstraat and incongruous views of the Oude Kerk, nothing else contradicts the culinary reliability of this modern European restaurant, aptly named after the patron saint of sailors and unmarried women.

Another reliable stop, the GEORGE family of restaurants scattered around the city are a depend-able, emergency go-to. Part brasserie, part diner, they serve up daytime favorites from burgers and French toast, to boeuf bourguignon and lobster linguine. Whether at the original GEORGE CAFÉ on Leidsegracht, the Italian-styled GEORGIO'S on Stadhouderskade, or the plushy GEORGETTE in fashion-focused PC Hooftstraat, you'll find each has a unique take on the same staples. Last but not least is IZAKAYA in the vibrant De Pijp area. Japanese cuisine often has a day-to-night vibe, and that's exactly the point here, with lunch served from the same dinner menu of small tantalizing dishes, taking you up to cocktail hour and beyond.

The greenhouses that provide the backdrop for the De Kas restaurant once belonged to the Amsterdam Municipal Nursery.

To the south of the city, George Marina has a menu known for its fresh fish and seafood dishes.

A city's clubs often give a clue to its soul and even though legendary venues RoXY and the iT have come and gone, there's no lack of opportunity to dance in Amsterdam. CLUB NL provides a cross-section on an intimate scale and has a tolerant, unpretentious door policy that is as good for I'm neither nor as I'm either or. Whatever your status, standing, or orientation, Club NL will respect. Since the 1980s, Amsterdam's LGBTQ community has found a home in the noncommercial foundation DE TRUT. Initially a squatted basement, it soon became an institution. Only open on Sunday evenings, it's run entirely by volunteers who keep the prices down. Its policy of no phones or cameras also provides a safe haven for all types and tastes, while the DJ skips through genres like profiles on a dating app.

Not every bar can boast that they have a replica of their establishment in its city museum, but then CAFÉ 'T MANDJE isn't your average venue. The café, the real one on the Zeedijk, owes its enduring existence to the owner's welcoming attitude toward the gay community of the time. From its 1927 heyday to its recent reopening by a family member, it's as if nothing has changed. Over at DOOR 74, the cocktails make the conversation. A small 1920s-inspired speakeasy with a secretive reservation policy and hidden entrance, you can cozy away the evening in an alcove or watch the professionals perform at the bar. Whether your taste goes to classic or experimental, it has an answer—or try your luck with its cocktail wheel selector game.

There's no lack of opportunity to dance in Amsterdam.

A modern city has to have its share of urban invention. In Amsterdam, this is clearly visible at DE HALLEN, the historic former tram depot in Oud-West, which has been transformed into a hub of street food stalls, a cinema, 55-room hotel, and public library. Another urban invention, the migratory BAUT—part restaurant, part culture club—moves location intermittently as part of its "forever temporary" philosophy. Giving new meaning to defunct spaces, its post-apocalyptic industrial look is a mix of hand-me-down 1980s office furniture and pawn-shop finds all assembled canteen style. The food, from an intelligently composed menu, is as unpretentious and unconventional as its locations.

Shaken and not stirred—Baut serves up a healthy repertoire of cocktails and mixers.

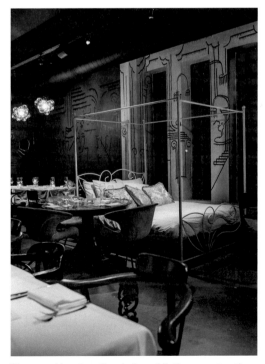

The great thing about Baut is that, while the menu stays the same, the décor changes with every venue.

Amsterdam is not big on showy glamour, but being more understated and less conspicuous doesn't mean that it lacks quality design. HESTER VAN EEGHEN'S original leather pieces, locally designed and manufactured in Italy, are an eye-catching testimony to taste. Around the corner in the Spiegelkwartier is contemporary design store MATTER .OF MATERIAL, which showcases innovative products by mainly Dutch talents such as Lex Pott, Christien Meindertsma, and Alex de Witte. To fully explain the diversity of Holland's modern design scene would take too long; for the short version, head over to X BANK behind the Dam. A curated superstore of fashion, art, and design from emerging and established talent, it's so good it could charge an entrance fee. If your tastes veer more toward outdoor nostalgia

and boys being boys, the answer might well be CONCRETE MATTER. From antique militia to basic workwear, its one-of-a-kind rugged apparel is hand-sourced and ranges from vintage lumberjack essentials to biker gear. For the more office-bound interested in rebooting their workspace with beautiful stationery, MISC STORE has a selection of desktop products that are stylish enough to take on a date.

Amsterdam is definitely more famous for its weed than its wine, but at the BOEREJONGENS coffee shops and dispensaries you can rely on product knowledge and informed advice from its "cannabis sommeliers," dressed in three-piece suits and bowler hats. Each of its four shops is even styled as a vintage pharmacy, with cigar lounge–style smoking areas to complete the picture.

Amsterdam is not big on showy glamour, but being more understated doesn't mean that it lacks quality design.

X Bank offers wares from 180 exclusively Dutch labels, representing emerging artists and established brands.

A prominent example of Amsterdam's progressive approach to urban redevelopment is found at the A'DAM TOWER, built in the late 1960s. Its rooftop lookout platform is where vertigo addicts can get one of the best views of the city by literally swinging over the edge of the building. Remedy yourself afterwards with a drink at Ma'dam's panoramic sky bar to calm your nerves. Next door, another architectural icon and a testament to Amsterdam's passion for film, the EYE FILMMUSEUM, takes pride of place. Besides a view from the banks of the IJ behind Centraal Station, it offers exhibitions and screenings of old, new, famous, and obscure films and filmmakers. Past and present captured in pictures are also found at the AMSTERDAM CITY ARCHIVES and around the corner on the Keizersgracht at FOAM, Amsterdam's photography museum. The latter constantly collaborates with the fashion, food, music, and design industries, and even publishes its own magazine for serious photo fanatics. Finally, if your destiny is to explore the city's selfie-worthy canals, joining THE PULITZER hotel's daily cruise is de rigueur. Not just for guests, this classic 1909 salon boat, fitted out gentleman's club–style, can easily be turned into a bespoke romance with champagne or a picnic around sunset.

Alongside numerous movie screenings, the EYE has a permanent exhibit detailing the history of cinema.

Travel the canals in polished-teak-and-brass style aboard Pulitzer's 100-year-old saloon boat "Tourist".

Whilst lacking the glitz and glamour of the Academy Awards, the INTERNATIONAL DOCUMENTARY FILM FESTIVAL AMSTERDAM (IDFA) deserves its position as one of the world's leading international cinema events. Gear yourself up for confrontational real-life stories, biographical portraits, and controversy, in styles ranging from artistic montages to new media. Although the festival takes place in several theaters, the handsome Tuschinski should be at the top of your hit list.

> Amsterdam also has that side to it that your mother warned you about. Once a year during summer, a two-day festival of freaks terrorizes the town.

As the capital of a country that was at the forefront of 1980s dance music, and that has since spawned world-class trance acts and producers, the force of Amsterdam's electronic music scene is strong. The annual five-day AMSTERDAM DANCE EVENT puts on a packed program across the city and is almost as renowned as the DJs who dominate it. Another must-attend festival is the 10-day CELLO BIENNALE AMSTERDAM, which mixes classical music with jazz, pop, world, and improv performances by upcoming artists, duos, and groups. This event brings composers and musicians together to showcase new works and workshops centered around what one cellist called, "the most beautiful piece of wood."

Amsterdam also has that side to it that your mother warned you about. Once a year during summer, a two-day festival of freaks terrorizes the town. MILKSHAKE, as it's called, is actually a celebration of freedom and love that sees drag performances, DJ parties, and other events take place around Westerpark, the area reappropriated from the city's old gasworks. Of equal intensity but spread out over shorter intervals is SPELLBOUND, an off-circuit performance party attracting a following from as far afield as Paris, Brussels, and Berlin. Hosted in the Occii, an independent cultural initiative with an innocent-looking Swiss chalet façade, events are random and not widely advertised but seriously worthwhile.

Behind the Westerkerk where the long queue to the Anne Frank House starts, you might spot someone laying flowers, or staring into the water

Fun and games at the Milkshake Festival, which takes over Westerpark for two days at the height of summer.

The Amsterdam Dance Event hosts 1,000 events hosted in as many as 200 venues across the city.

contemplatively—if so, you've reached the HOMOMONUMENT. A memorial to gay rights, the pink granite triangle that defiantly juts into the waters of the canal was inspired by the badge used to identify and persecute homosexuals in the Second World War. This quiet corner takes on a totally different atmosphere each year around the end of July when the whole city participates in Pride. The festival culminates in the spectacular CANAL PRIDE, which sees themed boats pulsating with performers throb down the canal to the cheers of supporters crowding the banks. The "gayborhood" of Reguliersdwarsstraat actually turns itself into a venue during this time, with cafes and bars spilling out along the streets, bustling with revelers.

A confused flock of seagulls might be the only clue that Amsterdam is actually located close to the sea. Or, to be precise, part of an extended and heavily populated river delta once on the shores of the Zuiderzee before the Dutch hobby of building dikes and reclaiming land from the water went epic. One of the closest beaches to the city now is BLOEMENDAAL. In summer, its sands are packed with daytime sunseekers and its numerous beach bars and restaurants throbbing with late night partygoers. Besides a stroll through Thijsse's Hof, one of the first indigenous gardens established, or De Kennemerduinen, a national park between the dunes, there's beauty to be found in the ever-gray seasons of the North Sea, which have inspired artists long before Van Gogh. So when you're done admiring the seaside as depicted by famous Dutch Masters in one of Amsterdam's world-class art museums, take the train and experience it for yourself.

The sandy beaches of Bloemendaal are just one hour from Amsterdam by train.

In summer, its sands are packed with sunseekers and its beach bars and restaurants throbbing with late night partygoers.

IN AMSTERDAM, PHOTOGRAPH-ING FREEDOM, THE EXPLICIT

Ferry van der Nat

"The DNA of Amsterdam is love, peace, and sex, and that remains forever," says photographer Ferry van der Nat of his beloved home city, the largest in Holland, even though it has a population of just 822,000 people. That aura is, of course, particularly present in the city's red-light district, the bustling heartland of Dutch sex work, but attitudes toward sexual freedom extend far beyond those narrow streets. "It's a very liberal place that embraces the LGBTQ community very much," Ferry says. "Amsterdam's always been a liberated city that attracts a lot of tourists; there's an international vibe here, and an anonymity."

The same is not true, however, of where the photographer grew up, "an hour away, near Rotterdam—there's a very big contrast in the mentality of the local people," he explains. It's a sentiment that echoes the experience of the many LGBTQs who grow up in the orbit of major cities without fully benefitting from their progressiveness.

Amsterdam's modeling, fashion, and photography circles are a key component of the city's forward-thinking spirit, and over the years, Ferry has become an important part of the scene. "I've worked with just about everyone by now—I probably know them all," he says, referring to the gay men in the industry who are based in Amsterdam. "I would definitely say I have made some great friends along the way. Of course there's a competitiveness, but I feel lucky to feel supported by other photographers I admire, so that feels very nice."

Ferry shares one of his most pivotal friendships with Jasper Zwartjes of Amsterdam's Ravestijn Gallery. "I started as a makeup artist many moons ago, and at one point I started to take Polaroids; from there, it developed naturally. Jasper sent a message telling me he appreciated my work and wanted me to come over and talk about representation. We curated my first exhibition at the gallery," he continues,

"and that was when I saw all my work together and realized this was the medium with which I wanted to become an artist."

Although he's shot for some of Amsterdam's most iconic magazines—*L'Officiel* and *Dutch Vogue,* to name but a couple—Ferry is best known for his intimate Polaroids of beautiful topless men, many of which can be found in his first hardback monograph, simply titled *Mr.* The images exude arresting beauty and unabashed queerness—qualities synonymous with the city and many of its locals, which is a link he is conscious of. When asked how Amsterdam inspires, influences, and is represented in his work, Ferry says: "That isn't easy to answer, but I would hope it has the same freedom and [sense of the] explicit."

So, being a gay male photographer, what is Ferry's foremost insight into Amsterdam? "We definitely have so many incredibly beautiful men!" he says.

*Ferry van
der Nat*

"Its DNA is love, peace, and sex."

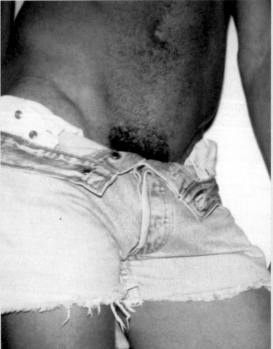

Prenzlauer Berg

Danziger Str.

Karl-Liebknecht-Str.

Str. des 17. Juni

Großer
Tiergarten

Unter den Linden

Leipziger Str.

Kurfürstendamm

Schöneberg

Potsdamer Str.

Kreuzberg

Skalitzer Str.

Karl-Marx-Str.

CLAIM IT

1. 25hours Hotel Bikini
2. Ackselhaus
3. Hotel Oderberger
4. Hotel Zoo
5. Soho House Berlin

SAVOR IT

6. Benedict
7. CODA
8. Lucky Leek
9. Markthalle Neun
10. ORA
11. Pauly Saal & Mogg
12. Tim Raue

CELEBRATE IT

13. Clärchens Ballhaus
14. Möbel-Olfe
15. Perle Bar
16. SchwuZ
17. Südblock
18. The Coven Bar

OWN IT

19. A.D.Deertz
20. Andreas Murkudis
21. do you read me?!
22. MYKITA
23. Spacehall
24. TYPE HYPE
25. Urban Industrial

EXPLORE IT

26. C/O Berlin
27. Hamburger Bahnhof
28. Künstlerhaus Bethanien
29. Schwules Museum

BERLIN

It's Gay, and That's a Good Thing

Although Berlin today is known as a gay-friendly city, the journey to get to there was long and tumultuous. As far back as the nineteenth century, there were gay venues popping up in districts such as Schöneberg and Kreuzberg (areas that are still central to the gay community today), and although illegal, the police tolerated them. The first ever gay and lesbian human rights organization was established, and numerous gay publications came into being.

During the 1920s, a decade of social and political liberalism, gay culture became woven into the fabric of the city. Berlin was effectively the gay capital of Europe, and the Reichstag was on the verge of legalizing homosexuality when the financial crash of 1929 derailed it. The rise of Nazism that followed not only wiped out decades of progress, but also led to the persecution and murder of thousands of gay people. It wasn't until the late 1960s, when same-sex relations were legalized, that the struggle for equality got back on track. In 2001, Klaus Wowereit became the first leading politician in Germany to come out with his now famous words, "I'm gay, and that's a good thing," before going on to win the mayorship of Berlin. Outside of Germany, he's perhaps better known for the phrase, "Berlin is poor, but sexy," a label that the city would come to wear with pride; other German cities may be wealthier, but Berlin has grit, style, and character.

Part of what makes Berlin so enjoyable to explore is that rather than being based around a central area as most other capitals are, it's more like a bunch of small towns, each with their own style and quirks. Of course, no introduction to Berlin would be complete without mentioning its hedonistic, non-stop nightlife. Whether you want to while away the hours in a gritty dive bar, elegant cocktail venue, or seemingly never-closing club, Berlin has it all.

During the 1950s, the exuberant HOTEL ZOO was favored by film stars and celebrities, and although its status waned over the years, a recent renovation spearheaded by designers Dayna Lee and Ted Berner recaptured the glamour of its decadent past—as well as adding animal motifs throughout that pay homage to the nearby Berlin Zoo. Just a couple of blocks away is 25HOURS HOTEL BIKINI. It was designed with an "urban jungle" theme in mind, which it nails thanks to the abundant plants and floor-to-ceiling windows that overlook the verdant Tiergarten park. The highlight, though, has to be the Monkey Bar on the 10th floor, which commands incredible panoramic views across the park, Berlin Zoo, and the city skyline.

> **If you're looking to stay away from the hustle and bustle of the city, Ackselhaus in Berlin's charming Prenzlauer Berg district is just the ticket.**

The quarters at members' club SOHO HOUSE BERLIN range from modest rooms to huge lofts adorned with antique furniture and DJ decks. As well as exuding luxury, this Grade II–listed building boasts some of the finest facilities in the city, including a heated rooftop pool and Cowshed Spa where you can indulge in some well-deserved pampering. It's also home to The Store, where even the tables that the products are presented on are available to buy—all part of curator Alex Eagle's concept of a home where everything's for sale, rather than your run-of-the-mill shop.

If you're looking to stay away from the hustle and bustle of the city, ACKSELHAUS in Berlin's charming Prenzlauer Berg district is just the ticket. To say the hotel is eclectic is a bit of an understatement: its 13 bespoke rooms each feature a unique theme, ranging from the bold and bright "Picasso" to the urban-industrial "New York." Also in Prenzlauer Berg is HOTEL ODERBERGER. A mix of rooms, apartments, and suites, it's housed within a beautifully restored historic building whose walls are adorned with art by Berliners (all available to buy). The centerpiece is the swimming pool that once formed part of the Oderberger Baths, which, having been abandoned for decades, reopened in 2016 alongside the hotel.

An ornate cast-iron bathtub takes center stage on the sixth floor of the luxurious Soho House.

Sparkling chandeliers suspended in birdcages hang at the center of the dining room at Hotel Zoo.

Breakfast is rightly considered the most important meal of the day, but this is even truer when you've been reveling in Berlin's bars and clubs the night before. Luckily, the city has plenty of great options, such as BENEDICT, which provides the ultimate breakfast experience. It's open 24 hours a day and has an expansive menu covering everything from stacks of thick fluffy pancakes to steak and eggs. When you start to get peckish again, head over to MARKTHALLE NEUN, one of Kreuzberg's most popular lunch spots. A number of independent vendors have set up shop in this huge hall to provide delectable international food, from jerk chicken to sushi burgers. One particular highlight is Street Food Thursday, which takes place—you've guessed it—every Thursday evening.

Not far from the Markthalle you'll find ORA, which began as a pharmacy in the mid-nineteenth century but these days is one of the district's finest eateries. When the current owners took over the establishment, they embraced its former life, restoring original features such as the wooden medicine cabinets and shelves, which are packed with antique bottles and liquors alike. Aside from being a great place to eat, Kreuzberg is also where one of Germany's most famous chefs grew up. The story of TIM RAUE is quite remarkable: he went from being a Berlin gang member in

Set within a former school for girls, Pauly Saal has plush green seating beneath incredibly high ceilings.

his youth to a two Michelin-starred chef. His namesake restaurant features a simple yet elegant interior and an Asian-inspired menu that's crafted with high-quality regional produce.

Another place that caught the eye of the Michelin inspectors is LUCKY LEEK. Many consider Berlin to be the vegan capital of the world, and though there are countless options to choose from, this is the place to go for fine dining sans animal products. The dishes here are so good that even staunch meat eaters will leave satisfied, and despite the wonderful food, prices remain affordable, earning it a Michelin Bib Gourmand.

Boasting one of the funkiest interiors in Berlin, PAULY SAAL is another worthy Michelin star recipient. All of its design flourishes, from the large rocket mounted above the kitchen to the dazzling Murano glass chandeliers, were created especially for the restaurant. It's not just a pretty face though; the modern cuisine is equally impressive, and it's a particularly good place to visit if you're craving seafood. Sharing the same building is a New York–style deli that could go toe-to-toe with any in the Big Apple. Born out of a lack of good pastrami in the city, MOGG has been delighting people's taste buds with its home-cured meats since 2012. Sampling the rich, velvety New York-style cheesecake is almost an obligation, being perhaps the best in the entire city.

For an unconventional culinary experience, try pastry chef René Frank's dessert bar CODA—awarded its first Michelin star in 2019. When it opened in 2016, the concept sure turned a lot of heads, but it soon proved itself a worthy entrant to Berlin's fine dining scene. It's not the place to come for standard fare. The tasting menus take your palate on a journey across all five of the tongue's basic taste sensations.

Refreshing mango and raspberry lassis are for sale beneath jolly striped awnings at Markthalle Neun.

The area around Kottbusser Tor is one of the most vibrant parts of Berlin, and one that has a long history of multiculturalism and political activism. It's here that you'll find two of the city's foremost gay bars. MÖBEL-OLFE is where to head if you want to rub shoulders with the locals and experience a classic Berlin dive bar, with its shabby-chic style and smoky rooms that stay packed into the early hours. Not far from here is SÜDBLOCK, which, in addition to being a great bar and a decent place to grab some brunch, hosts events that range from readings to drag performances. For something more upscale, check out THE COVEN BAR. After opening in 2014, it soon became one of the best gay bars in the city, as well as an excellent addition to the burgeoning cocktail scene in general. Berlin-based architect Thilo Reich designed an interior that's dark, industrial, and stylish, while its solid menu of cocktails and long drinks will keep you going well into the night.

The area around Kottbusser Tor is one of the most vibrant parts of Berlin.

Another gay venue that focuses on producing high-quality cocktails is PERLE BAR, which lies on a quaint, tree-lined street in Prenzlauer Berg. The use of seasonal ingredients is evident in its ever-changing menu, with each delicious libation crafted from top-quality liquors and wonderful homemade bases. For something a bit different, CLÄRCHENS BALLHAUS is probably as close as you can get to reliving the grandeur of 1920s Berlin. The restaurant and beer garden make for a good pit stop when shopping in Mitte, but it's the stunning ballroom that really draws the crowds. Whether it's swing or tango, a packed events calendar sees everyone, young and old, dancing the night away in the most splendid of settings.

When you fancy leaving the confines of a bar for one of the city's many gay-friendly clubs, you'll be spoiled for choice. The iconic Berghain is known the world over as one of the best clubs on Earth, yet it can be a bit hardcore for even the most intrepid traveler. Tucked away in a gritty part of Neukölln is a more accessible offering: SCHWUZ. Aside from being one of the best gay clubs, this expansive establishment offers a bit more musical variety than your typical Berlin club. Here, you'll find three main rooms with music ranging from indie to R&B to house.

Customers can choose from a wide range of cocktails at the Perle Bar in Prenzlauer Berg.

At Clärchens Ballhaus, diners sit beneath an impressive stucco ceiling in the venue's Hall of Mirrors.

ANDREAS MURKUDIS curated Berlin's Museum of Things for 15 years, and upon stepping into one of his two stores, you certainly notice a gallery-like presentation of products. The racks of 81 are adorned with high-quality clothes that include knitwear from Pringle of Scotland, whereas 77 focuses on beautiful interiors products such as scented candles from Japan and minimalist lamps from London. If you're looking to add some Berlin style to your home, a visit to URBAN INDUSTRIAL is recommended. The cavernous space is packed full of vintage and antique furniture that the owner, Jakob Wagner, has sourced from warehouses, schools, and factories that have closed down.

Industrial lighting, medical cabinets, and old school lockers are staples at Jakob Wagner's Urban Industrial.

For something a little smaller, concept store TYPE HYPE features a range of products based around typography. Whether it's a cushion or a bottle of wine, everything is adorned with a single letter or number and a design from one of five lines. DIN Berlin, for example, combines the clean lines of the DIN typeface with an elegant palette of black, white, and gold. Speaking of typography, there's no better place in Berlin to explore the world of print than DO YOU READ ME?! You won't find trashy gossip mags here, though; the shelves are packed with high-quality, independently produced books, journals, and magazines covering a range of subjects such as photography, design, and architecture.

Berlin also has a fantastic choice of record stores to satisfy crate diggers. SPACEHALL mainly sells new vinyl and is split into three sections, each of which could be a store in its own right. The front part is where you'll find things like soul and jazz, the middle section is geared toward rock, and the back room contains electronic genres.

Alphabetical home furnishings, stationery, bags, and accessories make purchases more personal at Type Hype.

You'll want to leave some room in your suitcase for new threads, too, as Berlin has some excellent menswear stores such as A. D. DEERTZ. Wibke Deertz's work stands out due to the way she combines her love of traveling with her creativity. The places she visits not only inspire her but are also where she sources much of her material, resulting in limited runs. Need some swanky eyewear to complete the look? MYKITA has you covered. This Berlin-based company hand-assembles all of its products from start to finish in Kreuzberg. There are two stores in the city where you're bound to find a style that suits you, whether you're looking for something beautiful yet understated, or idiosyncratic and guaranteed to turn heads.

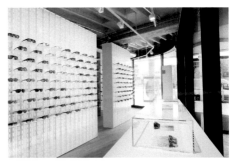

The sleek, industrial-looking interior of Mykita's store on Budapester Strasse.

For a showcase of some of the most important examples of contemporary art from the past six decades, stop by the HAMBURGER BAHNHOF, a former train station reimagined as an art museum. The building, with its arched ceilings, is as much a draw as the collection housed within it, spanning major movements in modern art, such as expressionism, minimalism, and pop art. Lovers of the photographic art form should be sure to visit C/O BERLIN, which puts on superb photography exhibitions throughout the year. Well-known names such as Annie Leibovitz, Sebastião Salgado, and Martin Parr have graced the walls of its 22,600 ft² (2,100 m²) exhibition space, although it's a great place to discover emerging talents, too.

Museums that focus on the subject of LGBTQ culture and history are hard to come by, yet Berlin features one of the world's most prominent institutions regarding such issues: SCHWULES MUSEUM. Here you'll discover a varied program of exhibitions that explore the struggles of the community throughout the years, both in Berlin and across the world. If you wish to delve a bit deeper than just exhibitions and installations, however, KÜNSTLERHAUS BETHANIEN offers

The lofty Hamburger Bahnhof houses temporary exhibitions as well as works from the museum's permanent collection.

a bit more than your regular art gallery or museum. Aside from hosting regular contemporary art exhibitions, there are open studio tours that give you an insight into the creative process.

C/O Berlin runs an impressive program in what was once Amerika Haus, hosting as many as 12 exhibitions through the year.

CHRISTOPHER STREET DAY (AKA Berlin Pride) is one of the biggest events in the city's calendar, drawing more than half a million people each year for a day of LGBTQ celebration. Events take place throughout the month, although the parade day is the biggest by far. Trucks crawl through the packed streets blasting out music and then the celebration goes on long into the night, with parties held around the city and unofficial raves popping up in parks. Every June, the KARNEVAL DER KULTUREN (Carnival of Cultures) takes place to celebrate multiculturalism and diversity, principles that are key to Berlin's identity. Aside from the main procession, you'll find the party stretches over much of Kreuzberg. There are stalls, too, where you can purchase handmade goods and sample delicious street food from around the world. Taking place every two years, BERLIN BIENNALE is one of Germany's most important contemporary art festivals. Since each Biennale has its own theme and curators, it's hard to know what to expect, although this is part of what makes it such an exciting and thought-provoking festival. During the Biennale, you'll find exhibitions and events taking place in various venues across the city.

Revelers celebrate Christopher Street Day in celebration of the 1969 Stonewall Riots in New York.

Unlike Berlin, you'll find that pretty much everything worth seeing is in HAMBURG's center, making it perfect for a day trip. The city's stunning architecture, which ranges from the baroque magnificence of St. Michael's Church to the gleaming Elbphilharmonie concert hall, makes for pleasant viewing as you explore Hamburg's winding streets and calming waterways. The bustling shopping street of Lange Reihe in St. Georg deserves a place at the top of your itinerary. When you arrive, the traffic lights that feature same-sex couples rather than a single man are the first indication that you've reached the center of the city's gay community, and it boasts a wealth of great stores, cafes, and bars. Gastronomy is high on the city's agenda, too, and as a port city you'll find a plethora of great seafood options, such as the Michelin star-winning Se7en Oceans. If you decide to stay the night, consider checking out Sternschanze, a hip Berlin-esque quarter that's home to some of the city's top nightlife.

Take a day or weekend trip to Hamburg, just two hours from Berlin by train.

IN BERLIN, PERFORMING QUEERNESS, TOGETHER-NESS

Jurassica Parka

Most modern cities can lay claim to a healthy gay scene, but the German capital of Berlin goes one step further. It's its own "gay universe," according to colorful local drag queen Jurassica Parka. "For gay men, Berlin's unique," she explains. "There are so many things you can do. The scene's much, much smaller in all other German cities, where there's just a bar you might go to. In Berlin, you can go out around the clock and stay in a gay universe only, if that's what you want."

As one of the world's most LGBTQ-friendly cities, it's little wonder that queer people, all in search of inflated diversity and freedom, flock here from around the world. But that wasn't the case for Jurassica. "I was born in Neukölln, so I don't really have an exciting history with the city!" she admits. "It's my home, my parents live here. I didn't come here—as many others did—to escape the countryside and start a new life."

Jurassica's long history with Berlin affords her some perspective on the ways in which the city's changed in recent decades. "When I was a kid, the Berlin Wall was still standing," she remembers. "A lot has happened since. I welcome the development of Berlin into becoming an international metropolis—you simply have to put up with the negative flavors of that." Cutting through the enthusiasm that is often tied to the city's recent boom, she adds, "I know Berlin by heart, and am a bit wary of the hype around the city, to be honest. Still, it is amazing that so many young people love this city so much." One positive change in particular, she explains, is how the city has become "much queerer—and that's great!" That shift is reflected in the fact that locals barely bat an eyelid when Jurassica hits the streets in her raucous drag persona. "Sure, people look, make stupid comments, but that doesn't happen a lot," she says. "Berliners don't really care. They're used to odd birds around their city." The drag scene has, she adds, "grown a lot in the last couple of years. And I'm really happy about that. Young talent is great and important."

Of course, the city's ever-lasting "queerification" also impacts the nightlife. "New places open all the time, places that are not gay or lesbian 'only' but queer or LGBTI," she points out. "That's very important. However, there are also places where only gays go, for instance, saunas or sex parties. That's also very important."

"Berliners are used to odd birds around."

She names Schwuz on Rollbergstrasse in Neukölln as one of her favorite hotspots: "It's a club and cultural activist center that's existed for more than 40 years and has achieved a lot." It's also where she started her career 15 years ago, when she was a DJ and party host. " As a self-employed artist, it's difficult to plan your career," she says. "Some people might be able to do that, but I never was. Berlin definitely has only advantages for me and my job. There are so many theaters, clubs, companies, and agencies here that both create and require creative work. I don't think I could live my job in so many ways in any other German city." The BKA Theater in Kreuzberg is another of her prized venues.

"I have different shows there," Jurassica says, "and they've supported me for a few years now. I can do whatever I want there—it's amazing!"

As for her time off, however, Jurassica explains, "for a few years now I haven't really been going out privately, except for a bar every once in a while maybe," like "Rauschgold bar on Mehringdamm for a few beers. Meeting friends and forgetting about the daily routine." Mostly, she likes to spend nights at home, in the heart of the city, near the red-light district at Kurfürstenstrasse, "on the top floor under the roof on Potsdamer Strasse with my husband Klaus. It's very well connected to all my favorite places in the city."

In place of her previous party agenda, she now lives a more homey life: "Sleeping in, taking a long walk with my husband and my dog—hopefully in good weather—maybe taking a stroll on Ku'damm, stopping somewhere for lunch. After that, I like to go home and cook a nice dinner. If it's a cozy one, we binge-watch a Netflix series."

The sense of Berlin's separate togetherness—of there being something for everyone—is perhaps reflected in the city's different *Kiezen*, meaning "neighborhoods, different centers," explains Jurassica. "There's not the one center, as in other cities, where everything happens. This city was divided by a wall for 28 years. This became part of the city's collective memory, I think."

CLAIM IT

1. Hotel Amigo
2. Hôtel des Galeries
3. La Maison Haute
4. Pillows Grand Hotel Place Rouppe

SAVOR IT

5. Au Vieux Saint Martin
6. Charli
7. Comme Chez Soi
8. La Fabrique
9. Maison Antoine
10. Mano à Mano
11. Noordzee

CELEBRATE IT

12. Café Charbon
13. Chez Maman
14. L'aube sur Aÿ
15. La Demence
16. Le Belgica

OWN IT

17. Hunting and Collecting
18. LuLu Home Interior
19. Maison Dandoy
20. Pierre Marcolini
21. Peinture Fraîche
22. Senteurs d'Ailleurs

EXPLORE IT

23. BOZAR
24. La Patinoire Royale
25. Magritte Museum

BRUSSELS

Europe's Provincial Yet Cosmopolitan Capital

Brussels has blossomed into more than a mere day trip from Paris or Amsterdam; deemed the veritable capital of Europe, it's both inspiring and technocratic. Unabashedly gay-friendly, this European hub welcomes a vibrant, creative, and tolerant community bolstered by a large foreign resident population from other parts of the European Union and beyond. Thanks to its geopolitical history, Brussels is cosmopolitan almost by default yet still manages to maintain an intimacy that other capital cities can't match. Although mainly French-speaking, Belgium is officially trilingual (French, Dutch, German). There are, however, so many expatriates that English has become an unofficial fourth language, effortlessly expanding a visitor's social repertoire. Soon, you'll find yourself with a beer in one hand and that of your new friend in the other, watching tourists taking pictures of a little boy peeing. Indeed, the ghosts of surrealism are alive and well in this city.

With a relatively large gay population packed into a tiny city, Brussels is both endearing and approachable. Its openness, though, is due to its small size not in spite of it. The capital of a country that was the second in the world to legalize same-sex marriage, that elected the first openly gay man to head a national government as Prime Minister, and is home to the International Lesbian and Gay Association, Brussels stands at the forefront of LGBTQ advocacy and cultural acceptance. From the gravity of the political institutions that reside within its borders to its playful comic book culture, Brussels circuitously frolics around any definitive cultural identifier, making it the perfect setting for a weekend getaway.

Steps away from the glorious Grand-Place is HOTEL AMIGO. Known for hosting prominent guests and dignitaries, the hotel is perfect for those who want to splurge on subtle yet well-designed rooms boasting views of City Hall. On the other side of the Grand-Place is HÔTEL DES GALERIES, residing within a nineteenth-century glass-roofed arcade lined with boutique shops, cafes, chocolatiers, and even a small movie theater. Designers Fleur Delesalle and Camille Flammarion have created an essentially Belgian space, intricately mixing ceramic works with contemporary furniture and earth-toned parquet flooring. Insider tip: do not miss the croquettes at its downstairs restaurant.

Mixing drinks at Hotel Amigo's Bar A, where guests relax in leather chairs on polished parquet floors.

Elegance pervades the rooms at Hotel Amigo.

While minimal in design, PILLOWS GRAND HOTEL PLACE ROUPPE embraces both warmth and charm. A delicate, subtle plushness infuses everything here, from the glass of champagne offered to incoming guests to its heavenly breakfast and cushy beds. If you're in need of a caffeine boost, across the street is Kaffabar, a gay-owned, aesthetically pleasing, and delightfully friendly coffee bar. You will hopefully catch Marc, the owner, and his adorable canine mascot Marcel.

Far enough away to explore a different side of the city, yet still close to the center is LA MAISON HAUTE. A treat for all your senses, it artfully blends the intimacy of a B&B with the comfort and ease of a hotel. If the scents emanating from the handmade soap shop on the first floor don't lure you in, then the tastefully designed rooms surely will. The owner and keeper, Sebastien, takes care of his guests from the moment they walk in, providing them with a snug ambiance, local knowledge, and a simple yet hearty breakfast.

Rue du Midi, one of several wide shopping boulevards in the city center.

Light and bright, there is a relaxed charm at Hotel des Galeries and, with just 23 rooms, an air of intimacy.

With a relatively large gay population packed into a tiny city, Brussels is both endearing and approachable.

The cuisine in Belgium is as diverse as its tumultuous history, and Brussels is no exception. Like the city's fashion, its food rivals various other culinary centers like London and Paris. Brussels, however, doesn't flaunt its culinary prowess, mainly because it doesn't have to—its food speaks for itself.

One good thing about the global hipster movement is its love for coffee and its fellow paramours, bread and pastries (along with the word "artisanal"). Start your day at CHARLI, near the lively area of Place Sainte-Catherine, which succeeds in offering unique coffee flavors accompanied by mouth-watering bread, croissants, and various other organic baked goods. Try the choux—you won't regret it.

When Parisian expats flock to a certain area in town, you know you need to follow, and the Châtelain neighborhood entices in a way that Brussels' city center cannot—it's likely you'll want to live here, not just visit. If so, your local weekend brunch venue would be LA FABRIQUE CHÂTELAIN, which serves up basic, freshly made dishes ranging from acai bowls to club sandwiches. For another casual lunch option, take a virtual trip to the Belgian seaside at NOORDZEE. This is one of those holes-outside-the-wall restaurants serving succulent oysters, moules, and fish of the season. Here you stand, not sit, while eating al fresco; savor the view of the cathedral while

Oysters anyone? Serving "fish for foodies" is the mantra of the team at De Noordzee.

sipping on a glass of champagne. For a slightly fancier lunch of quintessential Belgian cuisine, venture to family-owned AU VIEUX SAINT MARTIN, known for its filet américain: minced raw meat bound by egg yolk, mayonnaise, and savory spices, and always served with frites. Relish this delectable dish along with views of Sablon Square and its elegant passersby.

For a savory afternoon snack, try arguably the city's best frites at MAISON ANTOINE. It stands in the middle of Place Jourdan, a square surrounded by bars that allow you to bring in your fries to devour when you order a beer to wash them down. After, walk to nearby Parc Leopold to catch a glimpse of all the Eurocrats coming and going from the European Parliament.

For dinner, move away from the immediate area surrounding the Grand-Place and explore Ixelles, the birthplace of Audrey Hepburn and Brussels's most energetic area outside the city center. MANO À MANO is a small Italian pizzeria facing the neo-Gothic Saint-Boniface church in one of Brussels's most alluring squares. Foodies in search of a more upscale experience that shows off Belgian cuisine's prowess should dine at COMME CHEZ SOI. A two Michelin-starred restaurant with a rich family history, its petite space, art nouveau stained glass interior, and sophisticated haute cuisine are a microcosm of Brussels.

Earthy tones and simple, contemporary furnishings give La Fabrique its unpretentious, almost rustic air.

The flâneur might have been born in Paris, but he moved to Brussels a while back. It may be its size or it may be the people, but grabbing a drink here is a much more relaxed affair than in other European cities. CAFÉ CHARBON is one of those bars where you can sit all day while people-watching and drinking a Leffe Blond. A café, wine bar, and bistro, its relaxed, industrial setting rests confidently along a small cobbled street across from the enchanting Basilique Notre Dame de Bonsecours. Just around

> The flâneur might have been born in Paris, but he moved to Brussels a while back. Grabbing a drink here is a much more relaxed affair than in other cities.

the corner is Brussels's famous drag club CHEZ MAMAN, a must-see for any visitor. After knocking on the door, you'll be transported to a different world. Watch drag queens perform on a tiny bar while standing shoulder to shoulder with others singing along in English, French, or any other language the performer chooses. The space is intimate, making it conducive to forging new international relations.

Before Chez Maman, however, start your night out on Rue du Marché au Charbon where you'll find a row of bars. LE BELGICA is a tried and true haunt for gents, both local and foreign, to gather and grab a beer and, in the case of this bar, a Martinica. During the warmer months, men flush with confidence after a few drinks spill out onto the street to join their friends and meet new ones. If that doesn't sound glam enough, L'AUBE SUR AŸ serves a selection of more than 120 champagnes along with caviar, oysters, foie gras, and, of course, chocolate. This little gem offers a small slice of Brussels's take on joie de vivre, combining everyone's favorite aphrodisiacs with live music and performances.

> Watch drag queens perform on a tiny bar while standing shoulder to shoulder with others singing along in English, French, or any other language the performer chooses.

Take time to sample a traditional Belgian beer—not just a Leffe Blond, but also an Oud Bruin or a Flanders Red.

Head to Catclub for a relaxed dance vibe within large-scale industrial spaces.

A more innovative going–out venue is one that changes its location every event: that's CATCLUB. An eclectic dancing and music experience, it's set in artistic or industrial spaces such as Galerie Ravenstein or the old Citroën factory. There is a sense of cordialness at its nights, where club-goers truly appreciate the music and take delight in dancing with each other. If it's on when you're in town, dance like nobody's watching at European gay clubbing institution LA DEMENCE. Like Folsom in San Francisco, men of all ages, backgrounds, and proclivities have been coming for years to revel in a fun-filled party, explore their hedonistic side, or gawk at the characters around them.

While it's always important to stray off the beaten path, sometimes being a tourist is okay. Every so often, it's good to go with the cultural clichés that define a city—especially when they involve chocolates, waffles, beer, and fries. We all know about Swiss chocolate, but the Belgians are the real master chocolatiers. Skip Godiva and instead head to PIERRE MARCOLINI, sometimes dubbed "the Chanel of Chocolates." Then stop by the MAISON DANDOY tearoom for a delectable mélange of sugar and spice—the heavenly speculoos biscuit.

> While it's always important to stray off the beaten path, sometimes being a tourist is okay. Every so often, it's good to go with the cultural clichés that define a city—especially when they involve chocolates, waffles, beer, and fries.

Indulge your inner book fetishist at PEINTURE FRAÎCHE in Ixelles, an intimate shop with a carefully curated selection of photography, art, design, and fashion tomes. The design-inclined venture on to LULU HOME INTERIOR off nearby Rue du Page. Catering to Brussels's cosmopolitan residents, LuLu is filled with innovative, contemporary home goods ranging from furniture to dining sets. Its simple and tasteful aesthetic continues into the café where you can enjoy a coffee and pre-dinner snack from a menu developed by French chef Guillaume Gomez.

Belgium's most influential avant-garde fashion collective, Antwerp Six, which includes Dries Van Noten and Walter Van Beirendonck, put the country firmly on the map for sartorialists. So while not Paris, Brussels is an excellent place to update your wardrobe as well. Secure some gorgeous designer threads at HUNTING AND COLLECTING, one of Brussels's most popular boutiques. Afterward, pop in to SENTEURS D'AILLEURS to complement your new garment with a beautiful scent. An inviting olfactory paradise, it provides a vast array of products and fragrances that you won't find anywhere else.

An impressive range of contemporary ceramics are on display at Hunting and Collecting.

At Maison Dandoy at Galerie du Roi, sweet treats fill a counter that runs the length of the store.

The traditional-looking facade of Maison Dandoy-Galeries, in the heart of the city.

If it's culture you're after, but you don't fancy joining the line for an institution that houses five million pieces of art, visit the MAGRITTE MUSEUM. Exploring the works, life, and story of Belgium's most famous surrealist artist, René Magritte, this museum is fun and accessible. Standing on a hill in central Brussels, its top floors offer beautiful views of the city and Grand-Place.

Besides Magritte, Brussels is home to artists of all kinds who thrive on the city's creative energy and reasonable cost of living. From modern dancing to classical music, there's a wealth of venues where you can watch and engage with the arts. The BOZAR is the most famous of these, if not for its extensive events program, then for its nouveau architecture, which stands out even in a city renowned for this late-nine-teenth-century style. Like the BOZAR, the best gallery spaces enhance the art, and vice versa. As you explore Châtelain, veer just off Chaussée de Charleroi to discover LA PATINOIRE ROYALE, a small but exquisitely renovated building that was formerly a royal skating rink. Its remnants are visible if you look up at the wood-paneled vaulted ceilings, but instead of ice, it houses works by contemporary artists, both new and established.

Over 200 works are on display at the Magritte Museum.

In Brussels, the city itself is a tableau upon which artists can express their creativity. With the national mascot being Manneken Pis, it's no surprise that Brussels maintains a childlike, playful air. Walking through the city, one can't help but notice the giant comic book murals on the walls of various buildings. These are part of the COMIC BOOK ROUTE, a series of sites displaying motifs of the most famous Belgian comics. Start with the LGBTQ mural on Rue de la Chaufferette and then move on to the Smurfs in front of Central Station.

A mural by German artist Ralph König graces the wall of the Rainbow House, a social space for the local LGBTQI community.

When in Brussels, do as the Belgians do—drink beer. This country has been brewing for centuries and despite its size is one of the largest producers of the golden liquid in the world. The BXL BEER FEST is, as the name suggests, a beer festival that takes place during the summer. Unlike similar events in Belgium, it focuses on independent local and international producers attracting aficionados and amateurs alike. To temper its ardent beer intake, the city has passionately embraced the food truck scene, producing the largest event of its kind in Europe with the BRUSSELS FOOD TRUCK FESTIVAL. From waffles, fries, and quiche, to burgers, tacos, and patatas bravas, this festival is packed with fare from all over Belgium and the world. Every summer the canals of Brussels come alive with outdoor festivities, and BRUXELLES LES BAINS is the most anticipated of the season. The Bruxellois take advantage of the sun to wistfully reconnoiter the food stalls, sip on libations, and partake in various cultural events. Take in a movie in the outdoor cinema or watch Brussels's gay volleyball teams play. If visiting in winter, join art collectors, buyers, and lovers from around the globe at BRUSSELS ART FAIR, or BRAFA. Initially a national event, it has expanded its base to include international artists while still perfecting the art of quality over quantity.

Starting at the end of January, and lasting nine days, BRAFA marks the first major event in the city's art calendar.

ESCAPE IT

Escaping Brussels for a weekend is an easy affair, especially when another country is a hop, skip, and jump away—but you don't need to leave Belgium to feel like you're in a foreign land. It only takes a few minutes on the train for the conductor to code-switch from "mesdames et messieurs" to "dames en heren," and voilà, you find yourself in Flanders, Belgium's Flemish-speaking region to the north. Bruges is quaint but you might find yourself at a loss of what else to do after two hours of bobbing on its canals and exploring its charming streets. In less than an hour by train from Brussels, you can find yourself in the bigger, hipper, and more vibrant medieval city of GHENT. Meander to the vertiginous grandeur of St. Bavo's seventh-century cathedral with a *gestreken mastel* (a sweet local delicacy) in hand or discover Ghent's ancient quarter, Patershol, while embracing the city's magical history and awe-inspiring architecture. Warm yourself up with coffee and lunch at Vos Restaurant, then head to the SMAK Museum for your afternoon fix of contemporary art.

The ultra-modern City Pavilion is an open space that plays host to markets, concerts, and dance events.

IN BRUSSELS, DANCING FOR PROGRESS AND INCLUSIVITY

Gay Haze

Brussels, the Belgian and European Union capital, has a "blurry mix of influences because of its situation, its political history." This is how Guillaume Bleret, cofounder and organizer of queer dance party collective Gay Haze, thinks of the city. "Basically, it's at the meeting point of Latin and German heritage," adds the 38-year-old, who was born and raised close by, in a medieval town in the Walloon region.

He met his friend and eventual Gay Haze cofounder Diego Cozzi, 28, partying in the city 10 years ago. (Nightlife is a theme that comes up again and again during our interview.) "I grew up in Luxembourg City, two hours away by car," says Diego. "Brussels is now my city, my home, but my first choice was actually Berlin." Attracted to the German capital's raucous and agenda-filling club scene—a quality it shares with Brussels—Berlin, Diego says, is "where I met my boyfriend, who I'm still with." But he ended up moving to Brussels so they could be together

full time. "I started coming on weekends [at first]," he says. "That's how I got to know Guillaume."

The rest is history, almost literally: Belgium's rich culture of electronic music ("Have you seen the documentary *The Sound of Belgium*?" asks Guillaume) and thriving nightlife scene has enveloped the lives of both guys. And while the highest-profile member of Brussels's legendary queer nightlife is perhaps the world-famous, decades-running monthly gay super-party La Demence, their contribution is fresher, edgier—a Sunday afternoon/evening event they describe as a "wacky, colossal tea dance."

"It's alternative and liberally minded, with a provocative homo aesthetic," adds Guillaume. "People got quickly amused by the concept and we've gathered a loyal and reliable audience, no matter the sexual orientation. We've been lucky—there was clearly a free slot in the party scene. The disadvantage of maintaining such a project in Brussels is the lack of average capacity places."

But, if it's always growing, how do they keep Gay Haze inclusive and open? "It's a natural thing," insists Diego. He then quickly adds, "Maybe we don't go too crazy with the promotion. We keep it fun and spontaneous. And we play a certain kind of music not everyone will be into. Then there's the Sunday afternoon/evening thing. Not everyone can go crazy on a Sunday. The people joining really want to be there."

Guillaume is also a member of 24hBrussels, "an observation platform on nightlife, extending reflections from clubbers and party-goers to managers, club owners, night workers, neighbors' committees, transport companies, health workers … It studies the facts. What's missing or can be better? What's already great?" The project also fosters "cooperation" between party organizers, he says. "There's competitiveness as well as mutual support. Some people have to stoop very low in order to protect their prerogatives. This excessive vision of competition is luckily not winning all the time."

"It's alternative and liberally minded, with a provocative homo aesthetic."

Guillaume lives in Brussels's Anderlecht district, an affordable area that attracts creative types, and Diego stays 10 minutes away, nearer to the historical center. "Everything's close, it's easy to see people, there's loads of bars," Diego enthuses. His favorite spot is Fontainas, which has a charming café terrace and many LGBTQ staff. "It's an important spot for gay people— it's close to the gay street, the gay sauna, it's super beautiful, you can go alone and be sure you'll meet someone you know."

The guys admit, however, that they might hesitate before taking a partner by the hand in certain areas of the city: "To walk hand in hand with your partner is an act of bravery. You have to be ready to accept the gazes, the comments, the spits from people who will cross your way," Guillaume, paraphrasing Diego, says. "The gay scene is quite developed and visible," he further explains, "and from one street to another, you will go from a lack of safety to a very

liberal feeling." They cite same-sex marriage and the granting of adoption rights to LGBTQs as two examples of recent progress.

Nevertheless, this is truly a city with inclusivity in its roots. "Thanks to its presence at the sea, it was always a land of crossing, immigration, and prosperity," says Guillaume. "*Zinneke*," he continues, "is a Brussels word for hybrid. It's originally derogative but took on a meaning of pride and is symbolically used as an identity."

W Foster Ave

Kennedy Expy

Lincoln Park

W North Ave

Magnificent Mile

W Grand Ave

CLAIM IT

1 Chicago Athletic
   Association
2 FieldHouse Jones
3 The Publishing House
4 The Robey
5 Viceroy & Devereaux

SAVOR IT

6 Entente
7 Lost Larson
8 Passerotto
9 Roister
10 Southport Grocery
11 Vincent

CELEBRATE IT

12 DISCO
13 Elixir Lakeview
14 RM Champagne
   Salon
15 Sidetrack
16 The Second City

OWN IT

17 Asrai Garden
18 Blind Barber
19 Rotofugi
20 Stock Mfg. Co.
21 Volumes Bookcafe

EXPLORE IT

22 Auditorium Theatre
23 Center on Halsted
24 Museum of
   Contemporary Art

CHICAGO

The Midwest's Smoking-hot, Eternally Cool City

American architect Frank Lloyd Wright once said: "Eventually, I think Chicago will be the most beautiful great city left in the world." And while asking us to pick a favorite city is akin to picking one's favorite child, we certainly see why Wright would feel that way. The city is wrapped in an exciting mix of architecture and style, its people are gregariously charming—the perfect blend of New York chic and Midwestern warmth—and its food scene is an ever-changing kaleidoscope of global flavors elevated to heavenly heights. Chicago offers a haven for culture, a stage for the arts, unlimited access to the world's finest jazz and blues music, and a front-row seat to the state's natural beauty. It's also home to Boystown, one of the largest LGBTQ communities in the United States.

Rife with LGBTQ history, in the 1950s Chicago saw an explosion of gay bars including Tiny and Ruby's Gay Spot, opened by trumpeter Ernestine "Tiny" Davis and her partner, drummer Ruby Lucas, on Wentworth Avenue. In the 1960s, Chuck Renslow, an icon within Chicago's gay movement, opened Gold Coast as the country's first leather bar. Renslow went on to launch his men's "physique" magazines in the Windy City along with his partner, Dom Orejudos, and to create both the International Mr. Leather contest and the Leather Archives & Museum in Rogers Park. In 1961, Illinois made what was arguably its biggest step in advancing LGBTQ culture by being the first state to remove sodomy from its list of forbidden acts. It was a bold move that helped pull the gay movement closer toward the light, and today Chicago's commitment to help change society's view of the LGBTQ community is as fierce as ever. It's a city that is smoking-hot, eternally cool ... and yours for the asking.

For more than a century, entry into the CHICAGO ATHLETIC ASSOCIATION was reserved for a privileged few. Founded in 1890 by Marshall Field, Cyrus McCormick, and A. G. Spalding, among others, its members included one particularly well-heeled baseball fan named William Wrigley. Fun fact: when Wrigley joined a consortium that bought the Chicago Cubs baseball team in 1915, he chose to adopt the Chicago Athletic Association's crest as its logo—a decision that irrevocably bound the two for decades to come. While still definitively elegant, the hotel is no longer reserved exclusively for the ultra elite. Located a stone's throw from Millennium Park and now open to all, it features Cindy's, one of the city's best rooftop bars, a Shake Shack on premises, and an all-new, ruggedly chic urban look courtesy of design studio Roman and Williams. We can't imagine why anyone wouldn't opt to spend a night or two.

Another Chicago retrofit wonder resides in a Perkins, Chatten & Hammond–designed art deco stunner originally known as the "Northwest Towers." THE ROBEY, comprised of 69 tower rooms housed in the original building and multibed, loft-style accommodation located in the adjoining 1905 property, is gritty and elegant, rugged and refined. During summer, guests at The Robey, which straddles Chicago's historic Wicker Park neighborhood and the arty community of Bucktown, can conquer the concrete jungle while channeling their inner Johnny Weissmuller at the chic, rooftop pool. You can also indulge in creative, American fare by chef Kevin McAllister in Café Robey, people watch while sipping espresso upstairs in The Lounge, or sample cocktails from low-slung sofas at a higher altitude in the Up Room whilst watching the city's twinkling skyline come alive. One more remarkably unique place to set down your bags is FIELDHOUSE JONES. Part indie indulgence, part upscale dormitory, part new-age penthouse, this is a hotel unlike any other in a city that is nothing if not unique. With rooms ranging from classic "Trailblazer" to loft apartments to its signature "Campus" featuring four bunks, just choosing your accommodation at FieldHouse Jones is a fun activity that will have you calling dibs on the top bunk before the Windy City has had a chance to ruffle your hair.

For more refined respite, VICEROY in the posh Gold Coast neighborhood is noteworthy. Resting in the footprint of the 1920s-era Cedar Hotel, standing side by side with the city's most covetable mansions, and boasting both the Magnificent Mile and Lake Michigan as neighbors, the hotel pays homage to the moneyed world of Midwestern luxury. Designed by the hospitality masterminds at TAL Studio, the Viceroy delivers a delicious serving of art, style, and aesthetics, celebrating Chicago's vibrant landscape and lavish lifestyle with each detail and nuance. This is also where you'll find Somerset, the dining venue featuring cuisine from Michelin-starred chef Lee Wolen, and Devereaux, the 18th-floor rooftop lounge where the craft cocktails—not to mention the cultivated company—are as mesmerizing as the views of the city below.

And for the trendsetting among us, any Chicagoan worth his salt will tell you that West Loop is the place to be. A former warehouse district, it's home to the University of Illinois at Chicago campus and like any decent college town, has morphed into a treasure trove of hot nightspots and notable eateries. At the heart of this neighborhood is THE PUBLISHING HOUSE, a brilliantly reimagined bed and breakfast located in the former Free Methodist publishing house. Offering en-suite accommodation ranging from a cozy bedroom to a relatively sprawling suite, rooms here are a delightful blend of bare brick and warm oak, while its restaurant-quality breakfasts are reputed to be the best in the city.

With its boutique flair, The Publishing House combines a warm welcome with luxury.

If there is one thing Chicagoans know, it's food. From simple street fare to over-the-top gastro experiences, this is a city that refuses to go hungry–and with its plethora of dining options, it doesn't have to. Come to Chicago ravenous and trust us when we tell you that you'll be busy for breakfast, lunch, and dinner.

Start your day the right way day with breakfast (not to mention lunch and an occasional secret supper), at the café at SOUTHPORT GROCERY AND CAFE. A hidden gem rife with comfort food goodness, in-the-know Chicagoans flock for the all-day menu that ranges from bread pudding pancakes to house-smoked brisket and gravy served with cage-free (and locally sourced, of course) organic eggs. Plan to spend the entire day out? No worries—just swing by and pick up a custom-made lunch box to go. Another breakfast favorite is grab-and-go café LOST LARSON in Andersonville. This bakery bistro uses flour freshly ground from whole grains on a traditional stone mill to make its decadent pastries and open-face sandwiches served on otherworldly bread. No stranger to the baking game, before opening Lost Larson chef-owner Bobby Schaffer led the pastry programs for some very high-flying restaurants, including New York legend Blue Hill at Stone Barns and the Michelin-adorned Grace in Chicago.

After breakfast, start working up an appetite for dinner because it would be a shame to visit Chicago without indulging in the culinary creations of fine dining's golden boy Grant Achatz. Following on from the stellar success of Achatz's Alinea and Next, the chef brought ROISTER to West Loop in 2016—and it was awarded a Michelin star in its first year. Guests can choose between an à la carte menu served in the main dining room or a prix-fixe served family-style in a kitchen. If the thought of hushpuppies served with chicken liver pate, peach jam, and pickles appeals,

Roister won't disappoint. Another option for quintessential Midwestern fine dining is the Michelin-starred ENTENTE. Tucked away on Lincoln Avenue, the restaurant has a front room with small tables and bar, and a somewhat austere, albeit comfortable, rear space awash with natural woods— all the better to showcase the brilliant dishes coming from the kitchen. Chef Brian Fisher brought his A-game when he developed the restaurant's seasonal menu of game, seafood, meat, and vegetables. Begin your sojourn with a perfectly chilled flute of NV Domaine de la Louvetrie Atmosphéres before delving into a plate of Berkshire pork with Sea Island red peas, collard greens, Littleneck clams, and cornbread, or a divine, signature rice dish served with summer truffle, duck egg, pea tendrils, and fragrant shavings of Parmigiano Reggiano.

> If there is one thing Chicagoans know, it's food. From simple street fare to over-the-top gastro experiences, this is a city that refuses to go hungry.

An Andersonville notable is PASSEROTTO on North Clark Street, where Korean fare is served with Italian flair by chef-proprietor Jennifer Kim. Showcasing small plates and large dishes meant for sharing, as well as Korean feasts for two or more, the menu runs the gamut from cavatelli served with nori butter, beans, Japanese sweet potato, and pickled shallots to glazed short ribs served with kimchi made from a family recipe.

Lastly, if Peter Luger and Delmonico's had a love child, it might be VINCENT—think dark wood wainscoting, white tablecloths topped with kraft paper, and damask wall covering. The similarities end there, though. Far from your father's favorite three-martini haunt, Vincent is steakhouse fare vaulted to another dimension. Need more proof? Just one bite of chef Jake Chappel's bone marrow spaetzle with braised mushrooms, brandy, and petit mustard greens ought to do it. The wonder doesn't end at the kitchen, either. From the bar overseen by Brian Riester come craft cocktails such as "Smoke & Mirrors," a heady take on the Old Fashioned, or a gin, grapefruit, Lillet blanc, thyme, lemon, and egg white concoction called "Six Inch Voice."

The sophisticated interior of Lost Larson, which serves some of the tastiest breads and pastries in town.

No shrinking violet when it comes to nightlife, evenings in Chicago are sultry—even in the dead of winter. Among the city's more intimate venues are DEVEREAUX, the ultra-chic lounge perched atop the Viceroy; ELIXIR LAKEVIEW, a homage to elegance where sophisticated cocktails are served in a sleek, sexy lounge; and RM CHAMPAGNE SALON in West Loop where you can pop, clink, fizz, and sip bubbles between bites of dessert.

While legendary gay club The Warehouse (considered to be the birthplace of house) may have come and gone, you can still dance the night away at DISCO on West Hubbard Street. This is a self-proclaimed "nightlife sanctuary" where music, faux-fur sofas, and LED-illuminated dance floors—in short, everything we love about the 1970s—are celebrated with aplomb. It's where the cool kids like to freak out and work up a sweat, where the best DJs come to cut loose, and where celebrations like The Masquerade Macabre, a seductively dark Halloween fetish party, take place—all excellent reasons for opting out of yet another night of Netflix and chill.

Want something even more offbeat? Go all out at SIDETRACK, where you can dance like a little monster during the All Things Gaga revue, kick back at a Will & Grace viewing party, or spill it all at one of its LBGTQ storytelling events, held the first Tuesday of each month. Alternatively, laugh your socks off at THE SECOND CITY, the iconic comedy club that's served as an unofficial launch pad for the best comedians of our time.

Eighteen floors up, Deveraux offers sweeping views of Chicago's Gold Coast neighborhood.

Fans of comedy savor a night of improvization at Second City's Mainstage venue.

Reid Murdoch Building
Garage | 300 North LaSalle
Garage

While the Magnificent Mile offers a thousand ways to give your Platinum Card a workout, Chicago is rich with boutiques and shops that don't just speak to us—they scream our name. Anime and pop culture fans flock to ROTOFUGI in Lincoln Park with good reason: it's the in place for collectible toys and the home of Rotofugi Gallery, which features the next big artists in monthly exhibitions. A different kind of art can be found at ASRAI GARDEN. More than a florist, it's a wonderland of vintage-inspired gifts, bath goods, and botanicals all under one intoxicating roof. Or for an academically inclined afternoon, head to VOLUMES BOOKCAFE on North Milwaukee Avenue. An independently owned gem, here you can order a flat white or buttery chard while browsing the shelves.

Offering wardrobe basics with a modern spin, there's STOCK MFG. CO. where the devil is ensconced in the elegant details—like how many holes are in a button, how the fabric feels, and why those pants drape so damn well. And because there's nothing like a fresh haircut and shave to make even the sexiest outfit look better, stop by BLIND BARBER. A barber shop by day and speakeasy by night, in addition to its grooming services there's a wealth of bespoke preening products to peruse making it the perfect place to pick up a little something.

The facade of Stock Mfg. Co., a Chicago-made menswear store on West Fulton Street.

Fit, fabric, and quality are buzzwords at homegrown menswear store Stock Mfg. Co.

EXPLORE IT

With a collection of more than 2,500 pieces, Chicago's MUSEUM OF CONTEMPORARY ART is in a league of its own. Rather than designating a space to its permanent collection, MCA prefers to draw on it to present frequently changing, thematic shows, ensuring there's something new for people to see each time they visit. Fans of dance should head to the AUDITORIUM THEATER. A glittering historical landmark and a beacon for Chicagoans, it is

Fans of dance should head to the Auditorium Theater—a glittering historical landmark.

Grand gilded arches and a sparkling ceiling are hallmark features of the impressive six-story Auditorium Theater.

home to the Joffrey Ballet and hosts myriad events and performances throughout the year.

Finally, the CENTER ON HALSTED is the Midwest's most comprehensive center dedicated to advancing the community, health, and well-being of lesbian, gay, bisexual, transgender, and queer people, and has profoundly affected the cultural fabric of Chicago. Located in the heart of Boystown, it attracts more than 1,000 visitors each day in a safe and welcoming environment.

NORTHALSTED MARKET DAYS is Chicago's most illustrious summer party and the largest street festival in the entire Midwest. Founded in 1980, the two-day celebration now stretches through a full half-mile. Every August, Chicago also rocks when LOLLAPALOOZA, a four-day music festival, comes to Grant Park, bringing with it headliners such as Bruno Mars and Arctic Monkeys. The largest of Chicago's music festivals, however, is the CHICAGO BLUES FESTIVAL. The biggest free blues festival in the world, it runs for three days across four stages that have welcomed everyone from Bonnie Raitt to the late Ray Charles and B.B. King.

Above and opposite: Music fans chill out on the grass in Grant Park during the Lollapalooza festival.

ESCAPE IT

Just outside of the city, OAK PARK is one of the most architecturally significant villages in America. Boasting the largest geographically focused concentration of Frank Lloyd Wright–designed buildings, it was also the architect's personal residence and studio for the first 20 years of his career, from 1889 to 1909. A good way to familiarize yourself with the architect's unique design aesthetic is by starting your day with a tour around the Frank Lloyd Wright Home and Studio, followed by a visit to the houses designed by Wright and other prairie-style architects. A veritable prairie wonderland, Oak Park is a perfect place to while away a day.

The Arthur B. Heurtley House, Oak Park, is an early example of Frank Lloyd Wright's Prairie style.

The rapid-transit system serving the city is known affectionately as "L," short for elevated railway.

IN CHICAGO, DIRECTING DIVERSITY AND DYNAMISM

Mikael Burke

"The city's a vast quilt of unique neighborhoods; so many different people of different walks of life, all stitched together." As a successful theater director, proud Chicagoan Mikael Burke knows how to effortlessly set a scene, and never more so than when discussing his home city, the largest in the state of Illinois. "The resulting community is dynamic and exciting," he adds. "One moment you're in an urban metropolis, another minute you're on a quiet tree-lined street. You can take a train and feel like you're in a completely different world, but you're still in the heart of Chicago."

Mikael was born in Chicago but grew up in Nashville, Tennessee. After completing a bachelor's in theater at Indianapolis's Butler University, in 2009, he moved to the Windy City, where, "with some close colleagues," he started what he describes as "a small theater company." He adds, "We just followed our guts. Fast-forward a few years and that company expanded, merged with another small company, and sure enough I'd quit my side jobs and was making a living just making and teaching theater."

Since then, he has completed a Master of Fine Arts in Directing at Chicago's DePaul University, and he also holds two academic positions in the city: one as an Artistic Fellow at the Northlight Theatre and the other as a teacher at Roosevelt University, where he gives classes on script analysis and theater history. The stage is obviously still very much alive in his hometown. "I think we're on the cutting edge of new play development and it's a really exciting market to play in," he says. Chicago's theater scene is, for Mikael, "my artistic home—we're like a big family. I'm continually struck by the vibrancy of this community, its tenacity in challenging and upending harmful, non-inclusive production practices; for not only demanding but creating and fostering a theatrical landscape that's as rich, varied, and multi-faceted as the communities whom we reflect."

This Bitter Earth by Harrison David Rivers, a recent production Mikael directed, was an exploration of a gay, biracial relationship for About Face Theatre, which specializes in creating plays that advance the dialogue on gender and sexual identity in Chicago. He says the staging of stories about black queerness, in particular, is the biggest evolution in Chicago's theater scene of the last decade.

"The city's a vast quilt of unique neighborhoods."

"Much of my younger artistic years, you'd see work about white queerness, or heteronormative blackness," he explains. "But in recent years, black queerness has been given its own space to breathe. It's radical and exciting. My dream, though, is that soon we'll get to the point where stories about black and queer people are not explicitly about their blackness or queerness. I want stories where those identities are present, but simply circumstantial."

The drive for inclusivity permeates the city in general. "I've noticed Chicago at large has begun to recognize its white-centric biases and has started to make concerted efforts to shake up the status quo on that front," he says. It's a development that is occurring at a different scale in the city's famous queer scene, which is based around longstanding "gayborhoods" like Boystown and North Halsted. "For the most part," Mikael explains, "being a queer person in Chicago is pretty great, as we live in a pretty open and accepting city. However, I do think that—like in most American cities—being a cis, white, male queer person is more readily accepted than being any other queer person, POC or otherwise. There are many more queer spaces for white gay men than any of the rest of us. We're doing the work, but there's definitely room to grow on that front for sure."

The Windy City reveals itself over and over again to Mikael, and he is content to stay on while it continues to change around him. "One of the things that I love about Chicago is that the longer you live here, this city reveals more and more of what makes it completely irresistible. I have no intentions of leaving."

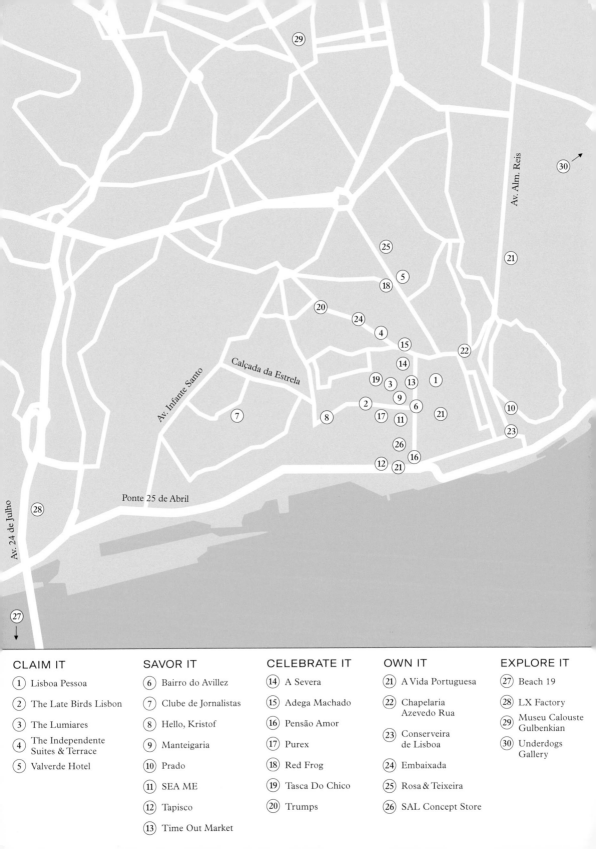

CLAIM IT

(1) Lisboa Pessoa

(2) The Late Birds Lisbon

(3) The Lumiares

(4) The Independente
Suites & Terrace

(5) Valverde Hotel

SAVOR IT

(6) Bairro do Avillez

(7) Clube de Jornalistas

(8) Hello, Kristof

(9) Manteigaria

(10) Prado

(11) SEA ME

(12) Tapisco

(13) Time Out Market

CELEBRATE IT

(14) A Severa

(15) Adega Machado

(16) Pensão Amor

(17) Purex

(18) Red Frog

(19) Tasca Do Chico

(20) Trumps

OWN IT

(21) A Vida Portuguesa

(22) Chapelaria
Azevedo Rua

(23) Conserveira
de Lisboa

(24) Embaixada

(25) Rosa & Teixeira

(26) SAL Concept Store

EXPLORE IT

(27) Beach 19

(28) LX Factory

(29) Museu Calouste
Gulbenkian

(30) Underdogs
Gallery

LISBON

A City of Contrasting Charms

An ancient city of harmonious duality and urban pleasures, Lisbon is Europe's reigning queen of contrast. Seven hills overlook cobblestone streets that lead to majestic squares and monuments, to sense-tingling pathways along the Tagus River, and to the tree-topped serenity of the ritzy Avenida da Liberdade. Yet, just around the bend, other adventures await, pulsing with the raw energy of the street art, folksy fado, and vibrant nightlife found in the rebel districts surrounding Bairro Alto. Add to that a burgeoning food scene that showcases dynamic seafood, and the result is a full throttle destination for travelers of all sorts, shapes, and sensibilities. While Catholicism retains a stranglehold on Portugal, the gay community has enjoyed an ever-growing acceptance since homosexuality was decriminalized in 1983. In fact, the country is one of only a handful worldwide that has a ban on discrimination etched right into its constitution. The proof of progress is evident in the rainbow-hued spray of developments: major cities host annual Pride parades, legal same-sex marriages have been performed since 2010, and the Queer Lisboa film festival is among the largest of its kind in Europe. In Lisbon proper, the LGBTQ scene is thriving with bars, shops, and clubs in bohemian stalwart hoods Bairro Alto, Príncipe Real, and, most recently, in the modish streets of Chiado.

Reminiscent of the most stylish cosmo capital townhouses, the boutique VALVERDE HOTEL on Lisbon's posh Avenida da Liberdade exudes modern-day meets bourgeois living, its six floors adorned with retro wood-veneer furnishings, patterned rugs, and touches of vintage decor. Adding to the opulent home-style feel, each of the 25 rooms boasts unique features that skillfully honor the Moorish heritage of the nineteenth-century building. The ground floor Sítio restaurant serves Portuguese staples and regional wines, but the real highlight is Pateo, a plant-filled courtyard offering five o'clock tea, classic cocktails, and seasonal poolside musical performances.

When the weather warms, guests enjoy exceptional views of the Tagus River and the Moorish São Jorge Castle at Mensagem Restaurant.

Built atop the Glória Funicular and overlooking the narrow walkways, tiled façades, and retro shops of Bairro Alto and Chiado, THE LUMIARES offers luxury suites in a former eighteenth-century palace. Rooms vary in size and feature monochrome headboards, woven artisan cushions, handmade tapestries, and indulgent toiletries from Claus Porto. Dining options include informal pastries at Mercado and, for discerning palates, traditional Portuguese fare at acclaimed chef João Silva's rooftop restaurant Lumi restaurant. A short jaunt away, THE LATE BIRDS is a fashionable boys-only guesthouse complete with poolside and courtyard gardens that allow guests to enjoy an affable stay or take part in private events in optimum comfort. Sandwiched between Bairro Alto and Príncipe Real, this homey location is comprised of 12 stark yet lived-in rooms adorned with eclectic items carved from various woods. Public spaces are equally striking and feature the owners' collection of treasures from around the world.

For views over the fabled red rooftops and multihued buildings found in the trendy Chiado district, check into LISBOA PESSOA, a minimalist four-star hotel celebrating the life and work of famed nineteenth-century Portuguese poet Fernando Pessoa. The rooms are minimalist with tasteful touches—blonde wood headboards, textured throws, and ultra-mod brass fixtures.

Serene by day and night, a courtyard patio offers a little private outdoor space at the Valverde Hotel.

When the weather warms, guests enjoy exceptional views of the Tagus River and the Moorish São Jorge Castle at Mensagem Restaurant, which is named after one of Mr. Pessoa's most famous works and serves traditional Portuguese fare and seasonal tipples.

If scenery is a must, THE INDEPENDENTE SUITES & TERRACE is among Lisbon's most enchanting options. Situated in a nineteenth-century edifice that faces the prime lookout belvedere Miradouro de São Pedro de Alcântara, this type of stay suits the adventurous traveler, one that prefers to discover the city through the lens of creative denizens. There is a hostel side that offers unisex bunk beds in spartan rooms with sprinkles of retro designs, but for a real feel of the local lifestyle, book one of the hipster-style suites. Short on amenities, guests receive an app loaded with all of the upcoming happenings in town and a choice of two eateries: The Decadente, providing typical tastes prepared with natural regional ingredients, and The Insólito, serving up outlandish fusion sides such as oyster ice cream.

Lisbon's vibrant landscape—equal parts sun, sea, and pastoral hills—makes for an endless bounty of nature's best, from vegetation to seafood to livestock. Though actively trading with neighboring nations since the Middle Ages, Portugal's focus on staple ingredients, with just a pinch of innovation, maintains a cuisine that is decidedly unique in look and flavor.

For a tantalizing introduction to Portuguese cuisine, start your exploration at former food market Mercado da Ribeira. Remodeled in 2014 as a mammoth gastro pavilion—a project sponsored by international city guide *Time Out*—the rechristened TIME OUT MARKET features more than 30 eateries, ranging from basic bites to talented chef-inspired creations to delectable desserts, alongside cooking demonstrations, workshops, artisanal crafts, and live musical acts. Noteworthy features include menus by star chefs Miguel Laffan, Miguel Castro e Silva, and Henrique Sá Pessoa; the homemade cakes at Nós é Mais Bolos; and a large selection of Portuguese wines from Garrafeira Nacional. For enterprising chef José Avillez—arguably Lisbon's reigning king of the kitchen—it was not enough to open a string of successful restaurants in hipster hood Chiado. In addition, he's introduced a variety of contrasting culinary concepts headquartered under one brightly lit roof. BAIRRO DO AVILLEZ houses four foodie hubs in an arched bi-level space freshened up with waggish tile illustrations and potted greenery. Casual Mercearia focuses on deli delicacies and cheeses, Taberna serves sandwiches and more traditional bites, and Páteo caters to seafood lovers— while jewel in the crown Beco offers an upmarket menu selection, at once Portuguese and international, accompanied by a cabaret performance.

Continue the gourmet quest at CLUBE DE JORNALISTAS, an eighteenth-century villa that today

From farm to fork, Prado excels at bringing Portugal's finest seasonal and regional produce to the city.

serves as a journalist hangout and has kept its vintage appeal through a cluster of singular dining environments that include a snooker room and period kitchen. Here, food gravitates toward the traditional, with an emphasis on fish, vegetables, and hearty meats.

The brainchild of young up-and-comer António Galapito, PRADO is new on the upscale scene. In this former fish factory's current inception—a swank high-ceilinged venue that spotlights a wall of Roman ruins—the concept is a collaboration of the finest seasonal products served on small tasting plates and biodynamic wines. In homage to the artisan fish shops and seafood eateries of years past, the SEA ME PEIXARIA MODERNA restaurant was created to remind patrons of Lisbon's love of sea-food. Its mix of Japanese cooking techniques and Portuguese ingenuity—boosted by its glass displays of the best indigenous aquatic life—is a perfect way to enjoy the culinary catch of the day. Another Portuguese staple, petiscos (Portugal's answer to Spain's tapas), takes center stage at TAPISCO, top chef Henrique Sá Pessoa's casual restaurant that unites two classic cuisines—Portuguese and Spanish—with-out an ounce of rivalry. The food is prepared in an open kitchen and never fused together as one would expect. Standout dishes from both countries are duly offered. Even the drinks are equally divided—this is the first eatery in Lisbon to serve Spanish vermouth.

Slow the pace at HELLO, KRISTOF, a Scandi-navian-style café with wood tables, racks of art house zines, a selection of coffee blends, and simple but tasty homemade granola, avocado toast, egg scramble, and cake. For fans of both sugar and indulgent new flavors, make a stop at MANTEIGARIA, a former butter shop turned pastel de nata (custard tart) factory. The crispy treat—a national specialty— is prepared on demand to enjoy freshly baked at the counter or gingerly packaged to take home.

The Time Out Market Hall—this huge communal dining space houses the city's best restaurants and bars.

Tucked away on a tranquil street minutes from the bustle of Avenida da Liberdade, the RED FROG takes patrons on a clandestine adventure back to the Roaring Twenties. In true speakeasy style, this dimly lit venue is only accessible after buzzing a bell beneath a wall-mounted frog. Once inside, barmen, dapperly adorned with bowties and suspenders, mix signature swills with names like American Gangster and Walking Dead to the affable beats of swing, jazz, funk, and rock standards. Kick it up a notch at PUREX, a rambunctious haunt for misfits of all stripes and sexual orientations. Located in the gay-happy Bairro Alto district, this fun-loving venue, which features wacky urban decor and seasonal themed parties, hosts a rotating lineup of local DJs that spin the latest electronic dance music near the rarest of bar commodities—a mini dance floor.

In its décor, history, and entertainment, you can feel the burlesque vibe that runs through Pensão Amor.

> Fado, hauntingly melancholic Moorish folk music, is one of Lisbon's most revered traditions. Born on the hilly backstreets of the Alfama district.

A onetime seedy boarding house for lonely sailors that docked at Cais do Sodré, the PENSÃO AMOR lounge and bar has since been reinvented as a curiously convivial nightspot. Visitors can opt to view live burlesque performances or gather for a tipple or two in a number of ambient spaces festooned with graffitied corridors, chandeliered ceilings, and mishmashes of rainbow-hued retro furnishings. For your dancing pleasure, TRUMPS— Lisbon's largest gay club—boasts a duo of dance floors, where you can gyrate to the sounds of pop and house beats. Popular with boys of a younger sensibility, though all are welcome, this treasured

nightspot was the spirited venue of the first international gay festival in Portugal.

Fado, hauntingly melancholic Moorish folk music, is one of Lisbon's most revered traditions. Born on the hilly backstreets of the Alfama district and, in recent years, heard in and about the popular Bairro Alto, this indigenous nineteenth-century genre is here to stay. Built in 1937 and sporting a whimsical façade stained with musician and guitar motifs, ADEGA MACHADO remains one of the oldest fado houses in town. Rows of storytelling vintage photographs are strewn throughout, but the intimate arched main room is where all the magic happens. A humble selection of local bites, paired with wine and a solid 45-minute performance, is available daily. Nearby, A SEVERA is the only Bairro Alto fado restaurant run by the same family since the 1950s. Though the setting is romantic, with candlelit tables and arched azulejos tile murals, the traditional Portuguese dining experience is not the main reason for your visit; it's the nightly string of solo singers and duos with 12-string guitarists that make the venue memorable. For a less formal, impromptu experience, A TASCA DO CHICO is a local institution in the world of fado. A gritty yet mirthful neighborhood bar packed floor to ceiling with framed photos of fado luminaries, it invites new faces to showcase their talents while patrons enjoy wine, conversation, and sausage and cheese nibbles.

Bar staff at the Pensão Amor dress up in sailor outfits in celebration of the venue's past history.

Made evident via its top quality textiles, leather, and bespoke artisan goods, Lisbon's rich cultural heritage meshes effortlessly with modern innovation. Specializing in impeccably tailored fashions, dapper gents flock to ROSA & TEIXEIRA for all their custom clothing needs. From the time-honored to the light side of edgy, this mythical shop offers suits for all occasions, along with casual collections and ensemble-enhancing accessories. For a nostalgic glimpse at yesteryear's household essentials, A VIDA

> For the ultimate unmistakably Portuguese souvenir, venture into the tiny Conserveira de Lisboa for a wide selection of gourmet canned fish in vibrant vintage tins. The true star on the scene is the regional sardine, as evidenced by the stacks of flavors on offer.

Twice weekly in Lisbon's Alfama district, dealers bring their antiques and bric-a-brac to the city's flea market.

PORTUGUESA sells toiletries, fragrant soaps, vintage advertisement posters, and other novelty curios packaged in kitschy, retro designs. Along a similar line, CHAPELARIA AZEVEDO RUA is a centuries-old millinery that still crafts hats and bonnets with artisanal flair. Founded in 1886, this classic shop is lined with wood and glass cases that display a wide collection of headgear, as well as scarves, umbrellas, and, for the nattily dressed man with a penchant for the dramatic, hand-carved walking sticks.

Housed in boho Príncipe Real's onetime Arabic palace Ribeiro da Cunha, EMBAIXADA offers a unique backdrop for scouring through Portuguese clothing, shoes, housewares, furnishings, and gastronomic items. The multilevel space makes full use of its former grandeur by meshing merchandise displays and public spaces with the building's original frescos, sculptures, marble columns, and floor tiles. Whimsically cozy in feel and face, the SAL CONCEPT STORE inspires home design aficionados with custom-made furnishings displayed in a voguish lifestyle setting. Operating in collaboration with the distinguished Branco sobre Branco atelier, this one-stop haven for unique interiors sells everything from boldly hued abstract furniture, decorative conversation pieces, and artwork to home scents and slick lighting.

Canvas pannier bags and panama hats are among the retro-looking gear for the dainty city tourist at Embaixada.

For the ultimate unmistakably Portuguese souvenir, venture into the tiny CONSERVEIRA DE LISBOA for a wide selection of gourmet canned fish in vibrant vintage tins. Kooky at first glance, this buzzy shop has artfully preserved the product and packaging of three iconic local brands: Minor, Tricana, and Prato do Mar. Although mackerel, tuna, and other aquatic morsels are sold in pickled, salted, spiced, and oiled varieties, the true star on the scene is the regional sardine, as evidenced by the stacks of flavors on offer.

For lovers of art in all its forms, Lisbon is a virtual goldmine of inspiration. Galleries and museums that range from classic to offbeat complement the city's colorful cultural aesthetic, and intricate tile murals, stately monuments, and street-style artwork greet visitors at every turn.

> ## Between viewings, take a breather in Museu Calouste Gulbenkian's surrounding manicured gardens, which are among the largest in Lisbon.

A well-rounded experience awaits at the MUSEU CALOUSTE GULBENKIAN, a popular attraction divided into two contrasting sections: the first houses a once private collection of international art pieces dating from antiquity to the early twentieth century, and the second offers over 10,000 modern Portuguese paintings, sculptures, and installations. Between viewings, take a breather in the surrounding manicured gardens, among the largest in Lisbon. In keeping with today's trends, discover emerging artists at UNDERDOGS GALLERY, a collaborative creative space hosting of-the-moment urban art projects and exhibitions designed to bring together key players from the contemporary art scene.

Compare and contrast at LX FACTORY, a former nineteenth-century textile mill transformed into a dynamic showroom for avant-garde architects, fashion designers, and media specialists to display their modish industrial wares. Trade your exhibitions for disinhibition at BEACH 19, a gay-friendly, clothing-optional stretch of golden sand just a short drive from the city center. Located on the south side of Costa da Caparica, this quiet haven's pristine beaches and pleasant climate make it a must-visit for the LGBTQ community.

The work of Lisbon-based visual artist Akacorleone is on display, among the exhibits at the Underdogs Gallery.

Proudly promoting equality and diversity for over 20 years, ARRAIAL LISBOA PRIDE is Portugal's largest and most highly anticipated LGBTQ event. Situated on the riverfront square Terreiro do Paço, the 12-hour free festival features a packed agenda of children's activities, craft wares, workshops, and street eats. Once the sun goes down, the convivial space transforms into a cavernous dance floor with pole-dancing shows, concerts, and inspired DJ sets. Summer kicks off with the month-long FESTAS DE LISBOA, a spectacular citywide celebration boasting outdoor live music parties, ornate decorations, and a lively parade commemorating St. Anthony, Lisbon's patron saint. During this festive period, the streets, particularly in and around the hilly Alfama district, are overrun with nightly impromptu fado performances, street musicians, and buzzing bar patrons taking their reveling into the wee hours.

A must for contemporary jazz lovers, JAZZ EM AGOSTO is an open-air extravaganza that features the multifaceted genre's most up-and-coming and revered talents from around the world. Held in the sprawling garden amphitheater of the Gulbenkian Foundation since 1984, this 10-day music fest is widely considered to be among Lisbon's best.

Waving the rainbow flag at Arraial Lisboa Pride, usually held in the month of June.

A leisurely 30-minute drive west of central Lisbon, CASCAIS, a former sleepy fishing village and fabled summer stomping ground of Portugal's King Luís I, has since evolved into a holiday hotspot for sun-soakers seeking a brief respite from urban living. Harboring a trio of scenic bays, the seaside resort town offers a collection of diverse golden beach scenarios. Praia da Rainha is the smallest and most secluded of the local sands, while Praia da Conceição and Praia da Duquesa offer roomier stretches and a slew of water-based activities. Enjoy a change of environment a bike ride away at Praia do Guincho, a windy beach with rugged terrains and wild, surf-perfect waves. During warmer months, the town center is abuzz with alfresco seafood dining, tony boutiques, and a fairy-tale square with theatrical pavement tiles resembling waves. Excursions of note include hikes to the westernmost point in Europe, Cabo da Roca, a savage, rocky landscape with raging waters, and to the Condes de Castro Guimarães museum—inside the Marechal Carmona gardens—a mock Gothic-style castle displaying artwork and furnishings from a local official's private collection. Among the more interesting displays is a six-teenth-century manuscript containing one of the oldest surviving depictions of Lisbon.

To the west of the city, the Praia do Guincho is known for the massive waves that roll in from the Atlantic Ocean.

CLAIM IT

1. 40 Winks
2. Ham Yard Hotel
3. Qbic
4. The Curtain
5. The Zetter Townhouse

SAVOR IT

6. Bistrotheque
7. Berners Tavern
8. Bob Bob Ricard
9. Dishoom
10. MEATmission
11. Morito
12. Noble Rot
13. Poppie's

CELEBRATE IT

14. Bloc South
15. Dalston Superstore
16. Roundhouse
17. Royal Vauxhall Tavern
18. Savage
19. The Glory
20. The Queen Adelaide
21. The Tiger

OWN IT

22. Bonds
23. Dover Street Market
24. Fortnum & Mason
25. Gay's The Word
26. Konditor & Cook
27. Liberty
28. Murdock
29. We Built This City

EXPLORE IT

30. Barbican
31. Hampstead Heath
32. Newport Street Gallery
33. Sadler's Wells
34. Sky Garden

LONDON

A Thoroughly Modern Metropolis

London is one of those extra special cities that thrives when the going gets tough. Despite an unsteady political climate, shared with many of the world's global cities, England's capital is currently at its best. Widely acknowledged to have the largest gay population in Europe, it adapts quickly, and caters for locals and guests in equal measure. With 300 nationalities speaking 270 languages, the city is more tolerant and diverse than ever—London is very firmly open.

The city has a rich LGBTQ cultural history, with many different neighborhoods catering to different gay agendas. Soho, Earl's Court, and Clapham still thrive with a mix of established venues and new spaces, while in the East End's Dalston and Hackney you'll find some of the most unique places in the world. Pride in London draws thousands to the city and, while it has suffered a similar straightwashing as other Prides, London has a mammoth program of other LGBTQ events all year round.

Home of the Queen and countless other queens, it is the birthplace of Byron, Bowie, and Beckham. From the Gothic revival of the Palace of Westminster to the macho, ultra-modernism of The Shard, London is famed for its architecture, alongside being a center for art, finance, culture, and music, of course. But in a city where everyone and his brother know about the old, how do you connect with the new?

Some smaller European metropolises struggle to offer the same experience as a single London suburb. It feels like four different cities: north, south, east, and west, all battling against each other. But scratch beneath its familiar surface and there is much to enjoy in the United Kingdom's capital, from an unrivaled world cuisine scene to a wealth of pansexual artists busily shaping the city's newest, hippest neighborhoods. A visitor who celebrates the old and embraces the new will be the most rewarded.

As you can imagine, London has its fair share of decadent dorms. Mix with Shoreditch's hipsters at THE CURTAIN, where residents can exploit the benefits of this slick, sexy members' club. More of a cultural hub than a regular hotel, it boasts a rooftop pool, bars, a dining room, and even a ballroom, while

Described as "The most charming hotel in England," 40 Winks only has two bedrooms.

the bedrooms have a modern industrial feel that will enhance any Instagram feed. The equally photogenic HAM YARD HOTEL, the latest addition to Firmdale Hotels' impressive portfolio, has an enviable location in the heart of Soho making it the perfect spot from which to explore London's sexy, seedy center. It also boasts individually designed rooms, as well as apartments, a roof terrace, screening room, and even a 1950s-style bowling alley.

THE ZETTER TOWNHOUSE in Clerkenwell mixes all the luxury of a super hotel with the intimacy of a B&B—something that's hard to come across in this mad metropolis. An award-winning Georgian townhouse, it's equal parts eccentric and welcoming, with rooms evoking memories of visits to aging relatives in the best possible way. The design-led interiors of QBIC offer laid-back cool with heart, for this is also London's self-styled green hotel. Credentials include recycled and reloved furniture, renewable energy sources, a bike loan service, and free drinks at the bar for guests who choose not to have their room serviced. All this at prices that won't threaten your wallet, which makes it particularly popular with solo travelers. Lastly, for a truly unique experience, 40 WINKS will tick your boxes and tickle your fancy. Described by Brazilian Vogue as "The most charming hotel in England," it only has two bedrooms, each individually decorated in an unrivaled, camp fashion. Feel like Diana Ross as you perch on the porcelain throne, complete with gold leaf walls.

Gold-leaf wallpaper and numerous curios and objets d'art set the scene in the living room at 40 Winks.

Navigating the London restaurant scene is a bit like navigating Grindr: too much choice. But, also like Grindr, often the old ones are the best, and Hackney's BISTROTHEQUE is living proof. It's the perfect brunch location—you can enjoy a traditional English fry-up with a contemporary twist, while resident ivory tinkler, Xavier, plays pop tunes on the piano making *Love Machine* and *Like a Virgin* sound like unearthed Elgars. Dinner ain't half bad, either. If it's unpretentious food you're looking for, MORITO is your man. This family of restaurants brings summer tastes to London in three locations, but the best is its latest opening in Hackney. A slick concrete interior provides an airy, laid-back feel that complements the restaurant's Mediterranean fare.

The West End offers a dizzying display of the finest restaurants in the world. Many have succumbed to BOB BOB RICARD's infamous "press for champagne" button as they gorge on the restaurant's exemplary fare. This dimly lit Soho icon, with its all-booth interior, serves more champagne than any other bar in the United Kingdom, apparently. Wash down its meaty,

The minimalist interior of Bistrotheque, set on the first floor of what used to be a clothing factory.

Want to try local cuisine? Well, London is the curry capital of the world.

mouth-watering menu with one of its 20 varieties of fizz. A short walk away, the BERNERS TAVERN's breathtaking dining room is popular with local and international celebrities—and it's easy to see why. This is the creation of renowned chef Jason Atherton, a former Gordon Ramsay protégé who could now teach the old dog a thing or two. Try the British seafood selection or the Scottish beef burger—the latter being a hilarious juxtaposition to this

Bagels packed with salt beef, dill pickle, and mustard are a hot favorite at Brick Lane's Beigel Bake.

decadent setting, which is lined with hundreds of framed photographs and paintings, from whimsical sketches to Old Masters.

Want to try local cuisine? Well, London is the curry capital of the world and has more Indian restaurants than Mumbai and Delhi combined. With five locations across the city, DISHOOM is a firm favorite, whisking you away to a bygone era of the British Empire with its rich interiors and playful menu. The Bombay breakfast is a delicious antidote to the English staple but the dinner menu, packed with sharing dishes, is the highlight. For that other staple, good old fish 'n' chips, POPPIE'S does it best. Its ambition was to recreate the wartime restaurants of the 1940s and 50s, and it succeeds with aplomb thanks to the staff uniforms, mishmash interiors, meals served in paper, and sauces spilling out of jars.

Elsewhere, amongst the achingly hip menswear and lifestyle stores of Lamb's Conduit Street, lies NOBLE ROT, a wine bar and restaurant serving locally sourced produce. A grown-up venue, the decor harks back to an older world, with dark wood panels and crisp white napkins. Food is strictly British, with hearty haute meals served alongside a wine for every palate. Finally, for the city's best burger, head to MEATMISSION. Enjoy Gilbert & George artworks as you sink your teeth into their heaven-sent meat (Meatmission's, not the artists') and don't miss the artery-clogging Hippie Fries, smothered in grilled onions and a delicious sauce.

With camp and kitsch, the Queen Adelaide attracts local art students, Romantics, and members of the fash pack.

To the east, where Hackney and Dalston compete for the title of London's hippest homo hub, unrivaled club nights reflect what it means to be queer in the city today. There are plenty of pansexual parties: DALSTON SUPERSTORE, a bar-cum-club on Kingsland Road, offers a diverse lineup, with everything from a Naked Boys Reading Brunch to sleazy Saturday night discos. Founded by London legend Jonny Woo, THE GLORY is the city's latest home of drag and performance, where you'll find a host of competitions and shows all through the week. Split over two levels, it also doubles up as a traditional pub with real ales where you can try it on with the locals.

Hosted by the polysexual Sink the Pink posse, SAVAGE is a debauched disco for all that's held weekly at Metropolis, once Bethnal Green's most notorious strip club. Its labyrinth of rooms and stripper poles lends itself well to a big gay disco. Pre-Savagers can be found mixing with London menswear designers at THE QUEEN ADELAIDE a few doors down—a spot full of old-fashioned charm. The bar's belly was also a former strip club; London can reimagine venues like no other city.

Allegedly, you're never more than seven meters away from a pub in London, and it has the best in the world. Options are plenty, but choose well: avoid big chains like Wetherspoon or anything with a suspicious Irish name above the door. THE TIGER in Homerton is a new venture that locals are fond of, with a gay-ish mentality, good food, and packed parties at weekends. For a more traditional experience, the ROYAL VAUXHALL TAVERN is a stalwart. Featuring performers who aren't influenced by the latest influx of dames, expect classic, bawdy, smut-filled drag. The RVT also hosts some of the most popular club nights, like Duckie, the most inclusive pop party in the city. And there's still plenty happening in the debauched arches of Vauxhall. BLOC SOUTH (East Bloc's seedy younger sister) is a firm favorite and hosts Brüt every Friday. A men-only muscle fest, the organizers have finally realized that there's a thirst for music that isn't just hi-NRG remixes of Céline Dion. If all that sounds too exhausting, the ROUNDHOUSE in Camden is one of London's greatest live music venues. The world's biggest stars have performed inside this unique Grade II–listed building.

London invented the department store, and LIBERTY is its best. Do you know why the perfume counter is always placed at the front? Traditionally, it was to mask the smell of horses dropping off insatiable shoppers. You won't see many horses these days, but Liberty's mock-Tudor façade is just the start of this icon's charm. Enter the scarf room and adore the architecture of the oak atrium, or go down below for a wide selection of the latest menswear from British favorites such as Oliver Spencer and Paul Smith to contemporary Parisian and Nordic designers. Another firm favorite is DOVER STREET MARKET, where a visit is essential even if you have absolutely no intention of buying an exorbitant Commes des Garçons kaftan. The vision of Japanese designer Rei Kawakubo, this multilevel concept store features ambitious visual merchandising in its maze of rooms. A celebration of creativity, the interior is a riot of color and materials—lose yourself in there for an hour or two; you won't regret it. A short sashay down Piccadilly lies the FORTNUM & MASON department store, home to the city's—nay, the world's—most decadent food hall. It supplies Her Majesty's provisions and Prince Charles's tea—did you ever read a more British sentence? Here you'll find high-quality produce, from fruit to foie gras, with 300 years of history.

The east offers an unrivaled selection of independent stores. The brainchild of Niko Dafkos and Paul Firmin, BONDS was set up to create a

Murdock London has outlets in Shoreditch, Soho, and several other locations.

All Murdock outlets have the same traditional barber vibe.

world around their travel-inspired fragrance line Earl of East London, which includes scented candles that make the perfect souvenir. Pick up other unique gifts at WE BUILT THIS CITY, a souvenir shop without a *Keep Calm and Carry On* magnet in sight. Instead, you'll find dog toys modeled on the United Kingdom's most notorious politicians, lust-worthy screenprints, and a host of other products perfect for Londonphiles.

A pilgrimage to GAY'S THE WORD, the United Kingdom's only LGBTQ bookstore, won't disappoint. The location for many pivotal moments in our history, it was the headquarters of the legendary Lesbians and Gays Support the Miners alliance that was well documented in the movie *Pride* (2014). With the constant threat of rising rents, the store has had more comebacks than Cher, but its future looks secure for now thanks to prolific campaigning.

For grooming, head to MURDOCK, where a handsome team will make you feel like a million dollars. Styled on traditional barbershops and offering cuts and treatments, this is a quintessentially British experience. While you're there, stock up on its wide range of beard oils and skincare products. Then there's KONDITOR & COOK, the city's best purveyor of sweet treats. Gay-owned and gay-run, you'll find saccharine snacks with salacious names like the Fudge Packer brownie and gingerbread men with erections. It's the cake version of a *Carry On* film, and we love it.

Niko Dafkos restocks the shelves with Earl of East London candles at his Bonds store in Hackney.

Nothing is more rewarding than a vast view of a city, and few places are more inspiring than the SKY GARDEN, an observation deck the size of an airport hanger at the top of Rafael Viñoly's 20 Fenchurch Street. The starchitect's bulging phallus, nicknamed the "Walkie Talkie" by Londoners, affords stunning views of the entire city. For a more natural vista, there's HAMPSTEAD HEATH. George Michael once sang "Let's go outside," and the Heath was one of the icon's favorite outdoor spaces. Here, he would allegedly, in his own words, service the community. For all its old-school connotations, though, the Heath is a magnificent green space offering an unrivaled view of the capital. At the north of the park is the stately Kenwood House, with its breathtaking interiors and stunning art collection, and to the east is the glorious men's bathing pool—so you can admire the male form in painting or in real life.

The arts program at the Barbican includes architectural tours of the vast, brutalist estate.

a hotspot for all things arts and culture. Its gallery has a reputation as one of the city's best exhibition spaces, with previous shows covering a diverse range of topics from Bauhaus to Viktor & Rolf, while its theater presents a rolling program of Shakespeare, modern plays, and dance. If it's the latter you're after, though, SADLER'S WELLS is the place to be. The world's leading center for international dance, its contemporary and classic performances are sure to inspire.

The Sadler's Wells theater in London's Clerkenwell neighborhood attracts high-class dance troupes from around the world.

London is a city packed full of inspiring art, and after you've been inside the big ones, there are heaps of others to explore. Damien Hirst built NEWPORT STREET GALLERY to house his ample art collection and even bigger ego, and it's one of the finest galleries in London. The space runs solo and group shows—a Jeff Koons retrospective is a previous highlight. Here's hoping Hirst will show off his Picassos, Emins, and Bacons soon. Secondly, the BARBICAN is a Brutalist behemoth worth a visit for the architecture alone, but the venue's center is

Many of London's historic sites can be seen from along the London River Walk.

London is the art capital of the world, and the ROYAL ACADEMY SUMMER EXHIBITION, held every year since 1769, is the jewel in its crown. This mammoth, all-inclusive show contains more than 1,000 works carefully selected from artist's submissions, with amateur works hung alongside pieces by world-famous names. The city's LGBTQ festival, MIGHTY HOOPLA, rewrites the rules of British music festivals with a colorful one-day riot of pop music, pleasure, personality, and performance. It's a shameless celebration of sexuality set in the city's glorious Brockwell Park.

London's Royal Academy summer exhibition runs for almost all of June, July, and August.

> George Michael once sang "Let's go outside," and the Heath was one of the icon's favorite outdoor spaces. Here, he would allegedly, in his own words, service the community.

For theater lovers, REGENT'S PARK OPEN AIR season is not to be missed and signals that summer has arrived. Since 1932, the outdoor theatre has hosted major plays and performances in its unique circular setting—just don't forget your brolly. Another truly unique scene awaits at SECRET CINEMA, an immersive movie experience that brings cult classics and contemporary releases to life. Transforming obscure London locations, previous screenings have included *One Flew Over the Cuckoo's Nest* set in an abandoned hospital, and *Moulin Rouge!* complete with busty strumpets and six-pack-blessed trapeze artists.

In recent years, the Mighty Hoopla, a bright and colorful festival, has attracted as many as 20,000 fans.

ESCAPE IT

Dubbed London-by-the-Sea, Brighton has attractions to rival London.

A mere hour away from the hustle and bustle of the capital, the great British seaside awaits. BRIGHTON is so much more than Brits in bathers, though; a warm, generous community awaits those who seek it out. Brighton Pride forms the center of the city's LGBTQ program and attracts big-name artists, but the city is at its best all year round, with count-less bars, restaurants, stores, and galleries that cater for all tastes. The city's liberal, bohemian attitude has long been attractive to LGBTQ folk and their friends, and remains firmly so.

IN LONDON, DRAWING THE EVER EVOLVING

Josh McKenna

Cornwall-born illustrator Josh McKenna makes minimal pastel-hued creations that balance bold, dynamic, and often homoerotic themes. It's a profession that destined him for the English capital. Speaking of the seaside town he grew up in, he explains, "I had to escape as soon as I could to explore my creativity and, in turn, my sexuality."

He recalls first landing in London as a young man. "Party days in nu-rave Shoreditch" with "likeminded characters: creative, adventurous, excited by life." But after a few years, he left. "I wanted to knuckle down and do something with my creativity," he says. "So I studied back in Cornwall. Later, as a somewhat grown-up graduate, I knew I had to be in London for the career opportunities. There, I had access to exhibitions, galleries, magazine publishers, creative platforms."

"I was pretty relentless," he says of his early days back in the city. "I'd make contacts and constantly update them with my work, probably at an annoying pace. But it seemed to work." Networking always came naturally in the neighborhood Josh calls home: the east. "From the grimier parts of Dalston to the lush greens of London Fields, where I live, it's full of other creatives doing exciting things," he explains.

He shares his Dalston studio with some of these artist types, including other illustrators. "Having them for feedback and opinions on a day-to-day basis is incredibly helpful," he says. "We connect with others in the building, meet for drinks, go to openings, exhibitions. It's at these events we bump into other illustrators, art directors, commissioners, publishers. You're reminded how small it actually is, how nice it is to find out what

everybody's up to." Josh calls London's illustration scene "fundamental," "like a family network," and "a place to be proud of your peers," and he talks of leaving "the feeling of competition within illustration at university."

All of this might make the Big Smoke sound like an artists' utopia, but the city's not without its downsides. "Money's always an issue in London," Josh says. "It's an expensive place to live, let alone to pursue a freelance career in a very overpopulated sector. I've always needed a part-time job to support my illustration. I pretty much worked seven days a week for a long time. It's only in the last couple of years I've been able to work solely on illustration, which at the beginning was daunting, but paid off massively."

Since then Josh has created perhaps his most signature work to date: a playfully queer

"London's a huge place but within this community, it feels very personal."

Instagram sticker of a broad-shouldered, red-heeled dancer, which went on to inspire a four-meter-wide mural for London's Pride in 2017. "Since its creation I've been propelled into doing amazing work for some really big clients," says Josh. "It's taking me to Sydney Mardi Gras too, so watch this space."

It's Londoners like that illustrated dancer—not unlike the creatures of the night you might see walking the streets of Dalston—that inspire Josh's work on a daily basis.

"We see some of the craziest characters on our lunch run," he says. "Big afros, colorful shirts, big butts, and sassy women on the market all make it into my work, as well as the trendy kids walking around."

He finds further inspiration, not to mention support, from within London's "close-knit" LGBTQ community. "It feels like that as a gay man I am part of a supportive, all-inclusive community that is there for one another. London's a huge place but within this community, it feels very personal. I've been here for

most of the last 10 years and seeing the sense of pride that gay people have in London compared to how it used to be has been a major change."

Nevertheless, Josh admits his relationship with London is changing. "I feel like it's time to try somewhere new," he says. "My work can be done remotely, I can be anywhere—this question comes when it's ice cold on my cycle to work." But wherever he goes, Josh will always connected to London. "It's ever evolving, as am I," he says. "It feels like we're doing it together."

Griffith Park

Glendale

West Hollywood

Santa Monica Blvd

Beverly
Hills

Santa Monica Blvd

Sunset Blvd

Wilshire Blvd

Santa Monica Fwy

Downtown

CLAIM IT

1 Hotel Covell

2 Kimpton
La Peer Hotel

3 Petit Ermitage

4 The Ambrose

5 The NoMad Hotel

SAVOR IT

6 A.O.C.

7 Alfred Melrose
Place

8 Bavel

9 Café Gratitude

10 Craig's

11 Norah

12 République

13 Sawyer

CELEBRATE IT

14 AKBAR

15 E.P.&L.P.

16 Moonlight
Rollerway

17 Precinct

18 The Chapel
at The Abbey

OWN IT

19 Cactus Store

20 Carlton Drew

21 County Ltd.

22 The Elder Statesman

23 Garrett Leight
California Optical

24 Melrose Place
Farmers Market

EXPLORE IT

25 Griffith Park

26 Marciano Art
Foundation

27 Phoenix Effect

28 Tom of Finland
Foundation

29 Will Rogers
State Beach

LOS ANGELES

Judge the Book by Its Cover

Los Angeles, the city of many unfulfilled dreams, is repeatedly defined according to what it is not—New York City. That is because there is a resistance to LA based on sometimes true but often unsubstantiated myths: LA is the land of frivolous celebrity, crowded freeways, shallow people, and, of course, no culture. To challenge or dispel these myths, one simply needs to approach LA differently. Do as the natives do—you may find it delusional, but it's not called La La Land for nothing.

Forty percent of West Hollywood residents are gay, making it the largest gay city in the United States. But the boys flock beyond West Hollywood, too, into areas like Silver Lake and Downtown that offer completely different aesthetics and vibes. And LA's diversity extends beyond sexuality—only here can you go to a Gay and Lesbian Armenian Society picnic and then jaunt over to Club Cobra, LA's best Latino gay bar.

The universal discourse of LA is, of course, film and television. Home to such classics as *Gone with the Wind* and *Brokeback Mountain,*the city is responsible for celebrating LGBTQ experiences globally by opening the celluloid closet. With its glorious warm weather, beautiful people, and remarkably great food, the constantly revived film capital of the world is beckoning—so put on your thigh-hugging shorts and embrace your inner superficiality.

Tucked away on a small residential street just north of Santa Monica Boulevard is West Hollywood's bohemian, artsy enclave, the PETIT ERMITAGE. Unassuming at first, in part because of its verdant, vine-enshrouded exterior, the hotel becomes a wonderland once you pass the alligator-with-fire-torch statue at the entrance. Owned by two brothers, Adrian and Severyn Ashkenazy, the pied-à-terre-style retreat is meticulously decorated with their family's own art collection, including pieces by Joan Miró and Salvador Dalí. From the hand-woven carpet to the antique roof tiles, each aspect of the hotel contains a story from the brothers' travels.

If you go down the street to the other side of Santa Monica Boulevard and veer to the edge of West Hollywood, just before Beverly Hills, you will find KIMPTON LA PEER HOTEL, which has created its own space for enjoying LA with its lively pool

Hotel Covell boasts a private sundeck at rooftop level, complete with loungers and bar.

The kitchen and sunroom of a two-bedroom master suite at Hotel Covell.

The suites at Hotel Covell combine French charm with New York aesthetics and a dash of playful seventies vibe.

bar, stylish rooms, impeccable service, and plenty of eye candy. Here, it is easy to imagine you are an LA native while at the pool sipping on kombucha from the breakfast bar. If you are more into a tall-building, big-city environment with a little more grit, then venture to Downtown Los Angeles (DTLA, to locals) and check into THE NOMAD HOTEL. Like its branch in New York City, the NoMad gives tribute to Los Angeles's surprisingly rich history—Europeans, please don't laugh—as the hotel takes residence in the historic building Giannini Place,

a former bank built in the Roaring Twenties. A mélange of Italian sophistication and Californian mellowness singed with art deco decor, this hotel is a gift for those who appreciate a space adorned with vibrant colors and disparate textures.

Just on the edge of Silver Lake—LA's more alternative gayborhood—lies a smaller non-descript boutique hotel off Hollywood Boulevard, HOTEL COVELL. From Parisian atelier to 1950s New York, each suite at Hotel Covell is uniquely designed in an apartment style, with walk-in showers, kitchenettes, and herringbone hardwood flooring. Don't miss the hotel's Bar Covell, a snug and welcoming abode with an impeccable selection of wine, all available by the glass.

If all that comes to mind when you think of Los Angeles is driving along the Pacific Coast Highway in a red convertible Mustang with the top down—not recommended, by the way, as you will burn your head when stuck in traffic—then naturally head west to Santa Monica. Embedded in a quaint residential neighborhood, THE AMBROSE is walking distance to the beach and the Santa Monica Pier. With its ever-so-charming craftsman-style interior, the hotel embraces natural colors and materials to reflect California's breezy approach to living, which is particularly present in this part of town. Here you can take notice of some of the techies surfing on Silicon Beach on their lunch breaks.

The best-kept secret in LA is its food scene. From Korean barbeque and Persian *koobideh* to Israeli falafel and Mexican pastries, the cuisine is multifaceted and authentic. "Ethnic" food is so embedded within any Angeleno's daily life that it is no longer "ethnic." NORAH in West Hollywood makes perfect use of LA's diverse heritage to create truly awe-inspiring dishes that blur the lines between the familiar and exotic. Afterward, hop across the street to Hamburger Mary's to play drag bingo.

Almost every guy remembers Jake from the television show *Melrose Place*. What people may not know is that there is an actual Melrose Place. It is not, however, an apartment building with a pool, but a small, elegant street with high-end shops. Spot the many Jake wannabes that are just as hot, if not hotter, at ALFRED MELROSE PLACE, a quintessentially LA coffee shop. Yes, here the coffee and pastries are good, but the scene, especially for visitors, is better. Order your coffee and stay around to watch the women with midriff tops and Kardashian-style hair look at their phones, gorgeous men talk to their friends about the music video they just produced, or the struggling screenwriter with his laptop and writer's block.

For brunch, head east to the hipsterville that is Silver Lake and enjoy the fanciful California fare at SAWYER. Light, bright, and airy, Sawyer has a serene feel and ingenious cocktail list. Although the restaurant focuses on seafood, particularly its lobster roll and fish tacos, there are definitely more traditional brunch options, like cornmeal blueberry pancakes, eggs benedict, and poached eggs with kale and quinoa. Ask to sit in the front of their dining area so you can watch the Sunset Boulevard strollers.

If you are staying in West Hollywood and want to go downtown for the day, stop by Larchmont Village, an Angeleno favorite. Here you will find the best place to eat if you are vegan or simply fancy vegan food, CAFE GRATITUDE. Apart from producing quality, healthy food, the restaurant's mission, as its name suggests, is to give thanks. In fact, ordering here involves stating an affirmation: the items on the menu have inspired names, like "Gracious" or "Fabulous," both of which are properly ordered by stating, "I am Gracious" or "I am Fabulous," respectively. Before you know it, you'll feel the urge to yell, "I am Irresistible" (coconut cream pie).

DTLA has a wide selection of dining options, and the list keeps on growing in this part of Los Angeles. Each restaurant attempts to push the limit by offering provocative dishes that are both novel and familiar, and the same goes for aesthetics. Case in point is BAVEL. Quartered within a naturally lit warehouse, it challenges the dark, ornate, and exotic design of other Middle Eastern dining venues. An LA city treasure, RÉPUBLIQUE is an all-day restaurant that becomes alive at dinner time with packed seats, lively chatter, and illuminated ambiance that keeps you in your seat wanting more. Originally built in 1928 for Charlie Chaplin, the space maintains its Hollywood charm with a Provençal twist, luring devoted customers in with its white brick walls and geometric tile flooring.

Similar to DTLA, West Hollywood also has a considerable number of quality restaurants. One of the more established eateries in this neighborhood is A. O. C., a Spanish-style casita with an enchanting courtyard engulfed by creeping figs and candlelight. Before or after stuffing your face with their tapas-style dishes, fervently imbibe their spicy yet refreshing Green Goddess cocktail, a concoction of green tea-infused vodka, cucumber, jalapeno, and absinthe.

Visitors often complain that they never see celebrities in Los Angeles. However, the one restaurant where you are likely to spot one is CRAIG'S in West Hollywood. Although its name makes it sound like a taco stand opened by an 18-year-old surfer dude, it is an upscale but still approachable steakhouse that various A, B, and even C list celebrities frequent.

Flooded with natural light, the main dining room at Bavel has a backdrop of bare brick walls.

The traditional Middle Eastern menu at Bavel includes such dishes as slow-cook tagines (pictured).

Los Angeles may not have the grandiose skyline that New York City does, but when sitting at a rooftop bar in LA, at least most of the year you will not beg for a blanket. Start your night up high at E. P. & L. P. where the unobstructed skyline allows you to take in the illuminated mansions of the Hollywood Hills. Sit back and watch the LA crowd love themselves as you consume the special mezcal, passion fruit, and chili lime cocktail as a pre-dinner drink.

LA may be known for its image-first Hollywood glamour tableau, but it has also mastered a carefree, light-hearted way of being.

Naturally, the gayest city in America has to have the most popular gay bar and club in the country. The welcoming ABBEY in West Hollywood is just that—and it also has restaurant, lest we forget—drawing crowds of men as well as a sizable female audience, despite recently banning bachelorette parties. The Abbey has gotten so big that it purchased the space next door and created THE CHAPEL, which has another bar and club space, and even more "professional" go-go dancers that entertain your eyes while you're not listening to your friends talk to you. Often described as The Abbey's scruffier, older brother, AKBAR is the Eastside's answer to West Hollywood. After a few drinks, you might finally realize that if you veer to your left at the entrance, there is a passageway that leads to a more humble club space. If you like disco and happen to be there on the first Saturday of the month, partake in some seventies hedonism at the club's Full Frontal Disco night.

If you're looking for a grander club where you can escape the more chiseled prettiness of West Hollywood, go to the largest gay club in DTLA,

Head to the L. P. rooftop bar for a tantalizing selection of specialty cocktails and bar snacks.

Just as the sun is about to go down, fans of the E. P. & L. P. enterprise jostle for seats at the rooftop bar.

PRECINCT. Dance, sweat, and drink in this more lewd club scene, where gay men of different shapes, sizes, and ages go to watch one of the best drag shows in town, dance to mixed and flipped eighties music, and, believe it or not, make friends.

To the world, LA may be known for its image-first Hollywood glamour tableau, but it has also mastered a carefree, light-hearted way of being that other American cities can't seem to. If you're looking for a less intense night out with a sense of community, drive a little further east to Glendale and go down memory lane at Moonlight Rollerway's RAINBOW SKATE NIGHT. A fun alternative to the bar scene, the LGBTQ roller skate night happens every Wednesday.

The distinctive signage of Akbar on Sunset Boulevard. "We are Akbar. Love it or leave it."

Formality is not LA's style: you don't have to wear a button-down or turtleneck—why would you anyway?—to go to a nice restaurant. COUNTY LTD. in Silver Lake is the ideal men's boutique if you gravitate to a more casual hipster look, and its clothes are made of top-quality material from around the world. Angelenos also flock here for unique home goods, from chairs and pots to clocks and cups. As expressed in its "T-shirts and

West 3rd Street is one of the few walkable stretches in town that is lined with various restaurants, bars, clothing shops, and design stores, which are all uniquely LA.

chairs" tagline, the store focuses on the male aesthete rather than a particular type of product. Although it is warm most of the year, many visitors don't know that it can actually become cold during the evenings in Los Angeles. When that's the case, visit THE ELDER STATESMAN and purchase one of their well-crafted cashmere sweaters.

Garrett Leight California Optical is known for its stylish, but pared down, ultimately functional designs.

West 3rd Street is one of the few walkable stretches in town that is lined with various restaurants, bars, clothing shops, and design stores, which are all uniquely LA. For a preppy look, or if you simply need a cute bathing suit, go to CARLTON DREW, a gay-owned men's fashion line designed by Drew himself. La Brea Avenue in LA's Mid-Wilshire area is another shopping district that is increasingly hailed as a pedestrian haven, and it has even more clothing and accessory options. Here, you can accessorize the window to your soul—or simply cover your botox—with handmade sunglasses from GARRETT LEIGHT CALIFORNIA OPTICAL, experts on eyewear products that are inspired by LA's nonchalant, quirky lifestyle.

"Desert" is a common misnomer applied Los Angeles. No need to fret, however, because you can still experience the desert aesthetic right here in LA at the CACTUS STORE. Located on a small street in Echo Park, the shop specializes in rare and bizarre varieties of cacti. On another green note, California, as the largest agricultural producer in America, has some of the best produce around. At the MELROSE PLACE FARMERS MARKET you can find the freshest local fruit and vegetables in LA. Although small compared to other farmers markets, on a Sunday morning it's one of the best places to people-watch, grab a croissant from a French bakery, or buy a jar of local honey.

Plants at the Cactus Store are often harvested from the real desert rather than raised in a nursery.

Whether you admit it or not, comfortably warm weather throughout the year is hard to resist. So although it is most popular in summertime, the beach is not necessarily a seasonal thing in LA, especially for the men who flock to WILL ROGERS STATE BEACH, the city's unofficial gay beach. Blithely dubbed "Ginger Rogers," it provides everything one imagines for an LA fun-in-the-sun outing, with fit, hard bodies playing beach volleyball and bronzed mature men relaxing in the sun. California, after all, did have a foreign-born governor who trained at Gold's Gym in Venice—clue: "Hasta la vista, baby." From CrossFit and yoga to spin and Pilates, Angelenos simply love their gyms. For those not taking exercise too seriously, working out has even become one of the top ways to socialize. PHOENIX EFFECT off Melrose Avenue is one of those independent gyms that many gay men flock to, taking workout classes offered by professional trainers. The less intense activity of hiking is equally embedded in the LA social/workout scene. There are many trekking options throughout the city, but the most reliably entertaining, with stunning views, is GRIFFITH PARK, a large stretch of hilly land that encompasses the Griffith Observatory, LA Zoo, and, of course, the Hollywood Sign.

If you don't want a vacation that consists of moving too much of your body, then fondle the very much underrated, constantly up-and-coming art scene in Los Angeles. There are many options for enjoying art in LA—but guess who opened up a beautiful art space in a former Scottish Rite Mason Temple? Guess. No, really, in 2017, the Guess denim mogul brothers, Paul and Maurice Marciano, founded the MARCIANO ART FOUNDATION, a collection of established, mid-career, and emerging artists that showcases LA's vibrant and ground-breaking art culture. In a small turn-of-the-century craftsman-style house in Echo Park, you will find a display of homoerotic art from a Finnish guy known as Tom of Finland. The house he lived in is now the TOM OF FINLAND FOUNDATION, a non-profit organization dedicated to promoting his work. The institution often hosts exhibitions and events for erotic art lovers, such as drawing workshops or Wednesday Tea Salons. Leather is always welcomed.

For those not taking exercise too seriously, working out has even become one of the top ways to socialize.

The Griffith Observatory sits on the south-facing slope of Mount Hollywood and provides spectacular views over the city.

To get the most out of your trip to the Southern California seascape, take a ride on the Pacific Surfliner.

Many cities throughout the world have a film festival that showcases LGBTQ actors, writers, directors, and stories. For obvious reasons, the one that has the biggest clout is Los Angeles's OUTFEST. Nowhere in the world does a film festival like this one get so much backing from local and international communities. Taking place every July, the festival is also a way to explore the city, especially if you enjoy watching films, since many of them are screened in various locations that pull many enthusiastic locals.

There is really no place like home in West Hollywood. Here, for the span of one particular night, you could see over 50 hairy, muscular men dressed in long auburn pigtails, blue gingham dresses with frills peeping out, and bedazzled red shoes. You may go crazy with all the Dorothy sightings, but you will still have a blast seeing the many creative and skimpy costumes at the WEST HOLLYWOOD HALLOWEEN CARNAVAL. In this iconic event, men go all out, taking no prisoners when it comes to their costumes.

In 2014, Los Angeles founded the QUEER BIENNIAL, a celebration of everything queer, from cabaret, dance, and literature to visual arts and music. Held in the city every year just before summer begins, each iteration poses a different theme, which is expressed through exhibitions and live performances throughout the city. The audience of the biennial seems to grow yearly, and the event is a tour de force for LA's queer cultural scene.

Apart from the television and film industries, the one feature of the city that anchors both the local community and its visitors is the HOLLYWOOD BOWL. At over 100 years old, it is LA's first and oldest outdoor performance center. No matter who is performing, the Hollywood Bowl is never without its best quality, the airy accessibility. For years, this has been the best place to watch internationally recognized musicians, from Ella Fitzgerald and Stevie Wonder to Robyn and Kylie—just imagine the sea of gay men.

The photography of Cleonette Harris includes portraits of queer USA, as featured at the Queer Biennale.

A quilt by Boston-based artist George Summers, an exhibitor at the Queer Biennale.

There is really no place like home in West Hollywood. Here, for the span of one particular night, you could see over 50 hairy, muscular men dressed in long auburn pigtails, blue gingham dresses with frills peeping out.

A two-hour drive is no big deal for people living in LA. In two hours or less, you could go to Santa Barbara or Laguna Beach, or, if stuck in traffic, from West Hollywood to Beverly Hills. When choosing to escape the city, however, LA men usually opt to go eastward, to the land of heat, more men, mid-century architecture, pool parties, and more heat. Since the early 1900s, PALM SPRINGS has been known as the "Playground of the Stars;" now, the desert oasis has blossomed into a veritable playground for gay men. Stay at the Parker Palm Springs, where the varicolored rooms of radiant orange, blue, and gold offer the perfect complement to its verdant grounds, which feature fountains, hammocks, pools, and a pétanque court where you can enjoy a well-earned glass of pastis after you're done playing with balls.

Palm Springs is a mecca for fans of mid-century modern architecture.

Palm Springs, known as the "Playground of the Stars," has blossomed into a veritable playground for gay men.

Palm trees are synonymous with the LA skyline, a fashion that dates back to the 1930s, when many of the trees were planted.

IN LA, STORIES OF SUNSHINE AND SHADOW

Michael Lannan

Screenwriter and producer Michael Lannan describes LA as "my forever home—on a deep, instinctual level it's where I feel like I belong." He also makes it sound fundamentally, joyously queer. For example, he talks of the gayness that permeates the air of Silver Lake—"or Echo Park, depending who you ask"—the Eastside neighborhood in which he resides. "In Spanish, there's this word *ambiente,* meaning environment," he says. "But according to a Mexican friend, it's also slang for a kind of gay energy that only gays can see. Silver Lake-Echo Park has *ambiente* deep in its landscape."

He calls the area "a historic queer heart of LA," home to "an easily overlooked monument: the Mattachine Steps, where LGBTQ activist Harry Hay held his homophile meetings in the fifties. There have been tons of gay bars going way back: the Black Cat

was the site of a pre-Stonewall police raid that some consider the first catalyzing event of modern gay rights." Then there's the city center's One National Gay & Lesbian Archives at the University of Southern California Libraries. "It's the largest queer archive in the world," Michael enthuses. "It's a great place to go for inspiration."

Michael's relationship with the City of Angels might sound inspiring, but it wasn't always this way. "Growing up in Southern California, I never liked LA much," he explains. "I dreamed of a place with more weather and skyscrapers. But I went to college in the Midwest, came out, read Mike Davis's *City of Quartz*. LA took on this new, exciting energy. It was now a place of mystery, sexual charge, and possibility. It also felt strangely forgotten: empty and crumbling, in the most romantic and mysterious ways."

Michael felt himself gravitating to LA over the next 10 years, "partially because it's where the entertainment industry is. It's such a strange, specialized field. There's nowhere else you get the same community of writers, performers, directors, and producers to share stuff with, commiserate and collaborate with. But also, it's such a big, vast wonderland of high and low culture, sunshine and shadow."

Michael settled in LA around the time HBO green-lit *Looking,* the seminal TV drama he cocreated, which follows the lives and loves of three gay men in modern-day San Francisco. There was, however, talk of setting the show in LA—specifically, in Silver Lake. "But if I remember right, HBO wasn't wild about the idea," he says. "They felt we'd eventually have to have a storyline about entertainment, and they didn't want

"It's such a big, vast wonderland of high and low culture, sunshine and shadow."

that. I didn't either, so maybe they were right."

Indeed, if queerness permeates LA, so does showbiz—sometimes simultaneously, as Michael illustrates when he speaks of LA's age-old LGBTQ spaces. "Sadly, a lot of classic gay bars have disappeared in recent years due to rising rents," he says. "There were some really special places like The Other Side piano bar and The Spotlight, a sleazy old Hollywood place. They had an atmosphere and community that will never be recreated, both spiritually and aesthetically. It

was so magical to step into a bar filled with older guys who'd actually slept with Rock Hudson or Anthony Perkins."

"At the same time it's important to keep looking forward," he adds. "There's lots of energy from young people, especially young people of color. Places like The Offbeat in Highland Park, the Bootleg Theatre in Hi-Fi, and the roving Dirty Looks events are creating new hubs of creativity and social life."

Among many lovely descriptions of LA, the ultimate comes as Michael addresses—of all

things—its trademark traffic problem. "I don't have a car, so getting around inspires me," he says. "I ride my bike—I love being connected that way. There's so much you miss from a car: gorgeous light, incredible architecture, amazing people." Even the flora seems to have star power. "Plants grow like crazy here. Whenever my friend comes out from New York, it blows her mind when a bougainvillea blooms brightly over a broken down fence next to the freeway—even though absolutely no one's taking care of it."

Calle de José Abascal

Paseo de Eduardo Dato

Calle de San Bernardo

Calle de Sagasta

Malasaña

Paseo de Recoletos

Calle de Bailén

Calle Gran Vía

Paseo del Prado

Calle de Segovia

Parque del Retiro

Centro

CLAIM IT

1. 7 Islas Hotel
2. Axel Hotel
3. Only You
4. Urso Hotel & Spa
5. Vincci The Mint

SAVOR IT

6. Angelita
7. CEBO
8. Celso y Manolo
9. Federal Café
10. Honest Greens
11. La Duquesita
12. Mercado de San Miguel

CELEBRATE IT

13. CHA CHÀ The Club
14. Hemingway
15. Macera TallerBar
16. Marta, Cariño!
17. Medias Puri
18. Sala Equis

OWN IT

19. El Moderno
20. García Madrid
21. Mercado de Motores
22. Oliver & Co.
23. Orquídea Drácula
24. Xoan Viqueira

EXPLORE IT

25. CaixaForum
26. La Casa Encendida
27. Matadero Madri
28. Museo Sorolla

MADRID

A Metropolis of Mirth and Mayhem

With its signature combination of brains and beauty, Madrid has firmly staked its claim on all of life's little pleasures. With a neo-classic façade that opens up to reveal a wealth of first-rate galleries, parks, and museums, as well as award-winning culinary delights complemented by a curated cocktail culture that extends deep into the night, the Spanish capital fully embraces all the multisensorial pleasures she has to offer.

Seemingly the oddest of bedfellows, deep conservatism and Catholicism happily coexist alongside real acceptance and diversity in Spain. The country's denizens, having experienced decades of oppression under dictator Francisco Franco, understand better than most that life should be lived to its highest potential—and as long as personal views on lifestyle don't infringe on others, pretty much anything goes. Defiantly, Madrid is one of the few cities on the planet where tolerance is king—a convivial safe haven where same-sex partners can casually stroll down the street hand in hand, or even steal a kiss, without so much as a sideways glance. Not just tolerant, Madrid truly welcomes diversity of all colors and proclivities. A leader in the fight for LGBTQ rights since the fall of fascism, the local gay community, which enjoys a strong presence in bohemian gayborhood Chueca, has of late, saucily spilled over into tastemaker districts Malasaña, La Latina, and Lavapiés.

For those opting to stay in the heart of ever-effervescent Chueca, ONLY YOU decadently combines a classic, colonial base with a modish mash of eccentric decor. Rooms are boldly styled, but it's the high-roofed courtyard-turned-lobby of this former nineteenth-century palace that captivates. Kitted out with retro-hip furnishings, oversized pottery, and art books aplenty, lounge lizards are encouraged to linger. For a tantalizing taste of local flavor, visit adjacent bookshop-slash-bar El Padrino, for regional wines, cold cuts, and—yes, please—cheese. Still close to the action, but deliciously juxtaposed between the buoyant Chueca and bourgeois Chamberí districts, lies URSO HOTEL & SPA, a one-time regal residence reborn as an elegant boutique stay. Spacious interiors ooze warmth and sophistication, from the oak-paneled Media Ración by Cuenllas restaurant adorned with stylized 1930s headline posters, to the skylit conservatory decorated with eighteenth-century painted paper and a lush vertical garden.

> ## For a tantalizing taste of local flavor, visit adjacent bookshop-slash-bar El Padrino, for regional wines, cold cuts, and cheese.

The foyer space at the avant-garde Axel Hotel in Madrid's bohemian Barrio de las Letras district.

A Gold Deluxe suite at Axel Hotel, which includes a beautifully decorated living room and an ensuite bathroom.

Fronting Madrid's main thoroughfare Gran Vía, but perfectly positioned around the corner from Chueca's vibrant urban scene, VINCCI THE MINT suits renaissance gents preferring a home-style stay in elegantly relaxed surrounds. Devised by Chilean-born interior designer of the moment Jaime Beriestain, the all-purpose lounge-bar-lobby comes to life with a mishmash of dark wood, leather, and multiple shades of green splashed across walls and furnishings. When the weather permits, venture upstairs to the verdant terrace where drinks and nibbles are served from a nifty pastel-hued food truck.

Next door, in the none-less-hip Malasaña district, 7 ISLAS HOTEL is what happens when design creatives marry art with industrial space. The bare-bones lobby, save for black steel storage lockers, doubles as a gallery space, while rooms are kept stark to highlight custom oddities such as intertwined leather and steel headboards, patterned rugs, and bronze-bathed wall hooks sculpted to resemble baby hands and feet. Don't miss 7 Craft Bar run by wunderkind mixologist Narciso Bermejo, who distills his own spirits then adds market-fresh fruit, vegetables, and spices to create weirdly wonderful signature cocktails.

A tad further afield from central happenings, the adults-only AXEL HOTEL merits a mention for its flamboyant facelift of a once refined, aristocratic mansion. A pioneering space for the LGBTQ community, the hetero-friendly hotel's decor fires on all cylinders, with pink hallways and, fittingly, rainbow-colored fabrics and furnishings. During the summer months, the rooftop sundeck doubles as a buzzy cocktail bar, while the kooky Las Chicas, Los Chicos y Los Maniquís bar and restaurant continues the fun indoors.

A culinary melting pot since the turn of the seventeenth century, Madrid expertly meshes regional Spanish dishes with international cuisine. A confirmed foodie destination, just about the only thing visitors have trouble swallowing are the late dining hours: lunch typically starts at 2 p.m.; while 10 p.m. suppers are the norm. To find your favorite eats, it's wise to go out—often—and embrace the mishmash of gourmet delights found at many a tempting table.

A good place to start is at the gourmand paradise MERCADO DE SAN MIGUEL. Revamped in 2018 and packaged in a dream of wrought iron and whimsy, this fabled gastro market features more than 30 stands of glorious product from the whole of Spain. On any given day, sample the best cheeses from Asturias, the finest seafood from Galicia, grains from the Mediterranean coastline, and, for your drinking pleasure, hard-to-find wines from every corner of the country. Fueled by a passion for Spain's underexplored provinces, brothers Mario and David Villalón take regional delights to new heights at ANGELITA. A bi-level bistro serving elevated cuisine paired with an eclectic list of fine wines, in the basement a speakeasy-style bar serves daring cocktails. Don't let the laidback tavern-style setting fool you, CELSO Y MANOLO is serious about serving hearty home-style fare made with organic ingredients. Chow down on rice dishes made from grains provided by a sixth-generation

The handsome wrought-iron-and-glass Mercado de San Miguel lies just a stone's throw from Plaza Mayor.

rice farmers and ecological eats whose protein is supplied via chicken, eggs, or beef. At the opposite end of the culinary spectrum, CEBO—awarded its first Michelin star in 2018—combines the typical with the innovative. The vision of enterprising chef Aurelio Morales, the menu, which is decidedly Mediterranean in spirit, brings staple ingredients such as fish and vegetables center stage while incorporating new twists on meat dishes in homage to his Madrileño roots.

> ## To find your favorite eats, it's wise to go out and embrace the mishmash of gourmet delights found at many a tempting table.

For health-conscious consumers on a budget, HONEST GREENS combines the best of both. Expect eco meats and veggie-infused dishes heightened with haute cuisine techniques served in a sleek, designer space that rivals any high-end eatery. Patrons construct their own bio-rich meals in three easy steps by selecting a protein, a salad base, and a garnish. For brunchers on the prowl, there's the brick-faced FEDERAL CAFÉ, an industrial-style coffee shop and eatery serving a nifty selection of eggs, bagels, and other brekkie staples, with smoothies and crafty coffee. Sugarholics can rejoice, too. Returning a folkloric bakery to its former glory proved to be a "sweet" task for master baker Oriol Balaguer. The original early-twentieth-century design intact, LA DUQUESITA's display cases are lined with rows of aromatic croissants—flavored with international ingredients—artisan candies, breads, pies, and, the pièce de résistance, a multitextured, four-layer chocolate cake.

Along with fresh fruit and veggies, numerous tapas dishes are on sale at the Mercado de San Miguel.

A Malasaña mainstay, MACERA TALLERBAR twists tradition with custom-tailored swigs. Narciso Bermejo achieves mystical mixology by infusing base liquors with a crushed fruit of choice. In a stark scene from an alchemist's dream, transparent uniform bottles with equally austere labeling line simple bar shelves. Pick up the pace at MARTA, CARIÑO!, a premier gay bar and club situated in Madrid's old Luchana Theater. Favored by the naughty and nice alike, this joint knows the secret to a perfect celebration: quality drinks, sublime entertainment, and the prettiest people. The voguish space, dipped in ruby red, has zones dedicated to dancing, dining, and the imbibing of artisanal aperitifs.

> In keeping with the spirit of hidden hangouts, enjoy a classic cocktail or two at Hemingway, the swanky speakeasy named after the legendary American scribe.

The indoor/outdoor plaza at Sala Equis has a relaxed vibe, screening films to be viewed from a deckchair.

For flair of a different face, MEDIAS PURI holds the key to secret soirées in the heart of Madrid. A retro lingerie shop on the surface, behind its façade is a cavernous clandestine club that keeps things interesting with three multigenre dance areas, mobile theatrical performers, and a hefty dose of the bizarre—it's not unusual to witness an impromptu poetry recital in the loo. In keeping with the spirit of hidden hangouts, enjoy a classic cocktail or two at HEMINGWAY, the swanky speakeasy named after the legendary American scribe as a tribute to his patronage. Ideal for nightcappers, the jovial joint is accessible through the service floor of the Nordic-style Casa Suecia restaurant.

Decadent and dramatic, the abandoned Bogart theater entertains once more as CHA CHÁ THE CLUB, an alternative hotspot featuring beats that range in genre from hip-hop to house to electronica. Access is selective, but for revelers that make the cut, a sexy scene bathed in carved woods and vaudevillian red velvet awaits. Along a similar vein, SALA EQUIS, a one-time cinema of the crudest persuasion, has been resurrected as an entertainment venue divided into three zones. Here, a cushy cocktail scene with sofas and hammocks gives way to a cozier velvet-lined bar, but the cherry in its crown is a 55-seat movie theater equipped with tipple tables that plays vintage films.

Media Puri boasts high-quality shows and three dance floors that can accommodate 1,000 party revelers.

Spain in general (and Madrid in particular) has a long-standing tradition of manufacturing quality artisan goods and textiles. Add to the mix a multicultural point of reference and desire to impress, and you're left with exceptional shopping options to treasure. One weekend every month, old pairs with new at the storied railway station Delicias, home to the Museo del Ferrocarril (Train Museum), as it transforms into the MERCADO DE MOTORES. A joyful second-hand flea market, it offers retro wares, antique collectibles, handmade trinkets, and art pieces, all of which you can scour while sampling gourmet bites and beers over the sounds of peppy live performances.

As popular as they are practical, concept stores do more than present like-minded local designers in one location—they best inspire curated lifestyle goals. One such shop is EL MODERNO, a Madrid must for design-led homewares, jewelry, stationery, and an assortment of artisanal goods you never knew you always wanted. A true romantic, Valencia-born graphic designer XOAN VIQUEIRA moved to Madrid with the very best of intentions: to be with the man he loves. He also opened his namesake shop, selling tees, sweatshirts, underwear, espadrilles, dinnerware, and framed posters depicting romantic cartoon couples for an array of sexual orientations.

For the modern man with a penchant for understated flair, GARCÍA MADRID designs suits, jackets, and daywear with a little something extra. Always impeccably tailored, its clothes thrive on the unexpected: an offbeat print or motif; an unusual cut or shock of color. For signature scents on the cutting-edge, OLIVER & CO offers daring unisex fragrances conceptualized in-house. Free of animal-based products, perfumes are mixed with organic spices, florals, aromatic oils, woods, and manmade molecules, all packaged in minimalist monochrome bottles. For a final flourish, self-appointed "plant doctor" and creative Felipe Carvallo's original arrangements never leave his laboratory, ORQUÍDEA DRÁCULA, without full instructions for their care. Florals can be reshaped, potted and painted (with harmless products) to refresh any room in the house, and if your greenery yellows, hurry back for some expert, in-patient mending.

Spain has a long-standing tradition of manufacturing quality artisan goods.

Shoppers browse the aisles of vintage clothing at a monthly flea market, the Mercado de Motores.

Xoan Viqueira dresses his store window with his distinctive designs for a wide range of clothing, accessories, and homewares.

An architectural marvel in its own right, the state-of-the-art CAIXAFORUM by architects Herzog & De Meuron appears to sit atop the remains of an abandoned electric power station near the art triumvirate made up of the Prado, Reina Sofia, and Thyssen-Bornemisza museums. Seemingly suspended in mid-air, the brick and cast-iron building features an eye-catching vertical garden wall and houses a multimedia cultural center hosting works from the ancient to present day, music festivals, and educational workshops. Nearby, LA CASA ENCENDIDA is Madrid's foremost cultural center for all things avant-garde. Visit this space for emerging young artists hailing from a vast array of fields including film, dance, music, and contemporary art. Plus, for the coolest, most in-the-know cats, the chromatic rooftop terrace and bar is among the city's best unkept secrets.

Rescued from its tawdry beginnings as the city's slaughterhouse, MATADERO MADRID has since become a mini metropolis housing and promoting all walks of artistic expression. Most creative mediums are actively represented here via dynamic spaces dedicated to literature, architecture, film,

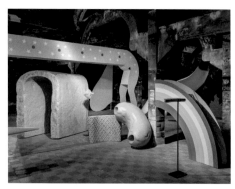

One of several scenes from *Ride, Ride, Ride* a solo exhibition created by Teresa Solar at Matadero Madrid.

music, performing arts, and design. Alternatively, take a walk on the mild side at MUSEO SOROLLA. Dedicated to the life and work of prolific Spanish painter Joaquín Sorolla, this venue invites visitors on an intimate tour of the artist's former grandiose residence. Although more than 1,000 paintings are on display, it's the personal ceramics, jewelry, sculptures, and antique furniture that provide a true glance into the privileged world of genteel living.

Nave 16, the main exhibition space at Matadero Madrid, a 43,000 sq ft (4,000-sq m) space that hosts major exhibitions and concerts.

What began as the city's first organized protest for LGBTQ rights, MADRID PRIDE has since blossomed into Europe's largest celebration of gay love and acceptance. Held annually in and about Chueca, the weeklong event attracts more than two million visitors, pumped to participate in convivial activities, concerts, and competitions. Despite an agenda that updates every season, the

> Once the weather cools, take it inside with LesGaiCineMad, the most revered LGBTQ film festival in the Spanish-speaking world. Expand your knowledge of Spanish cinema beyond Almodóvar with screenings of queer-themed—and often subtitled—independent films.

Stiletto Race, Mr. Gay Pride España, and the hedonistic mayhem that best describes the massive Pride Parade remain among the most memorable mainstays. Another summer highlight, NOCHES DEL BOTÁNICO offers a superb lineup of local and international musicians backdropped by the city's bucolic Alfonso XIII Royal Botanical Garden. Running from late June throughout July, the outdoor fest spotlights a wide spectrum of established acts from the world of electronica, jazz, pop, rock, and Latin music.

Once the weather cools, take it inside with LESGAICINEMAD, the most revered LGBTQ film festival in the Spanish-speaking world. Expand your knowledge of Spanish cinema beyond Almodóvar with screenings of queer-themed—and often subtitled—independent films. Alternatively, attend the ARCOMADRID fair, a collaborative playground for contemporary artists and collectors from around the globe, uniting power players with established and emerging talent from more than 20 countries. Featuring a different theme every year, visitors can sample from a comprehensive program of Q&A sessions, exclusive exhibits, and curated pieces in a neatly compiled three-day package.

Crowds of people throng in Madrid's Plaza de Cibeles during the city's Gay Pride celebrations.

Visit the ARCOmadrid in February/March to invest in the latest trends in contemporary art.

A scenic two-hour drive north of Madrid, dotted with generations-old wineries, medieval hamlets, and following the lengthy Duero River, the RIBERA DEL DUERO region's superior vintages are certainly worth the effort. Producing some of the most intense red wines in the world, this area's secret lies in the fertile soil and high elevation, which allow for the slow ripening of Spain's indigenous Tempranillo grapes to potent perfection. Dedicated oenophiles naturally gravitate toward elite wineries such as Vega Sicilia and Dominio de Pingus, but for a well-rounded experience that needn't break the bank, sample the goods at one of the many neighboring vineyards. For a memorable moment, make a stop at Abadía Retuerta, a modern cellar boasting a Romanesque monastery reinvented as award-winning boutique hotel LeDomaine. Afterwards, visit ancient Peñafiel village's provincial wine museum and the must-see 600-year-old castle built atop a tenth-century fortress.

Take a wine-buying tour of the region to the north of Madrid, traveling as far as Rioja, some 185 miles (300 km) northeast.

Producing some of the most intense red wines in the world, this area's secret lies in the fertile soil and high elevation.

Above: The pantile roofs of Madrid's inner-city streets.
Opposite: Street musicians offer a lively performance for passersby.

San Rafael

Av. Ribera de San Cosme

Av. Paseo de la Reforma

Condesa

Roma

Calz. Chivatito

Av. Paseo de la Reforma

Av. Constituyentes

Av. Benjamín Franklin

Insurgentes Sur

CLAIM IT
1. Casa Prim
2. El Patio 77
3. Hotel Villa Condesa
4. La Valise
5. Nima Local House

SAVOR IT
6. Amaya
7. Contramar
8. Eno
9. Forte
10. Lorea
11. Milán 44
12. Rosetta
13. Por Siempre Vegana
14. Pujol

CELEBRATE IT
15. Baltra Bar
16. Guilt
17. Jules Basement
18. La Botica
19. Saint
20. Teatro Bar El Vicio

OWN IT
21. Bi Yuu
22. El Bazaar Sábado
23. Onora
24. Stendhal Store
25. The Pack
26. Voces en Tinta
27. Xinú

EXPLORE IT
28. ArtSpace
29. Casa Luis Barragán
30. Museo Dolores Olmedo
31. Museo Memoria y Tolerancia
32. Museo Nacional de Antropología

MEXICO CITY

North America's Complex, Ever-changing Megalopolis

For a city that dates back to the ancient Aztec Empire, it's hardly any wonder Mexico City has had to reinvent itself over the centuries. Not all that long ago, most travelers considered the metropolis a dangerous no-go, with stories of crime and violence defining the destination. But today, Mexico City is in the midst of a cultural renaissance. You can amble through revitalized neighborhoods and public spaces that show marks of a rich, storied past.

Regarding its gay scene, Mexico City can hold its own against other iconic welcoming and pulsating destinations around the globe. Same-sex marriage has been legal since 2010, discrimination is outlawed, and the annual Pride parade brings with it an epic weeklong celebration. Zona Rosa is the capital's most famous gay neighborhood, offering everything from fabulous glitter and glamour parties to low-key pubs and cocktail bars. For something a bit quieter but still trendy, there are also the nearby gay-friendly neighborhoods of Roma and Condesa.

Then there's the home of legendary artist Frida Kahlo, for many, an icon in the LGBTQ community for her openness around—and expression of—female sexuality. Travelers can take a pilgrimage to her famed home Casa Azul and learn more about her impact on the LGBTQ art scene. Equally fascinating—yet undeniably campy—no briefing on Mexico City would be complete without mentioning *lucha libre*, where exotic wrestlers take to the ring in flashy costumes and drag. The fights are a unique look into popular Mexican culture—and an all-around good time. Finally, as you're experiencing the best of Mexico City, keep an eye out for the many beloved murals, vivid and colorful portrayals of Mexican politics and society throughout the centuries. With all Mexico City has to offer the discerning gay traveler, don't be surprised if you find yourself trading in the country's famed tropical beaches for an extended cosmopolitan affair.

If you like your hotels as rich in history as the locale you are visiting, then CASA PRIM is an obvious choice. Located in buzzing Zona Rosa, the building dates back to the early twentieth century, when it served as a home and university—before being transformed into the luxurious five-star boutique hotel it is today. The old-world feel of the original architecture remains: as you relax in the lobby, it's surprisingly easy to picture the carriage-parking zone it once was. Even better, the best of Mexico City's gay nightlife is right at your doorstep. But if you prefer an escape among the tree-lined boulevards and hipster cafés of the nearby neighborhood Condesa, then you can't go wrong with iconic HOTEL VILLA CONDESA. This 15-room hotel combines antique furnishings with modern comfort in a restored art deco mansion. Complimentary bikes make it easy to get out and explore the fashionable area.

The ground floor entrance at El Patio 77 opens onto a green and serene public space.

Rooms at El Patio 77 are simply decorated and furnished with vintage objects.

EL PATIO 77, another historic home turned romantic B&B, is Mexico City's first eco-friendly guesthouse. Upcycled and repurposed furniture adorn the rooms, each of which is named after a different Mexican state. Take time to enjoy the ever-changing art on display throughout the space, and don't miss the traditional Mexican breakfast served in the courtyard.

Located amid Roma's modern art galleries, trendy shops, and independent eateries is the stunningly innovative LA VALISE. The small three-suite boutique hotel is flawlessly designed, effectively taking the idea of a concept hotel to an entirely new level. The crown jewel of the rooms is La Terraza, a suite that goes so far as to feature a king-size bed that can be easily rolled onto the private terrace for a romantic evening under the stars. Also in the heart of design-savvy Roma, NIMA LOCAL HOUSE delivers an intimately luxurious hotel experience that begins with a refreshing welcome cocktail and extends into the perfectly curated details of each of its four rooms. Expect highly personalized service and all the upscale amenities you would anticipate from a five-star hotel. The rooftop terrace is a particularly magical retreat. Here, enjoy a glass of wine and unwind after a day of exploring nearby must-visit attractions, like Chapultepec Castle.

Breakfast outdoors in the leafy courtyard at the Nima Local House Hotel.

It may not be a well-kept secret—this spot has topped many lists of the world's best restaurants—but thankfully PUJOL more than lives up to its notoriety. Celebrity chef and owner Enrique Olvera uses traditional local ingredients in ultra-modern ways to create acclaimed contemporary Mexican cuisine. Tucked behind a large wooden fence in upscale Polanco, Pujol's new location comprises multiple light-filled rooms that balance sophisticated minimalism and mid-century modern design, enhancing the already delightful dining experience. From octopus with habanero ink to upscale street snacks, the flavors here will leave your taste buds salivating long after your last bite. Don't go without trying their signature Mole Madre, Mole Nuevo (part of the eight-course tasting menu), a dish that flaunts a layer of mole sauce aged for more than 1,000 days. ENO, another creation of chef Enrique Olvera, offers the same quality ingredients as Pujol in a more casual café atmosphere. Expect gourmet breakfast and lunch menu items that incorporate fresh local and seasonal products. There's a tangible neighborhood hangout feel at all three of Eno's locations around the city, making them buzzing spots to mingle with locals and their pets.

Fuel up for a day of exploring Roma with the local coffee and fresh artisanal bread at FORTE. Owner and barista Rafa Rivera's passion for his craft shines through in each cappuccino and croissant he serves. For more pastry goodness, hop over to PANADERÍA ROSETTA, a European-style bakery with a divine pastry and sandwich menu. The guava and ricotta Danish is a must-try. And while you're in Roma, keep an eye out for the unassuming LOREA, an up-and-coming restaurant located in a stylish two-story townhouse. The open kitchen whips up smart takes on classic Mexican favorites. It serves only one set menu, but chef Oswaldo Oliva can customize meals to suit dietary restrictions. Go now, while it's still an under-the-radar gem.

If you haven't hopped on the Baja Med movement, you're missing out. Effortlessly fusing classic Mexican staples with Mediterranean and Asian influences, AMAYA takes the art of Baja Med to an entirely new level. Unsurprisingly, owner and chef Jair Téllez is no stranger to award-winning restaurants—you'll also find him at the city's beloved MeroToro. Most of the dishes at Amaya are designed to share, and the rabbit, tartar, and gnocchi are consistent crowd pleasers. Also an avid winemaker, Téllez expertly crafted the restaurant's long natural, organic, and biodynamic wine list, which includes selections from his own ranch in Tecate. Then there's CONTRAMAR—not really off the beaten track but undeniably delicious. From the white tablecloths to the sizeable marine mural to the chic *Chilangos* packing in for mezcal and the freshest seafood in the city, the restaurant offers an iconic dining experience that lives up to the hype. Here, both locals and tourists enjoy extended lunches of freshly grilled fish, tuna tostadas, and other seafood specialties.

It's impossible to eat your way through Mexico City without taste-testing the fare at traditional *taquerías*. An integral part of Mexican street food, this kind of venue promises delicious, authentic, and inexpensive tacos and burritos. There are plenty of options throughout the city, but both vegans and meat lovers alike shouldn't skip POR SIEMPRE VEGANA in Roma. Here, you'll find vegan takes on classics like *al pastor* and *loganiza*. Open until midnight, it is also a great spot to curb your late-night cravings.

Does anything get more hip than a mixed-use urban market complete with a yoga studio, hair salon, supermarket, and a smattering of chic restaurants? That's what you'll find at MILÁN 44, another cool new addition to the emergent Juárez neighborhood. A glass façade, exposed concrete beams, and natural design concepts call out to passersby, who pop in for a full meal or a quick local microbrew at the rooftop *cervecería*.

Hugely popular with locals, Eno gets very busy, but the staff keep things moving.

Expect a modern take on traditional Mexican dishes at Eno.

For something sleek and stylish in Polanco, Mexico City's poshest neighborhood, head to the gay nightclub GUILT. There's a premium cover charge, but once inside, you'll find two tantalizing dance floors with an attractive crowd that goes strong until the early morning hours. Guilt's only open on Saturdays, so plan accordingly. SAINT, which is also in Polanco, is where you go when you've dressed to impress. Located in a stately building complete with exposed stone, stained-glass windows, and chandeliers, this small but glamorous gay nightclub offers many themed nights, including drag shows with well-known queens like Lorena Herrera. It also puts on an infamous party every Friday.

Hidden away under a nondescript taco shop in Polanco, the speakeasy-inspired JULES BASEMENT is the obvious choice for sublime cocktails and intimate conversation. Enter through an industrial cooler door to discover a gorgeous watering hole decorated in chic black and white. The cocktail list is extensive, but don't shy away from requesting a bespoke drink from the mixologists, and if hunger strikes, tacos can be couriered down from up-stairs. The space is small and popular, so make a reservation. BALTRA BAR, a hip cocktail bar that finds inspiration in Charles Darwin's fascination with the Galapagos Islands, is a refuge in Condesa that showcases expert mixology in rustic ambiance—vintage maps and taxidermy dominate the decor. Colloquially known as "The Island," the menu here is divided up into the four seasons, consisting of new, creative takes on familiar classics that are regularly rotated into the selection. You'll have no trouble finding mezcal bars throughout Mexico City, but LA BOTICA, one of the oldest *mezcalerías*—and a long-time hangout in the gay community— boasts over 50 different variations of the hugely popular smoky agave liquor. Waiters act like sommeliers, providing tasting notes on the various mezcals sourced from around Mexico.

Mexico City is teeming with social entrepreneurs, independent artists, and young visionaries. You'll find them exploring Mexican tragedies through art and music at TEATRO BAR EL VICIO, which the writer Salvador Novo founded under the name "Habito" in 1954 as an artistic forum. Today, the theater hosts quality cabaret performances that explore important topics in a cozy, intellectual atmosphere.

The Queer Room hosts electronic music nights with local and international DJs. Check Facebook for events, as the program is not regular.

If you only visit one *mercado* in Mexico City, make it the EL BAZAAR SÁBADO. This open-air flea market is one of the best spots around for local handicrafts made by Mexican artisans, offering everything from intricate woodwork to dazzling textiles to Frida Kahlo–inspired trinkets. You'll find it in the leafy, cobblestone-paved neighborhood of San Ángel, complete with quaint colonial homes and cozy sidewalk cafés. While you're here, don't forget to stop in at the eighteenth-century bazaar house to enjoy quesadillas and mezcal margaritas. ONORA, a fantastic store for home goods inspired by the rich heritage and culture of Mexico, offers a curated display of one-of-a-kind handicrafts with modern flair. Think indigenous-inspired pillows, lacquered wooden cutlery, and handwoven copper baskets. You'll find it with the other upscale shops in Polanco.

For snazzy menswear that's making a difference, visit THE PACK, an apparel shop dedicated to the production of clothing that has a positive impact on society. Choose from an array of trendsetting items made from only the most environmentally sustainable materials—conscious and stylish alternatives to fast fashion that are bound to garner compliments back home. Then there's STENDHAL STORE, an innovative concept boutique specializing in urban and androgynous Mexican clothing brands. Expect to find sleek, minimal designs perfect for any occasion.

Before a night out on the town, stop by XINÚ to pick up a new fragrance. To create its one-of-a-kind sensory explosions, the brand sources inspiration from the unique botany of the Americas and uses only the highest quality natural ingredients. The stately, plant-laden showroom warrants a visit in its own right. From here, lose yourself at VOCES EN TINTA. Fittingly located in Zona Rosa, it is an LGBTQ bookstore and coffee shop that also hosts workshops and presentations.

A handwoven Mexican rug not only makes a statement but also promotes sustainably minded collaborations that include traditional artisans from around Mexico—when purchased from BIYUU, that is. Browse through organic rugs inspired by modernist Mexican architecture that are expertly handcrafted by those with an eye for innovation and style, or if you want a piece to match your favorite color palette, get a personal design made to order.

The owners of Stendhal select their goods carefully so that everything can be worn by all sexes.

A central display of perfumes and their botanical ingredients takes center stage at Xinu.

The MUSEO NACIONAL DE ANTROPOLOGÍA is the most visited museum in Mexico City for a reason. Idyllically situated in lovely Bosque de Chapultepec, the extensive institution displays one of the world's largest collections of archaeological artifacts from pre-Hispanic Mayan civilizations. Here you can get the rundown on Mexico's storied history, and be sure to visit the upper floors, which offer a glimpse into the life of today's indigenous descendants. The MUSEO MEMORIA Y TOLERANCIA explores the consequences of indifference, discrimination, and violence. Specifically, the "Memory" exhibit details massacres such as the Holocaust and other genocides, while the "Tolerance" section explores discrimination, human rights, and diversity. The museum also regularly hosts exhibitions surrounding LGBTQ issues, on the concepts of identity and sexuality, for example.

Art enthusiasts won't want to miss MUSEO DOLORES OLMEDO. A muse and an avid collector of Diego Rivera and Frida Kahlo, Olmedo's sweeping estate turned museum boasts a fantastic collection of these artists' works, including the world's largest collection of Kahlo paintings. Don't pass up a chance to walk through the elegant gardens, where you'll likely find peacocks and hairless dogs meandering around. For an avant-garde art gallery experience, ARTSPACE is home to an eclectic mix of work by queer artists from around Latin America. The art here explores sensuality, beauty, and queer identity.

Famed architect Luis Barragán greatly influenced architecture around the globe, spurring forward the movement of "emotional architecture"—the creation of spaces that merge traditional and modern elements to encourage thoughtfulness. His home, CASA LUIS BARRAGÁN, is a mesmerizing masterpiece preserved just as the architect left it after his death. Advance reservations are required to tour the residence and studio.

ArtSpace is home to an eclectic mix of work by queer artists from around Latin America.

The focus at ArtSpace is on works that challenge preconceived ideas of identity, gender, and sexuality. Visits are by appointment only.

For over 40 years, Mexico City has held its annual PRIDE festival every June, and it's now the largest of its kind in Latin America. The week-long celebration and demonstration for the increased acceptance of Mexico's LGBTQ community is a wildly fun time. Join over a million people in Zona Rosa for parades and festivities, which culminate in an all-night party in the Zócalo, the city's main square.

> ## The week-long celebration and demonstration for the increased acceptance of Mexico's LGBTQ community is a wildly fun time.

Each year, SALON ACME opens a space to show case some of the Mexico's most talented emerging artists—specifically, those who are not yet represented by galleries. Contemporary artists throughout the country submit their proposals to the salon, which makes this an excellent event for discovering up-and-coming talent and supporting the continued growth of the arts in Mexico. For something a little different, keep an eye on QUEER ROOM'S Facebook events calendar. The club hosts regular parties that feature international DJs and continue into the early morning hours.

The Salón ACME gallery exhibits in three once-elegant houses in the city's Juárez district.

About 60 young hopefuls exhibit their works at Salón ACME, where pieces can sell for 1,300 USD.

If you're going to take a day trip from Mexico City, it had better be to the City of the Gods, better known as TEOTIHUACÁN. Once Mesoamerica's greatest city, the impressive complex of pyramids provides a magical snapshot of the lives of the ancient Aztecs who inhabited it from around the thirteenth century. Climb to the top of the Pyramid of the Sun—the third-largest pyramid in the world—for sweeping views of the complex and surrounding area. No one knows who built the mesmerizing ancient city, though scholars are confident that it dates back to 100 BC and was home to some 200,000 inhabitants at its peak. As one of the most significant settlements in Mesoamerica, Teotihuacán extended its artistic and cultural influence through-out the region, and well beyond. You'll want to plan in at least three hours here if you don't want to rush through the museum and pyramids.

Teotihuacán, "the place where the gods were created," lies just 30 miles northeast of Mexico City.

Central Park

Manhattan

Brooklyn

Broadway
10th Ave
Park Ave
5th Ave
1st Ave
Brooklyn Bridge

CLAIM IT

1. 1 Hotel Brooklyn Bridge
2. Franklin Guesthouse
3. Pod 39
4. Pod Brooklyn
5. PUBLIC Hotel
6. The Bowery Hotel

SAVOR IT

7. American Cut Steakhouse
8. Avant Garden
9. Big Gay Ice Cream
10. Frankel's Delicatessen
11. Gotham West Market
12. Hunan Slurp
13. Legacy Records
14. MeMe's Diner
15. Pietro NoLita

CELEBRATE IT

16. Attaboy
17. Baby's All Right
18. Club Cumming
19. Industry Bar
20. Sleep No More
21. Stonewall Inn

OWN IT

22. Bureau of General Services— Queer Division
23. Coming Soon
24. DE VERA
25. Front General Store
26. MAST
27. STORY

EXPLORE IT

28. Dia Art Foundation
29. The High Lir
30. Leslie-Lohma Museum

NEW YORK CITY

A Melting Pot of the Iconic and Current

It's the city that never sleeps, the city most dream about visiting once in their lifetime, and a very condensed space home to millions. New York City can practically sell itself on name recognition alone, and visitors to the Big Apple can base their visits solely on television shows like *Sex and the City* and various blockbuster movies and still manage to have a once-in-a-lifetime trip. NYC is also the birthplace of the global LGBTQ rights movement—its iconic Stonewall Inn was where the infamous 1969 riots took place. Now designated a National Historic Landmark, it is still open for business, providing an opportunity to step back in time and pay tribute to the events that took place there. Walk in the footsteps of trailblazing New Yorkers like Edie Windsor, Marsha P. Johnson, James Baldwin, Alice Austen, and Langston Hughes, who all helped mold the NYC queer experience. Stroll past the locations of what were once legendary night clubs, like Studio 54, Palladium, and The Roxy, and walk around Chelsea and the West Village, which historically were two of the main hubs of LGBTQ culture in NYC, while also taking the time to discover the new and vibrant scenes in Hell's Kitchen and Williamsburg.

But there's more to NYC than self-guided walks through history, Times Square, and oversized celebrity chef restaurants that cater to the masses—who are there more to say they were there than to eat something extraordinary. The city is quite literally filled with things to see and do, all in a compact space that gives the impression of a never-ending sidewalk of skyscrapers. If your trip is planned correctly, New York City can still provide those quirky tourist obligations, but in addition, it can elevate your experience to a whole new level of awesomeness.

The FRANKLIN GUESTHOUSE is a boutique hotel that provides guests with a healthy serving of the authentic Brooklyn experience. Located in Greenpoint, the guesthouse is an easy train ride from Manhattan and popular Williamsburg. The unpretentious vibe of the neighborhood, combined with the modern elegance of the guesthouse, makes for a unique stay. Or if you prefer to be a bit closer to Manhattan, try 1 HOTEL BROOKLYN BRIDGE, located on the waterfront with expansive views of the eponymous bridge, East River, and Manhattan skyline. A local artist involved in the design of the hotel used lots of natural elements and reclaimed materials found in Brooklyn. For something in Manhattan with a difference, THE BOWERY HOTEL is located in NYC's hipster hangout, the Bowery, a place where no one would have thought to look for boutique hotels in the past. The bedrooms are light and reflect the classic style of the city's apartment living, while the lobby bar and public areas are art deco inspired.

For affordable luxury, try PUBLIC HOTEL, a property accredited to legendary hotelier Ian Schrager, the man behind NYC clubbing institutions Studio 54 and Palladium. The hotel features a destination restaurant by world-famous Jean-Georges Vongerichten, a rooftop bar with some of the best views of downtown, a hidden garden with a magnolia tree, Japanese maples, and rhododendrons, and a progressive multimedia performance space that is reinventing NYC nightlife. Lastly, for an affordable option where amenities are still impressive, the POD HOTELS are a good choice for those looking not for standard hotel room features but instead maximized small spaces that minimize waste and save you a buck or two. Pod 39 is located in Murray Hill in Midtown Manhattan, just steps away from Grand Central Terminal and five subway lines. Pod BK is in the heart of Williamsburg and offers incredible views of the Manhattan skyline from its four rooftop decks.

Pod Hotels are a good choice for those looking not for standard hotel room features but instead maximized small spaces that minimize waste and save you a buck or two.

Catching the sights of Midtown Manhattan from the rooftoop bar at Pod 39.

Start your culinary experiences at LEGACY RECORDS, a new restaurant in Hudson Yards that has a great space without the uptight feeling normally associated with NYC eateries. The high ceilings, leather-topped tables, and pricey menu items would normally indicate fancy attire, but there's no dress code here. Make a reservation and opt for the duck pasta and house-made gelato. Over in Tribeca, the AMERICAN CUT STEAKHOUSE pays homage to the traditional New York dining experience it is named after. The eatery has won several awards for its menu and restaurant design. In Hell's Kitchen, the day and night GOTHAM WEST MARKET is the first of its kind in the neighborhood. Offering a variety of unique eateries, the building also houses NYC Velo, a bike shop that does rentals and full services. As the options here are bountiful, it's the perfect place for foodies who are undecided on what to eat.

When visiting SoHo, PIETRO NOLITA is a must. Tucked away on a quiet street lined with century-old red brick buildings, the Italian eatery stands out for its contemporary decor that heavily features the color pink. The pink paradise is reminiscent of what one would expect to find along the waterfront at Santa Margherita and Portofino, near Milan, where one of the owners is from. Tasty Chinese noodle houses are abundant in the city, especially in the East Village, but HUNAN SLURP stands out among the rest. The narrow wood-lined space, which resembles a subway tunnel, was redesigned by a Cirque du Soleil set director, with multicolored orbs and extraordinary light fixtures that dangle

Authentic dishes from Hunan Province are on the menu at the minimalist Hunan Slurp.

from the ceiling. Sharing is caring here, so it's best to come with a plus one or small group, although its communal tables offer solo diners an opportunity for company. One branch of BIG GAY ICE CREAM is also located in the East Village, with its two other locations in the West Village and South Street Seaport. What started out, in 2009, as a seasonal ice cream truck has since soared in popularity, prompting the owners' decision to go brick and mortar. Their contemporary take on old-school ice cream parlors comes with high-quality ingredients and traditional flavors mixed with decadent guilty pleasures and unexpected tastes.

Don't discount Brooklyn when looking for that perfect dining experience! The borough has been quietly building its own spectacular collection of restaurants that are worth a subway journey or ride share to get to. Start with FRANKEL'S DELICATESSEN. Located on the Greenpoint–Williamsburg border, it is a retail shop and Jewish deli counter with around 15 seats. You can't do New York without visiting a deli, and if you had to pick only one, this modern take would be the one to choose. Expect everything from lox and latkes to brisket and pastrami. And don't forget about the bagels, a staple of any true NYC delicatessen. MEME'S DINER, located in Prospect Heights and known to be queer-friendly, is all about pairing cheese balls with a martini—because it can, and it does. Its unique menu matches farmers-market produce with bodega standards. Think comfort foods elevated to the next level. On any day of the week, vegetarians can rejoice at AVANT GARDEN, a restaurant franchise with an East Village location that focuses on serving vegetables that taste like vegetables, not some sort of meat. Even if you aren't on the veggie or vegan train, it is an experience worthy of your time, as you might come to realize that vegetables don't have to be served as a side dish and can instead easily be the main attraction.

With a slick interior that borders on glitzy, Legacy Records has two main dining rooms, a café, and a bar.

In a city filled with endless nightlife options, it might be hard to narrow down your choices. Beyond what you might already know, try some of the city's more diverse locations, like ATTABOY, a cocktail bar in the Lower East Side that can be tricky to find. There's no sign and the window suggests the space is a tailor shop. But after ringing the doorbell at 134 Eldridge, you'll know you are in the right place. There's no menu at this bar, so come knowing what you like to

> ## The Stonewall Inn is a must-visit, even if it's just for a quick stop to pay homage to the courageous queer folk that paved the way for today's LGBTQ community.

The Stonewall Inn remains little changed since its night of fame in the late 1960s.

A plaque commemorates the role the Stonewall Inn played in the history of the lesbian and gay liberation movement.

drink, or which spirit you gravitate toward, and let the masters behind the bar take it from there. The speakeasy-like bar can fill up quick, but the doorman is great about calling or texting once space opens up. INDUSTRY BAR is a blend of three types of gay bars one would expect to find in Manhattan: casual T-shirt lounge, tank-top mega club, and cruising spot. The partitioned rooms sprawl across a single floor, making it easy for anyone to check out the different zones. Of course, the STONEWALL INN is a must-visit, even if it's just for a quick stop to pay homage to the courageous queer folk that paved the way for today's LGBTQ community. Expect tourists during the day and a lively scene at night.

CLUB CUMMING, brought to us by actor Alan Cumming and promoter Daniel Nardicio, is a reimagined cabaret, comedy, and party hub, often frequented by celebrities, although the club is a star on its own. It's a one-of-a-kind performance space, the sort of place that draws on past traditions while being planted in the present. Another diverse spot to check out is the McKittrick Hotel, which is home to the immersive theater spectacle SLEEP NO MORE, in addition to the rooftop bar Gallow Green and jazz-inspired speakeasy Manderley Bar. The hotel is renowned for hosting elaborate costume parties and legendary events, including The McKittrick Masquerade, an event worth planning a trip around. Williamsburg also has a scene of its own, with BABY'S ALL RIGHT dominating the top of the list of bars to visit. Think experimental live shows, laser lights, and an anything-goes spirit. The place is very Williamsburg, in the best way possible.

A scene from *Sleep No More*, a production that takes a film-noir approach to Shakespeare's Macbeth.

The showroom at Mast is stacked with cocoa beans and chocolate bars.

When it comes to shopping, start at STORY, a 2,000-square-foot retail space located in Chelsea that offers an eclectic range of wares. The store comes across as a serial pop-up, keeping customers coming back for more. Founder Rachel Shechtman often collaborates with guest curators and architects, such as fashion icon Iris Apfel and Instagram illustrator Donald Robertson, to create incredible themed spaces for people to shop in. Here it's about surprising and delighting the customer. Nearby, THE BUREAU OF GENERAL SERVICES— QUEER DIVISION is an all-volunteer queer cultural center, bookstore, and event space hosted by

The Lesbian, Gay, Bisexual & Transgender Community Center. The space, like its name, is profoundly unique and worth visiting, as it's rooted in giving back to the LGBTQ community.

Established in San Francisco in 1991, the DE VERA gallery has been in NYC since 2003, showing finely curated selections of Venetian glass, Japanese lacquerware, ivory carvings, eighteenth-century religious figures, and antique jewelry. COMING SOON, located at the intersection of the Lower East Side and Chinatown, is a furniture design and gift shop founded by Helena Barquet and Fabiana Faria in 2013. Over in Williamsburg, MAST, which sells its chocolate bars in boutiques, stores, and restaurants around the world, offers visitors a glimpse into its chocolate factory, where they can see the artisanal "bean to bar" process in action—and end up inside its store that brims with unlimited sugar-filled goodies. FRONT GENERAL STORE is Brooklyn's best-kept secret, filled with endless options for shopping. Make sure to plan in enough time to rummage through the space so you can uncover those perfect finds that are usually hard to come across.

EXPLORE IT

Formerly an abandoned railway spur, the elevated THE HIGH LINE was repurposed as an unusual and immensely popular green space. The linear park runs along the Far West Side, from the Meatpacking District to the new Hudson Yards development. Prepare yourself for amazing vistas, and, since it's always packed, epic people watching. The LESLIE-LOHMAN MUSEUM was created by its founders to preserve LGBTQ identities and is a wonderful place to visit. The institution is a cultural hub for the queer community and the world's only museum dedicated to exhibiting and preserving art that focuses on the LGBTQ experience. With more than 30,000 objects in its collection that span three centuries of queer art, the museum is truly unlike any other.

The NYC LGBT HISTORIC SITES PROJECT is a tour to add to your list. It is the first initiative to document the historic and cultural sites, in all five boroughs, associated with the lesbian, gay, bisexual, and transgender community. The ever-changing tour continuously adds sites that reflect the diversity of the LGBTQ community, dating from the city's founding in the seventeenth century to the year 2000. Throughout the city, the DIA ART FOUNDATION provides various opportunities to

appreciate art. Dia maintains site-specific projects in the city, including Max Neuhaus's Times Square (1977), a harmonic sound texture that emerges from the north end of the triangular pedestrian island on Broadway, between 44th and 45th Streets. This incredibly unique art installation can be experienced 24 hours a day, seven days a week. DIA:CHELSEA provides a space for temporary exhibitions, performances, lectures, and readings, while DIA:BEACON, located in a former factory on the banks of the Hudson River in Beacon (a two-hour drive from the city), is a museum that presents Dia's art collection, which dates between the 1960s and the present.

The Leslie-Lohman Museum.

For quintessential New York City, try your luck on tickets for BILLY JOEL'S MADISON SQUARE GARDEN (MSG) residency. Since 2014, the iconic singer has played one show per month at the garden, amounting to an unprecedented run of more than 50 sold-out shows. His MSG performances are often marked by surprise guest appearances from fellow rock legends that join the "Piano Man" onstage for a song or two. Much like Billy Joel's residency, NYC PRIDE is an institution and one of the world's most vibrant Pride Month celebrations. During Pride Week, the boroughs mark the anniversary of the Stonewall riots of 1969 and celebrate the victories of the gay rights movement that followed. Expect to find events like a family movie night, a rally on the Hudson River waterfront, and a rooftop rave, all of which lead up to the huge march that heads through Chelsea and the West Village.

In celebration of the LGBT community, performers give it their all on the runway at the Latex Ball.

> **During Pride Week, the boroughs mark the anniversary of the Stonewall riots of 1969 and celebrate the victories of the gay rights movement that followed. Expect to find events like a family movie night, a rally on the Hudson River waterfront, and a rooftop rave.**

For something unexpected, if the timing matches your schedule, get tickets for THE LATEX BALL, one of the most popular balls on the NYC ballroom circuit. Over the past 28 years, the event has become renowned within LGBTQ communities around the world. It is put on in part by the Gay Men's Health Crisis and gives out approximately 10,000 dollars in awards over the span of six hours. The festivities that surround the ball have also expanded beyond the one-time event, with affiliated balls thrown throughout the weekend. Latex aside, the NY ART BOOK FAIR, the leading international gathering for the distribution of books, typically draws in more than 35,000 people each year. Besides being free to the public, the fair also offers opportunities to attend gratis programs, including artist-led discussions, performances, workshops, and curated exhibits.

Christopher Street—scene of the first major demonstrations by gay people in the face of police harassment.

Starting with the opening ceremony, numerous events, conferences, and parties take place during Pride Week.

While Memorial Day is summer's official kickoff, Labor Day marks its end. Between these holidays, expect easily reachable city escapes to be at maximum capacity, so plan in advance to make sure you can snag accommodation. For the refined traveler, think THE HAMPTONS, where the beaches are extremely picturesque. Find tranquility here on pristine and typically uncrowned shorefronts, in addition to the scenic state parks and unique towns that range from rustic to posh. The Hamptons are known for their sophisticated nightlife, award-winning wineries, and, of course, being home to the rich and famous.

For something a bit less high end, consider a trip to FIRE ISLAND, an unspoiled location without pretentious vibes. You won't find any cars here. Instead, there are wooden boardwalks and people that pull red wagons filled with groceries. Its two main communities are the Pines, which resembles

Visitors to Fire Island head to the stunning sandy beaches of Robert Moses State Park, or to the Fire Island Lighthouse.

New York's Chelsea, and Cherry Grove, which is a bit more diverse and down to earth. Visitors to Fire Island typically fluctuate between the two towns, following unofficial schedules of events that take them from one place to the next.

The relaxed vibe of Brooklyn's Williamsburg neighborhood, just across the East River.

Boulevard Haussmann

Champs-Élysées

Rue des Richelieu

Boulevard de Sébastopol

Boulevard Saint-Germain

Marais

Le Jardin de Luxembourg

Av Daumesnil

CLAIM IT

(1) Bourg Tibourg

(2) Hôtel Grand Amour

(3) Hôtel Monte Cristo

(4) Le Meurice

(5) Le Roch
Hôtel & Spa

SAVOR IT

(6) Septime

(7) Café Pouchkine

(8) CARBÓN

(9) Chez Georges

(10) La Tour d'Argent

(11) Le Temps des Cerises

(12) Pharamond

(13) Café de la Nouvelle Mairie

CELEBRATE IT

(14) Au Passage

(15) Le Dokhan's

(16) Les Souffleurs

(17) Le Syndicat

(18) Maxim's

OWN IT

(19) Anatomica

(20) Astier de Villatte

(21) Buly 1803

(22) Deyrolle

(23) Etat Libre
d'Orange

(24) L'Éclaireur

(25) La Compagnie
des Hommes

EXPLORE IT

(26) Astronomy Tower
of the Sorbonne

(27) Coulée verte
René-Dumont

(28) Fondation Louis Vuitton

(29) Grande Mosquée de Paris

(30) Musée de la Chasse
et de la Nature

(31) Muséum national
d'Histoire naturelle

PARIS

More than a Cornucopia of Clichés

Whether it's due to the rose-tinted glasses of visitors or the ceaseless self-marketing of the city, the fact remains that Paris has an iconic appeal that has lasted for centuries. Its panorama of façades and monuments are lodged firmly into the global consciousness, its romantic appeal is almost cinematic, and its inspirational power near cathartic. It's easy to be seduced by Paris, but when faced with such abundance, the challenge of choice inevitably becomes a little overwhelming.

It's said that Paris is a northern European city masquerading as a southern one, and as such has made itself into a bastion of sophistication and desirability. The city has welcomed foreigners and countrymen from all persuasions, tapping into the exotic, new, and talented. From writers and artists to royalty and refugees, Paris formed the creative center for gay luminaries such as Colette, Cocteau, and Genet, and has even elected its own openly gay mayor, twice. From all of that, and its careful instinct for self-preservation, this worldly capital continuously reveals itself like Cimetière du Père Lachaise resident Oscar Wilde's Salome in her dance of the seven veils.

Considering that Paris is more a collection of districts with unique identities, life on the street can vary quite considerably and so too can the view. For a uniquely stay, the chic HOTEL DUPOND-SMITH is a haven of tranquility. Rooms are tastefully stark with sleek design touches—from notables such as Philippe Starck and Hermés—a palette of neutral tones, panelled wood walls and an occasional splash of bold color. But the true appeal of this boutique beauty, located in a seventeenth-century mansion in the lively Marais, are the marvellous bespoke memories on offer via an attentive staff ready to indulge your every whim. Past the tempting stores of Rue du Faubourg Saint-Honoré, lies LE ROCH HÔTEL & SPA from where you can almost breathe in the exclusivity of the Place Vendôme jewelers. The hotel's dialed-down style is a counterpoint to such glamour, but the relaxing tonal simplicity of its light-filled rooms and spacious bathrooms with tubs is a true scarcity in

Eating in at the Le Roch Hôtel, diners sit in plush comfort with dark surroundings.

many Parisian hotels. Add to that a hammam and swimming pool and any water babies will feel right at home here.

Further afield is HÔTEL GRAND AMOUR, the second venture of artist André Saraiva. Made up of individually decorated rooms, it's furnished with his personal collection of designer pieces, but without the distractions of televisions or telephones. A quiet refuge in the colorful and up-and-coming 10th district, the fashion-media crowd that hangs around its bistro further flavors the place with a healthy dose of alternative chic. Personalized and home-style hospitality is also vividly evident at HÔTEL MONTE CRISTO, which is inspired by the global adventures of French author Alexandre Dumas's book but updated for today's traveler. Although the rooms are average by Paris standards, they are cozied up with custom tapestries, rich velvets, and dark woods that are suggestive of a ship's secret cabin and past voyages to faraway shores.

A color palette of intense blues, greens, grays, and browns brings a suave harmony to Le Roch.

Le Marais has been the Cinderella of Paris's gay scene since the 1980s but has stepped up her game considerably in the last decade. Popular fashion brand density has doubled and so has the amount of well-heeled visitors, but there are still a few hideaways where one can observe the spectacle without venturing into the fray. Case in point, BOURG TIBOURG. With its overly sumptuous period interiors discreetly disguised behind an anonymous façade, this boutique hotel takes traveling incognito to a new level of luxury.

The rooms at Bourg Tibourg have been styled luxuriously with antique furnishings and textiles.

On the edge of the Haut Marais, between the galleries and concept stores, is CARBÓN. Renowned for its wood firing, everything here is equally hot, from the raw wood furnishings to the hay-smoked duck breast. The voguish idea of sharing informs the restaurant's Argentinian-inspired dishes, while the intimate basement bar serves small plates to accompany your clandestine cocktails.

The literary scene around the Sorbonne in the Latin Quarter comes alive at CAFÉ DE LA NOUVELLE MAIRIE, where the handsome and knowledgeable staff suggest intelligent choices from the extensive wine selection. A near tourist-free bistro overlooking a small neighborhood square and with an equally unpretentious menu, it's a kind reminder that for some people, it's just another day in the city.

The amazing interior at Pharamond, featuring painted mirrors, tiled floors, and a gastro vibe.

> Naturally as the capital of a gastronomically famous country, Paris gets to draw on the best and Pharamond in Les Halles, the erstwhile produce market.

These many layers of Paris are most evident in its older areas, where small villages are planted like a time capsule into larger districts. One such spot is Saint-Paul, where you'll find LE TEMPS DES CERISES. Open every day of the week, it's a thoughtfully modern take on the classic bistro but with lighter alternatives, and, like the nineteenth-century commune song sung by Yves Montand after which it is named, quintessentially Parisian.

Naturally as the capital of a gastronomically famous country, Paris gets to draw on the best and PHARAMOND in Les Halles, the erstwhile produce market, has been importing the comforting gourmet traditions of Normandy since 1832. The interior is a plush mix of original and 1900s pastiche, while its selection of unique private salon rooms is a must for small private groups. Another restaurant that honors Paris's bistro heritage is CHEZ GEORGES near Place des Victoires with its menu, decor, and attitude almost frozen in time. Its enduring allure as a living reminder of the history of authentic French fare is due to the unchanged quality of its dishes and a complete lack of improvisation.

The importance of culinary tradition in France has also created the international benchmark: the Michelin star. A restaurant that epitomizes what this accolade means is LA TOUR D'ARGENT on the Quai de la Tournelle with its striking view of Notre Dame. During its 400-year history, the restaurant has seen the introduction of the fork to France and countless celebrities come and go, but has maintained its legacy by balancing quality and fashion. In contrast, the Michelin-starred SEPTIME is a young and fresh eatery exercising the same equilibrium in a modern vein. The ambiance and serving is kept simple, while the daring tasting combinations woo both foodies and critics alike. Its popularity makes a dinner reservation tricky, but a place at lunch or its trendy sister seafood restaurant, Clamato, is more than a consolation.

Down Boulevard des Capucines, not far from the Palais Garnier, where ballet pin-up Nureyev first tasted the freedom of gay Paris, is another Russian import: CAFÉ POUCHKINE. Looking out on L'église de la Madeleine, Pouchkine brings an element of Catherine the Greatness to the French salon du thé in extravagant period interiors. Don't miss its delicate modern pastries, which include a matryoshka doll in layers of caramel, ganache, and tonka bean.

Le Syndicat is admired for its emphasis on French spirits and its range of inventive house creations, which bring a French twist to the classics.

Life isn't always a cabaret, and in those times you should make for AU PASSAGE. An all-day bar meets wine lovers canteen, it offers a limited selection of delectable small dishes. Linger over a glass of the best surrounded by a relaxed, spontaneous crowd to lighten your mood. LES SOUFFLEURS on Rue de la Verrerie is an evergreen, late-night refuge for local artists, models, designers, DJs, and poets. Downstairs from the narrow bar is a cramped vaulted dance floor where guest events and DJs introduce you to the established and the new. Openness is the keyword here, so if you'd rather not, then don't—although it's equally likely that you'll be dragged into a discussion about speculative capitalism as invited back to someone's home.

To experience a little less now and more yester-year is quite easy in Paris, and tucked away in the five-star LE DOKHAN's hotel is a small but serious champagne bar. Here, a gentle candlelit intimacy is only broken by regular tastings and a sommelier that knows his way around more than 200 bottles, from the famous to the barely known. And it doesn't get more famous than MAXIM'S: a social center on Rue Royale since La Belle Époque and now part of Pierre Cardin's empire, it boasts a restaurant, museum, shop, and brasserie. It also brings the house down with the popular monthly LGBTQ party BIZARRE LOVE TRIANGLE—think electro goes breath-less with a decadent crowd.

Progressive is sometimes difficult to spot between all the history, but behind the Porte Saint-Denis a kind of garage-industrial-cool cocktail bar is finding furtive fame. LE SYNDICAT specializes in rare French liquors combined with unexpected local ingredients, but that's where tradition ends and a street-chic crowd enters.

It's almost as if Baron Haussmann planned Paris's shop-lined boulevards exclusively to trap consumers with their tantalizing window displays, and although he was forced to resign for this extravagance, we are still the proud heirs of this vision. Besides the grand avenues, there are plenty of alternative places to spend your money. One of these is L'ECLAIREUR, which has three concept stores scattered throughout the Right Bank's side streets. Each has its own style, specialty, and designer collections, and testifies to Paris's marriage of fashion, art, and design dynamism. For more homewares, accessories, and gifts, visit ASTIER DE VILLATTE'S tiny, brim-filled store on Rue Saint-Honoré. Invest in its handmade ceramic pieces, which mimic the traditions of eighteenth-century Parisian ceramic studios, its range of scented products, or complementary works by other artisans.

This nostalgic revivalist spirit is also to be experienced at BULY 1803 near the École des Beaux-Arts. An antique perfume brand brought back to life, it sells an assortment of cosmetics, grooming accessories, and scented products made from secret recipes in an elegant replica of a nineteenth-century pharmacy. A different olfactory explosion happens at ETAT LIBRE D'ORANGE on Rue des Archives in Le Marais. The brand has created scents for icons such as Rossy de Palma, Tilda Swinton, and Tom of Finland, and blends provocative combinations with names like "Sécrétions Magnifiques," inspired by bodily fluids in ecstasy.

As far as comfort is concerned, ANATOMICA brings a whole new dimension to footwear. The owner's philosophy that clothing must adapt to the shape of the body and not the other way round is what drives the reputation of this Franco-Japanese specialty store, which stocks hard-to-find quality labels together with its own line of tailored wares.

Everyone knows that Paris has enough fashion to go around twice—and at the vintage boutique LA COMPAGNIE DES HOMMES you can do exactly that. Stocked with designer brands and some special editions in between, you'll soon have reason to reply, "What, this old thing?". While window-shopping is not a crime, the Parisians take great care of their displays and one shop that is hard to pass by is DEYROLLE on Rue Du Bac. An institution since 1831 and created from the passion of a family of born naturalists, it's still home to their taxidermy, curiosity, and love of nature.

The nostalgic interior of Buly 1803, with its wall-to-wall wooden cabinetry and beautifully worn tiled floor.

The bar at L'Éclaireur has a fantastic interior, with surreal art inspired by the work of Piero Fornasetti, also on sale in the store.

Celebrating thirty years since it first opened its doors, L'Éclaireur is credited as being the city's first concept store.

Who doesn't love the Eiffel Tower or Sacré-Coeur? One may visit either for the view, but the lesser-known ASTRONOMY TOWER OF THE SORBONNE in the center of the Latin Quarter boasts an equally commanding vista. The night-time viewing here is perfect for taking in the spectacular City of Lights without the long queues or elbowing tourists.

The unexpected lurks around every corner of Paris and a tour of the MUSÉUM NATIONAL D'HISTOIRE NATURELLE won't disappoint. Take in France's oldest cedar of Lebanon or the alpine garden in the Jardin des Plantes and the last-surviving specimens of extinct species on earth in La Salle des Espèces Menacées et des Espèces Disparues. Here in ornate glass cases, the true finality of the vanished and disappearing natural world stares you in the face. Head across the road to the ornate 1920 neo-Mujédar-styled GRANDE MOSQUÉE DE PARIS, where you can stroll through the tiled archways and

Hôtel de Mongelas, one of the two buildings housing the collections at the Museum of Hunting and Nature.

Take in France's oldest cedar of Lebanon or the alpine garden in the Jardin des Plantes and the last-surviving specimens of extinct species on earth.

take refreshments in its souk-like tearoom to complete your exotic adventure. Another trail leads through the MUSÉE DE LA CHASSE ET DE LA NATURE in Rue des Archives. Think less museum, more secret society where an eclectic selection of contemporary art, antiques, and the private collection of its conservationist founders are housed in the uniquely themed rooms of a seventeenth-century hôtel particulier built by architect François Mansart (he of the mansard roof).

Although Paris has many parks providing relief from its busy streets, a standout is the COULÉE VERTE RENÉ-DUMONT, an elevated park occupying an old railway line that crosses through the 12th arrondissement. It is a peaceful bridge of greenery, which allows for a carefree three-mile stroll above the rooflines and away from the traffic. In another park, part of the Bois de Boulogne, rises the contemporary silhouette of the FONDATION LOUIS VUITTON. A modern architectural gesture designed by Frank Gehry and sponsored by LVMH, it contains a network of large contemporary art galleries that are connected by glass-covered garden terraces on overlapping levels.

The Museum of Hunting and Nature examines humanity's complex relationship to animals through the ages.

The approach to the main entrance of Frank Gehry's glass-clad, shiplike Fondation Louis Vuitton.

The CITÉ DE LA MUSIQUE in Parc de Villete has a packed agenda of multidisciplinary music performances. Its oblique, silver, Jean Nouvel-designed symphonic hall for the Philharmonie de Paris is an experience in itself and hosts concerts, musicals, and exhibitions in between regular season performances by world-class acts.

Like cliché, the French have given us the word soirée.

Befitting a major cultural center like Paris, there's naturally plenty on the events calendar. Appropriately center stage is the Grand Palais, a venue for exhibitions since it's inauguration in 1900 for the Exposition Universelle. These days, it hosts the internationally renowned PARIS PHOTO, which builds on the city's love for imagery. Not only for professionals, the annual fair represents the art of photography through exhibitions, books, and films from the world's leading figures. Another event, Foire Internationale d'Art Contemporain, AKA FIAC, brings the most famous contemporary galleries together under the Grand Palais's glass-domed roof. With a program including talks, screenings, and performances adding to the main exhibit, it's no wonder this event has become an important part of a city eternally associated with art.

Like cliché, the French have given us the word soirée, which has come to apply to an evening gathering of like-minded guests for music or conversation. It's also an apt description of MERCREDIX, the Wednesday night sister of the gay party-circuit's VENDREDIX. Held at Comptoir du Marché on Rue du Château d'Eau, the mood is more afterwork happy hour meets man of your dreams and starts getting busy around a civilized 7 p.m.

The façade of the Philharmonie de Paris is clad in thousands of tessellating bird-shaped tiles.

The stunning Grande salle Pierre Boulez, at the Philharmonie de Paris.

ESCAPE IT

If there is anything French that is as famous as Paris, it has to be champagne, and although it flows amply in the capital, there's no reason not to take to REIMS in the Champagne region. A short day trip through the picturesque countryside, stock up at the tasting rooms of the illustrious champagne houses and local épiceries before visiting Reims Cathedral. Famous as the place where French kings were crowned, its façade is illuminated by a light show after sunset in summer and is a spectacular sight to round off your day.

The countryside around Reims is full of vineyards belonging to the world's best Champagne houses.

NE Lombard St

NE Martin Luther King Jr Blvd

NE 33rd Ave

Forest Park

Irvington

NE Broadway St

Pearl District

SE Stark St

Downtown

SW Sunset Hwy

SE Division St

CLAIM IT

(1) Ace Hotel

(2) Caravan
The Tiny House
Hotel

(3) Hotel Eastlund

(4) Jupiter NEXT

(5) Sentinel

SAVOR IT

(6) Ava Gene's

(7) Canteen

(8) Coava

(9) Han Oak

(10) Hat Yai

(11) Kachka

(12) Langbaan

(13) Nomad.PDX

(14) Tasty n Sons

(15) Tusk

CELEBRATE IT

(16) Coopers Hall

(17) Crush

(18) Departure

(19) Dig A Pony

(20) Expatriate

(21) Multnomah
Whiskey Library

(22) Stag PDX

OWN IT

(23) Ampersand Gallery
& Fine Books

(24) Beam & Anchor

(25) Machus

(26) Monograph
Bookwerks

(27) Serra Dispensary
Downtown

(28) Union Way

EXPLORE IT

(29) Disjecta

(30) Forest Park

(31) lumber room

(32) Mississippi Studios

(33) Revolution Hall

(34) Washington Park

PORTLAND

Leading the Way to a Greener Future

In the past few years, Portland, Oregon, has quickly gained the attention of international cultural tastemakers from Brooklyn to Tokyo for its twenty-first-century model of healthy urban living. This modest former logging town now inspires many young creatives to start new lives in the heart of the Pacific Northwest. The region's vast wilderness, moderate climate, and fertile valleys, along with its DIY West Coast entrepreneurial spirit, provide an ideal setting for one of the worlds most exciting farm-to-table food scenes and a relaxed, progressive culture firmly committed to social equality and environmental sustainability.

While the west side of the Willamette River in the downtown area has excellent hotels, a high density, and many noteworthy attractions, the more expansive and relaxed east side is where you'll find much of Portland's culinary, outdoor, and creative pulse. Hop on a bicycle using the city's tech-savvy bike share program, Biketown, a partnership with locally based Nike, and discover why the city is so widely admired for its quietly utopian ambitions.

The Portland-headquartered ACE HOTEL has enjoyed great success in applying its site-specific, neo-bohemian design philosophy to a growing number of destinations, from Palm Springs to London. Room amenities at this trendy and historic West End lodging include custom murals (fawns, graffiti, mountainscapes, trolls, cats), shared or private baths, LPs and turntables, claw-foot tubs, and locally made and vintage furniture.

The posh SENTINEL, part of the trendy Provenance Hotels group, offers a classic, inviting sensibility that includes lively rock and roll–era photography, room-service Salt & Straw ice cream, and rooftop beehives that produce Bee Local Honey. The building also featured in local auteur Gus Van Sant's queer epic *My Own Private Idaho*. For those seeking a livelier, more casual east side roost, the JUPITER NEXT is a recent expansion of the quintessentially Portland Jupiter brand. The new site features sharp, contemporary angles, cool-hued concrete floors, and a state-of-the-art design that reflects the new tech-friendly face of the booming lower East Burnside district. When you're in a raucous mood, walk across the street to the original complex, an ingeniously updated mid-century modern motor lodge that features a top-notch music venue, bar, and restaurant, Doug Fir Lounge, whose lumber-chic aesthetic evokes the dreamlike Pacific Northwest of *Twin Peaks*.

Another relative newcomer to the east side, HOTEL EASTLUND'S updated mid-century boutique vibe, wrapped in floor-to-ceiling windows, delivers on multiple fronts. Its slightly uninspiring location is a blessing in disguise: being almost perfectly equidistant from most of the city's attractions and notable neighborhoods, it attracts a range of people. With the on-site Altabira City Tavern, the Eastlund also boasts one of the city's best rooftop restaurant views and beer selections. But for something a little different and *very* Portland, CARAVAN – THE TINY HOUSE HOTEL comprises a cluster of six tiny, uniquely designed cabin-like houses decorated with local art, hand-knitted quilts, and Adirondack chairs, which surround an outdoor gathering space, fire pit, and converted school bus that serves gourmet grilled-cheese sandwiches. Located in the heart of the Alberta Arts District—one of Portland's most charming bohemian neighborhoods—it is just steps away from some of the area's best food options, including the prime vegan dishes at Tin Shed Garden Cafe and the grocery range at Alberta Co-op Grocery.

A lofty foyer at Jupiter Next combines reception with a communal space for lounging in urban comfort.

Rooms at Jupiter Next have a stunning view—most of them looking out across Portland's historic Central Eastside.

The region's vast wilderness, moderate climate, and fertile valleys, provide an ideal setting for one of the most exciting food scenes.

The east side food scene is an embarrassment of riches that comprises dozens of micro-neighborhoods scattered throughout Southeast, Central Eastside, Northeast, and North Portland. A culinary incubator, the Ocean complex hosts some of the city's hottest pop-up restaurants. Peter Cho and Johnny Leach's HAN OAK serves prix-fixe Korean BBQ dinners on the weekends and a Sunday brunch that might include braised pork belly waffles, blood cakes, and pork-and-chive dumpling soup. NOMAD.PDX, a former traveling supper club turned brick-and-mortar standout, is one of the leading purveyors of contemporary Oregon cuisine, and it also showcases the origins of its wide range of locally sourced and foraged ingredients. Hidden away from the dining room, the intimate Ash Bar is itself worth a dedicated visit for its inventive cocktails and inspired bar food, such as black truffle sashimi and *dashi chawanmushi* (Japanese custard) served with foraged mushrooms.

Chef Ryan Fox prepares dishes in the kitchen at Nomad.PDX.

Fans of brunch in all its guises will not be disappointed at Tasty n Sons.

Art and textiles from Belarus adorn the walls at Kachka.

The chef and restaurateur John Gorham owns one of the city's most consistently outstanding food empires—it includes the fantastic Toro Bravo and Mediterranean Exploration Company. His TASTY N SONS offers "new American diner" cuisine with a satisfyingly eclectic Pacific Northwest spin, as well as an international brunch menu featuring Burmese red pork stew, North African sausage, and chocolate potato doughnuts. Northeast Portland's HAT YAI is the latest addition to chef and restaurateur Akkapong "Earl" Ninsom's growing list of excellent Thai restaurants, which includes the phenomenal and ever-popular LANGBAAN. On the pared-down menu of refresh-ingly accessible comfort food, don't miss the hearty plate of fried chicken, roti, and Malayu curry. For an all-around unforgettable, warmly lit, and leisurely dining experience, look to AVA GENE'S. Standouts among the delectable Italian dishes include sheep cheese and cherry tomato *pane* (flatbread), *sagna riccia* (ruffled pasta) with lamb ragù, and any of the light market-fresh vegetable plates.

At the southern end of the noteworthy 28th and Burnside restaurant district, the simple and modern CANTEEN turns out an inspired vegan menu of fresh juices, smoothies, bowls, and salads using local organic produce. The deceptively hearty quinoa, black bean, and baked maple tempeh Portland Bowl provides delicious, healthy sustenance for exploring the east side. Not far from here, you'll find TUSK, a bright, contemporary space that serves a locally sourced Middle Eastern–inspired menu, including Asian pear salad with matsutake mushrooms and wild rice, and steelhead trout and roe with delicata squash. First-generation Belarusian-American chef Bonnie Morales (née Frumkin) struck a deep chord in the east side food scene with KACHKA, a warm, lively hangout that serves Ukrainian sour cherry dumplings (*vareniki*), clay pot rabbit with porcini and potato pancakes, and a stellar selection of spirits, including the house's own horseradish-infused vodka.

The locavore approach to Portland's food movement also applies to its beverage scene, which features exceptional artisan producers of coffee, beer, wine, spirits, juice, tea, kombucha, and even drinking vinegars. The inner Southeast, in particular, is home to some outstanding single-source coffee roasters, including COAVA COFFEE ROASTERS, whose industrial-chic brew bar is housed in an open concrete-shell warehouse space that bridges the gap between café and tasting room.

Since many of Portland's pleasures revolve around food, you'll be happy you did lots of walking, hiking, and other outdoor activities during the day—so you can enjoy extra bites during your nighttime exploring. One of the benefits of the state's extensive alcohol laws is that most bars have a full menu and, as a result, some of the city's best food can be found at great local hangouts. Home to more microbreweries than any other U.S. city, Portland is the country's craft beer capital, and it's also the

> Since many of Portland's pleasures revolve around food, you'll be happy you did lots of walking, hiking, and other outdoor activities during the day.

gateway to one of the nation's most acclaimed wine regions. Sample some of Oregon's and Washington's finest wines—from Willamette Valley pinot noir to Walla Walla Sangiovese—at COOPERS HALL, a large, festive urban winery and taproom (with an excellent draft beer selection) in a casually elegant converted warehouse in the Central Eastside's fast-growing nightlife district.

With wood-paneled walls, candle chandeliers and reading lamps, plush leather and upholstered seats, and a decidedly British gentlemen's club ambiance, MULTNOMAH WHISKEY LIBRARY operates more like a restaurant than a bar. Solicitous and knowledgeable bartenders ferry around custom-built minibars and help guide you through the

astounding list of nearly 2,000 spirits, from local—and pleasingly peaty—Clear Creek single-barrel whiskey to expertly crafted mixed drinks. Pair your elixir with chef Ben Grossmann's estimable farm-to-table cuisine.

Soak in the relaxed neighborhood vibes of the Alberta Arts District at Asian-inspired EXPATRIATE, which serves remarkable international bar snacks and cocktails in a cozy space filled with well-suited DJ grooves. Here, chef and co-owner Naomi Pomeroy, whose famous meat-centric restaurant Beast is across the street, has concocted an adventurous fusion menu that includes Burmese tea leaf salad, Laotian tuna belly tacos, and fried wonton nachos.

Celeb LGBTQ chef Gregory Gourdet's spectacular rooftop pan-Asian eatery and cocktail lounge DEPARTURE is the downtown location to go to see and be seen. On the top floor of the swank Nines Hotel, which occupies a stately terracotta-glazed former Meier & Frank department store, its futurist-style lounge pays homage to mid-century modern visions of the luxury and excitement of early commercial air travel.

Portland has one of the most progressive queer scenes in the country, and CRUSH is its shaggy, unpretentious crowning achievement. A week in the life of this Buckman neighborhood bar might include a body-positive cuddle group meet-up, a genderqueer, clothing-optional dance party, a Latinx club night, or a friendly lightsaber duel on the sidewalk. Crush truly lives up to the city's proud spirit of inclusivity, embracing the community in its full spectrum of colors. One of the most eclectic bars in town, DIG A PONY serves creative cocktails and light meals in a restored 1920s pharmacy with a ski chalet–inspired wood interior. With an extremely unpredictable event calendar, a combination of queer parties, celebrity spelling bees, and live music abounds, and DJ nights are held for just about any genre you can think of. There's a little bit of everything, and somehow it works.

Compared to any city in the country, Portland's sex-positive culture boasts the highest per capita ratio of strip clubs. In addition, the recent success of the gay gentlemen's club STAG suggests that erotic dancing—when done right—has a viable future in the LGBTQ community. The bar draws in a wide cross-section of people: here, business professionals, club kids, service industry workers, and college students rub shoulders and intermittently interact with the performers.

Customers can chose from 900 whiskeys alone at the exclusive Multnomah Whiskey Library.

A good place to start shopping is downtown's West End, around Harvey Milk Street (recently renamed to honor the iconic gay rights advocate and politician). Sandwiched between the Ace Hotel and legendary Powell's Books, UNION WAY houses a cohesive selection of contemporary retail spaces, including clothiers, leather goods shops, and even a ramen parlor. With its sharp focus on formally inventive menswear from emerging designers, the beautifully appointed MACHUS is not to be missed, especially if you're a contemporary fashion or design enthusiast. You'll find it in the increasingly trendy lower East Burnside area, a locale that has been transformed by a series of high-profile, angular residential towers and a number of other stylish retailers.

One of Portland's most vibrant cultural hubs, the 20-block Alberta Arts District hosts an art walk on the last Thursday of every month. It's also home to two first-rate specialty bookstores. Besides hosting monthly exhibitions, the clean, minimalist AMPERSAND GALLERY & FINE BOOKS showcases rare vintage artwork and photography in old map chests and, on its shelves, a deftly curated collection of art books. Two blocks west, MONOGRAPH BOOKWERKS is a cozy den of a shop filled with rare new and used books spanning art, architecture, fashion, graphic design, photography, and counterculture.

In recent years, Portland has developed an enviable knack for exporting its signature lifestyle— a product of the ideal pairing of nearby mountainous forests with world-class cultural amenities. Taking the art of curated retail to impressive heights, the home decor shop and studio BEAM & ANCHOR is, along with the magazine *Kinfolk*, among the primary exporters of the city's artisan aesthetic, its objects evoking the themes of historical craftsmanship, Americana, rugged wilderness, global awareness, and contemporary urban living.

In 2015, Oregon became one of the first states to legalize the sale of marijuana for recreational use. Cannabis dispensaries immediately sprung up all over Portland and are now much easier to find than gas stations or even liquor stores. Downtown, the flagship SERRA DISPENSARY DOWNTOWN dispensary is a shining example of the new face of modern cannabis culture. Look out for special edition delicacies designed in collaboration with some of Portland's top culinary world luminaries, such as Ava Gene's Joshua McFadden and the team at Woodblock Chocolate.

The handsome store frontage of the Serra dispensary in downtown Portland gives way to modern displays within.

The Serra dispensary sells a range of cannabis products, including flowers (pictured), edibles, and pre-rolls.

The people of Portland draw much of their inspiration from their intimate relationship with the lush, dramatic natural surroundings. Just west of downtown, 5,100 acres of urban woodland reserve—an area that comprises FOREST PARK and the adjoining 410-acre WASHINGTON PARK—feature 70 miles (130 km) of recreational trails, the breathtaking Japanese Garden, the International Rose Test Garden, and several other noteworthy attractions.

To get a sense of the city's artistic pulse, visit North Portland's DISJECTA, a 6,000-square-foot (560 sq m) contemporary art hub that showcases emerging local and national talents—with a strong emphasis on female artists. Recent projects have focused on digital media, aesthetic presentations of gender, and virtual reality. Art enthusiasts will also find plenty to see in the dozens of galleries found downtown, in the chic Pearl District. But for a quick sampling, take a jaunt to LUMBER ROOM, which presents rotating exhibits inside a stunning loft space hidden in the heart of the former warehouse district.

The city's vibrant live music scene has the added benefit of drawing big name talent to small, charismatic venues. In the heart of North Portland's Mississippi District, MISSISSIPPI STUDIOS, a cozy renovated church with an Old West charm that extends to its covered patio and firepit, books some of the world's best indie artists. Check its calendar for some of Portland's best monthly queer dance parties. REVOLUTION HALL is an old converted brick high school that now houses a mid-size state-of-the-art performance space, two bars, and a spacious roof deck. In addition to featuring some of the most exciting live acts that roll into town, the auditorium showcases other events, like famed sex columnist Dan Savage's HUMP! Film Festival, which presents a selection of five-minute amateur porn films.

The people of Portland draw much of their inspiration from their intimate relationship with the lush, dramatic natural surroundings.

Among other attractions, Portland's Washington Park is home to a zoo, an arboretum, and a Japanese garden (pictured).

One of the most artistically fertile recent developments in Portland's LGBTQ community is its evolving queer BALLROOM CULTURE. In 2014, the internationally renowned dancer Kumari Suraj began throwing small kiki balls—the younger, more casual sibling of mainstream balls. Organized in collaboration with vogue instructor Daniel Girón, and students and friends, these events have helped to lay the foundations of the city's growing ballroom community. Portland's iteration of this century-old queer tradition heavily emphasizes the inclusivity of the full gender spectrum, celebrating all body types through nonconforming gender categories, and raising money and awareness for LGBTQ causes. PORTLAND BALLROOM (PDXB) is a loosely formed organization that hosts some of these balls. If you're new to the scene, it's recommended that you learn a little ballroom history and etiquette online before attending.

One of the city's most visible gay events is the yearly RED DRESS PDX party, an event at which all attendees—regardless of gender—wear red dresses to raise money for LGBTQ youth and people living with HIV/AIDS. PEACOCK IN THE PARK is a long-running LGBTQ variety show held in early summer in Washington Park that features drag performers, dancers, and live music. Catch the "world's oldest working drag queen,"

Darcelle XV (born in 1930 and still operating his own legendary eponymous show bar) performing at this all-ages, family-friendly community favorite.

Held in early May, Portland's QDOC, the only U.S. festival dedicated exclusively to LGBTQ documentaries, showcases the latest award-winning docs from Sundance, Berlin, and the like. Filmmakers and their subjects often lead lively discussions about the most pressing issues facing the community, from civil rights to aging and reshaping one's identity.

The Red Dress Party has been held annually since 2001. Now it attracts more than 2,000 attendees.

ESCAPE IT

In this city, you don't have to walk far to breathe fresh tree-scented air, but, to expand your options, it's best to bring hiking shoes. After all, Portland is a gateway to Oregon's rugged coastline, the dramatic Columbia River Gorge, and soaring Mt. Hood. Although it's about a 90-minute drive,

Crown Point is one of several spots for spectacular views of the stunning Columbia River Gorge.

you owe it to yourself to make at least a day trip to the Pacific coast. For a rewarding hike, OSWALD WEST STATE PARK contains the scenic Short Sand Beach, with two magnificent headlands to choose from. The trail to Cape Falcon leads to sea cliffs, where you may be treated to whale, dolphin, or sea lion sightings. And the steep hike across the 1,680-foot (512 m) Neahkahnie Mountain offers a truly singular view of the coastline.

During the warm summer months, Portlanders regularly flock to the clothing-optional, gay-popular beach at Rooster Rock State Park, in the spectacular Columbia River Gorge. The dramatic natural setting and relaxed social vibe make it a great place to meet handsome, friendly locals. Less than a 30-minute drive from Portland, the park is also close to several great waterfall-packed hikes through the gorge.

Villa Borghese

The Vatican

Rione I Monti

Trastevere

Viale Giulio Cesare

Via del Quirinale

Via Venti Settembre

Corso Vittorio Emanuele II

CLAIM IT

1 Elizabeth Unique Hotel
2 G-Rough
3 Horti 14
4 The Shire
5 Villa Spalletti Trivelli

SAVOR IT

6 Come il Latte
7 Coromandel
8 Faro
9 Glass Hostaria
10 Lanificio Cucina
11 Mercato Testaccio
12 Panificio Bonci
13 Roscioli

CELEBRATE IT

14 Goa Club
15 Jerry Thomas Speakeasy
16 Muccassassina
17 Salotto42

OWN IT

18 Bocache & Salvucci
19 Cartoleria Pantheon
20 Chez Dede
21 Tartufi & Friends
22 Mercato Vintage Ecosolidale

EXPLORE IT

23 All Saints' Anglican Church
24 MACRO
25 Palazzo Massimo alle Terme
26 Sacripante
27 Sant'Agnese in Agone

ROME

The Epitome of History, Art, Culture, and Cuisine

First-century BC poet Albius Tibullus might just have been onto something when he dubbed Rome the "Eternal City." Even after 3,000 years, Rome never ceases to enchant the millions of visitors who walk her cobbled streets each year. World-famous ancient ruins transport travelers back to a time of chariot races and gladiators, while the dolce vita lifestyle inspires leisurely walks through ornate piazzas—decadent gelato in hand. Lose yourself in Rome's rich history of great art and culture by day, and, in the evening, rub elbows with stylish Romans at alfresco pizzerias or over unpretentious aperitivos (predinner cocktails and snacks).

It's worth noting that homosexuality in Ancient Rome differed markedly from that of other cultures around the globe. Romans had no concept of homosexuality or heterosexuality, and it was commonly believed that men could be attracted to all genders. What was important was patriarchy and masculinity: sex between men was acceptable, provided one was the older partner and did not take the passive role. Homoerotic poetry and art further promoted same-sex love and desire, with famed poets such as Juvenal, Plutarch, and Petronius celebrating male–male relations. It wasn't until the fourth century and the rise of Catholicism that homosexuality became repressed. Yet even as the seat of the Catholic Church, Renaissance Rome brought with it prized homo-sexual artists who would forever leave their mark on the world, including on the very walls of the Sistine Chapel. A gay-lensed stroll through the Vatican museums shines new light on famed artworks as Michelangelo's, Da Vinci's and Caravaggio's passionate depictions of male nudes and love poems give a snapshot of Renaissance Italy's liberal take on gay relations. Few cities pack as much history, culture, and cuisine into their DNA as Rome, proving that even with the crazed traffic and sometimes overflowing trash bins, there's an undeniable romance to Italy's illustrious capital city.

Tucked away on Quirinal—one of the Seven Hills of Rome, just moments from the famed Trevi Fountain—VILLA SPALLETTI TRIVELLI is a villa hotel as opulent as they come. There's a distinct historical flair here, with smart antiques, marble-laden bathrooms, and luxurious fabrics defining the decor. A well-equipped gym, lush gardens, and Turkish baths promise plenty of spaces to relax in after a busy day. Don't miss the honesty-based aperitivo bar, which features wines from the owner's family estate.

For a true "made-in-Italy" feel, the design at the G-ROUGH hotel pays homage to innovative artists and designers like Giò Ponti and Silvio Cavatorta. Original vintage pieces lie throughout the 10 stylish rooms, attracting design-savvy hipsters and those who prefer to check in at a coffee bar rather than a lobby—there isn't one here. Located in a historic building near Piazza Navona, the hotel provides easy access to one of Rome's most popular and colorful gathering points, the bohemian Trastevere neighborhood. At HORTI 14, you'll have Trastevere's cool craft beer pubs, ivy-laden trattorias, and popular cobbled paths right at your fingertips. Sip prosecco on the rooftop terrace while enjoying the lush surroundings, seemingly far removed from the chaos of the city outside.

Save time for a glass of Italian wine.

Via Veneto is one of Rome's most famous streets, with historic cafés, rooftop bars, and one of the city's largest public parks, Villa Borghese. It's also where you'll find the boutique hotel THE SHIRE, which offers unparalleled views of the Aurelian Walls. Request the Corner Suite: the hotel's flagship room has exquisite glass windows looking out to the street. Then there's the ELIZABETH UNIQUE HOTEL, a fitting name for this elegant design hotel hidden away in a renovated seventeenth-century palazzo on the renowned Via del Corso. Galleria Russo curated the art throughout the hotel, and, should a piece pique your interest, nearly all of the works are for sale. Save time for a glass of Italian wine in the library-style lounge, which oozes romance with its open fireplace, or merely wander through the hotel and enjoy the antique wallpaper and historic architectural details. And don't forget to indulge in a luxurious breakfast at the hotel's Bar Bacharach & Bistrot, a spot that boasts an idyllic terrace surrounded by jasmine-scented gardens.

A Suite Apartment at the G-Rough hotel combines rough plastered walls with plush furniture and a beautiful tiled floor.

Grand tour etchings grace the walls of the suites at Elizabeth Unique Hotel, where midnight blue and gold are key colors.

It's worth noting that homosexuality in Ancient Rome differed markedly from that of other cultures around the globe.

For an authentic taste of Italy's famed pastries and pizzas, PANIFICIO BONCI is the obvious choice. Traditional Roman pastries line the deli counter, and its creative pizza combinations are made from only the freshest ingredients, including organic vegetables and stone-milled heirloom wheat. Chef Gabriele Bonci claims to sell some 1,500 different pizza varieties each year, so it's no surprise he's earned himself the moniker "the king of pizza." The takeaway bakery is small and popular—don't be surprised if you see a line snaking out the door. ROSCIOLI is headed by one of Rome's most prominent baking families, which dates back four generations. Part deli, part wine bar, and part unconventional restaurant, here you can expect a vast selection of deli favorites along with traditional pastas and main courses. With some 300 kinds of cheese, over 2,000 wine labels, and a vast range of cured meats and other antipasti, it also makes for a perfect pit-stop before a relaxed picnic in the park.

A seamless fusion of authentic Italian dishes and innovative global flavors, GLASS HOSTARIA is an eclectic yet ultra-modern restaurant in the center of picture-perfect Trastevere. Directed by Rome's only female Michelin-starred chef, Cristina Bowerman, it is all about a unique approach to the classics, with menu items like potato gnocchi with sea urchin or beef filet with chocolate, mushrooms, and aged foie gras. Then there are Rome's delightful markets—culinary experiences in their own right.

Frangipane with cherries and wasabi served up at Glass Hostaria.

The sleek, ultramodern interior at Glass Hostaria, with installations in glass cases.

MERCATO TESTACCIO is one of Rome's oldest. Though it recently moved to an ultra-contemporary space, the original food stalls—some of which have been in the same families for generations—moved with it. The foodie paradise is perfect for picking up fresh produce or for enjoying a leisurely lunch at one of the many stands. Be sure not to miss the two stalls run by Glass's very own Cristina Bowerman, Romeo and Cups, which serve fresh soups, salads, and sandwiches. After the market, be sure to stroll around the working-class neighborhood of Testaccio, considered by many to be representative of the "real" Rome.

A self-proclaimed production center and creative laboratory that is known for its alternative parties, LANIFICIO CUCINA is a bar, restaurant, and workspace located in a restored wooden mill along the Aniene River. Industrial piping, upcycled furniture, and floor-to-ceiling glass windows set the scene. Check their events calendar for everything from international DJ performances to cutting-edge exhibitions to vintage art shows.

While most Italians quickly down their espressos at café counters, spaces that cater to a more leisurely crowd are popping up. FARO, for example, is a laid-back coffee house with a mission to combine a relaxed atmosphere with an education in java. Try the single-origin tasting menu to learn more about the expressive flavors in each cup—but skip the sugar. Here, coffee aficionados and newbies alike are encouraged to sample unsweetened brews to effectively enhance the entire experience. For the best brunch in Rome, head to the wonderful COROMANDEL. Located near Piazza Navona, the elegant restaurant is known for its French toast, eggs benedict, and other classic brunch goodies. But if breakfast doesn't strike your fancy, it also serves a lovely dinner. The silver cutlery holders, opulent china, and dark wood interior combine to create a luxurious tone.

Italians love *la passeggiata*, a traditional evening stroll—especially one that includes a gelato. Don't be tempted by the tourist shops where the gelato is three feet tall and pumped with air, artificial flavors, and sweeteners. The best *gelaterias* use all-natural ingredients so the divine simplicity of the flavors can shine through. COME IL LATTE is always a good option, with fresh homemade cones and seasonal gelatos made using only the freshest milk. Try the caramel with pink Himalayan sea salt flavor or stick to classics like pistachio. For those with dietary restrictions who still want to indulge, there are also a few lactose-free varieties.

Today, gay culture is scattered throughout Rome. You'll easily find a small gay street—aptly named "Gay Street"—alongside the Colosseum, an excellent place to start your bar hopping. Cruising bars and dance events are hugely popular, but be aware that you'll need an Anddos card for admittance. You can pick one up at the entrance of most venues and use it for your entire stay.

For an entirely unique bar in a gorgeous setting, visit SALOTTO42, a book bar looking out to the exquisite temple of Hadrian. It's not hard to figure out that a former model owns the small cocktail lounge—distinct attention has been paid to detail and style. Try one of the interesting takes on the classic Aperol spritz as you people-watch in the Piazza di Pietra, or if you're there in the morning, gorge on its famous Sunday brunch. Rome's original craft cocktail bar, THE JERRY THOMAS SPEAKEASY, is a small password-required, intimately lit hangout complete with fine cocktails served by mustached waiters. Aptly named after bartending legend Jerry Thomas, the bar specializes in forgotten Italian liquors along with pre-Prohibition classics.

Rome knows how to keep the party going long after the sun goes down. Whether you're looking for all-night gay dance parties in the shadow of the Colosseum or cozy wine bars where you can intimately snuggle up, you'll have more than a few options. If you only go out for one night on the town, make it a Friday at the legendary MUCCASSASSINA. Dating back to the early nineties, the party started as a way to finance the Mario Mieli association for the fight against AIDS and homophobia. Today, the institution's famed Friday night dance parties attract all sexualities to the three-story Qube club. GOA, another of Rome's long-standing clubs, is a haven for electronic music, with world-famous DJs and an industrial-inspired design that attracts a fashion-forward crowd. As its events are held every two to four weeks, you'll have to check its program before going. AMIGDALA is also a night worth syncing with your schedule. The queer indie dance party brings together electro music and innovative visual effects in one-of-a-kind, ever-changing venues. Short films, art and photo exhibitions, and a litany of other cultural projects make it much more than just a dance party.

Gay culture is scattered throughout Rome. You'll easily find a small gay street—aptly named "Gay Street"—alongside the Colosseum.

The dynamic, graphic interior at the Goa Club, Rome's oldest and best-loved techno venue.

Shoe shopping reaches the next level at BOCACHE & SALVUCCI, where stunning footwear is tailored to the buyer's ideal shape, color, and style. Owners and designers Gian Luca Bocache and Roberto Salvucci take their crafts seriously, providing an artisanal, bespoke shoe-shopping experience in an elegant yet comfortable styling room. The "little masterpieces" take from 20 man-hours to two months to create, resulting in stately wardrobe essentials that won't go unnoticed. CHEZ DEDE's flagship store in Palazzo Antonelli Capponi is a retail shopping experience as hip as they come. The exquisite concept store feels more like a home than a commercial building, making it that much easier to lose yourself among the luxury art, fashion, and furniture items. The sophisticated husband-and-wife owners bring their innate sense of design and stylish world travel–influenced aesthetic to the expertly curated boutique.

At Bocache & Salvucci, each pair of shoes is made by hand from start to finish in the store's workshop.

> You can also shop for vintage treasures on any weekend at the Mercato Vintage Ecosolidale, where all the proceeds go to charity.

Foodies will delight in Rome's vast options for cuisine-based shopping, an experience epitomized by TARTUFI & FRIENDS. The shop is well aware that few ingredients elevate a dish like prized Italian truffles. Whether it's honey, pasta, liqueur, or pâté, at this adorable store there's a truffle-infused something for all taste buds. Stop in after a visit to the Spanish Steps—the gourmet boutique is conveniently located at their base. While you're there, try the taste-testing truffle menu for an introduction to these highly sought-after delicacies.

In our increasingly digital age, there's a certain romance to beautiful stationery—especially when it comes to handcrafted leather-bound notebooks, pens made of Murano glass, and gorgeous Florentine-style writing paper. Founded in 1910, CARTOLERIA PANTHEON still has everything you need for your desk or creative soul, and it's all made in Italy. You can also shop for vintage treasures on any weekend at the MERCATO VINTAGE ECOSOLIDALE, where all the proceeds go to charity. Located off of Via Ostiense, far removed from kitschy tourist stalls, it's an off-the-beaten-path market that's making a difference.

The exquisite interior at Bocache & Salvucci, a haven of luxury, heritage, and timeless style.

Good news: Tartufi and Friends also sell a limited range of truffle-based delights to take away.

Rome has enough timeless monuments, museums, and ruins to fill your itinerary to the brim. But be sure to leave time for a few quieter, offbeat attractions that might offer unique glimpses into Roman life and culture. One such underrated museum is the PALAZZO MASSIMO ALLE TERME, an ode to classical art complete with breathtaking sculptures and stunningly vivid frescoes, including an example from the Villa of Livia, the country house of one of Augustus's wives. The collection of ancient Roman art, dating from the late Republic through the fifth century AD, offers an unparalleled look at the city's cultural evolution. For those wanting to experience Rome's churches, while they are popular tourist attractions by day, the classical concerts held in them at night provide an even more memorable encounter. Many are free, though the outstanding acoustics might lead you to believe otherwise. ALL SAINT'S ANGLICAN CHURCH and SANT'AGNESE IN AGONE are smart spots to start with.

Located in a former brewery, MUSEO D'ARTE CONTEMPORANEA ROMA (MACRO) might be set in a nondescript building, but inside you'll find fascinating and edgy installations. In an attempt to transform the museum into a living organism available to all, the space also hosts ongoing workshops and performances on important cultural issues, and entrance is always free. Far removed from the traditional art gallery experience, SACRIPANTE is a "non-gallery" for art lovers interested in history, design, and culture—as opposed to pretentiousness. The word Sacripante is synonymous with scoundrel, a fitting name for an institution that houses what the owners dub "low-brow" art. The on-site cocktail bar lets you enjoy the gallery while sipping on a boozy libation.

Get a new perspective on important Roman institutions with an UNTOLD HISTORY TOUR, a set of excursions that shines a light on past gay and lesbian culture—and its impact on the present. The UNTOLD HISTORY VATICAN TOUR, perhaps the most popular circuit, brings a fresh perspective to iconic Vatican imagery and the gay artists who left their long-standing mark on the sacred space.

The fabulous cocktail bar at Sacripante. Like many of the rooms at the gallery, the quirky furnishings are set against raw concrete walls.

Italy's biggest PRIDE festival takes place in Rome every June. Equal parts political activism and exciting antics, it is an unforgettable party that doesn't lose sight of the essential message.
Each year, the period from October to May brings around GORGEOUS I AM, better known as G I AM. The gay dance party has been going strong since 1995, and, when it's on, it still takes place every Saturday night. Over the summer months, head to GAY VILLAGE, an open-air pop-up event that features concerts, dance floors, and live theater performances. It's open Thursday to Saturday until the early morning hours.

The Gay Pride march traditionally follows a route from Piazza della Repubblica to Piazza Venezia.

Rome's Gay Pride march takes in a number of the city's landmarks, including the Colosseum.

Despite resistance from the Vatican, tens of thousands of revelers attend the Gay Pride march in Rome.

ESCAPE IT

Escape to the Italian seaside with a quick train ride to idyllic SPERLONGA, a classic day trip for Romans over the summer months. Here you'll have plenty of beach companions lounging under their umbrellas close to the azure sea, but the sandy beach and crystal-clear water make up for having to share the space. When you're not lazing in the sun, meander over to the historic center, all pastel colors, lovely arches, and sweeping bougainvillea. The sleepy village offers plenty of sidewalk cafés and picture-perfect piazzas, ideal for people-watching while you sip on a refreshing gin and tonic. Don't miss an amble down to the Grotto of Tiberius, a fascinating cave with a rich history dating back to the ancient Roman coastal road of 184 BC.

The Truglia watchtower has come to symbolize the pretty seaside village of Sperlonga.

North Beach

Pacific Heights

California Street

Geary Blvd

Market Street

Folsom Street

Mission Street

Folsom Street

3rd Street

24th Street

The Castro

CLAIM IT
1. Hotel Drisco
2. Inn at the Presidio
3. Proper Hotel
4. The Laurel Inn
5. The Ritz-Carlton

SAVOR IT
6. Californios
7. Foreign Cinema
8. Liholiho Yacht Club
9. Monsieur Benjamin
10. Nopa
11. Sightglass Coffee
12. Tartine Manufactory
13. The Big 4
14. Zuni Café

CELEBRATE IT
15. ABV
16. Bar Agricole
17. Lookout
18. The Stud
19. Trick Dog
20. Twin Peaks Tavern

OWN IT
21. Heath Ceramics
22. Loved To Death
23. MAAS & Stacks
24. Park Life
25. Unionmade
26. Welcome Stranger

EXPLORE IT
27. GLBT Historical Society Museum
28. Minnesota Street Project
29. Precita Eyes Muralists
30. YBCA

SAN FRANCISCO

The Beguiling Charmer by the Bay

From moody, foggy mornings that morph into brilliant, sunlit days and the depths of Alcatraz's mysteries to the enchanting "painted ladies" houses punctuating its streets, San Francisco is an enigmatic gem and a traveler's dream in Northern California.

This is a city that has evolved from being the heart of the gold rush to the soul of the summer of love. For decades it has welcomed the LGBTQ community into its fold: from 1908, when The Dash—where waiters cross-dressed and a dollar could buy you a sex act in a private booth—opened as one of the country's first gay bars, to the early 1960s, when San Francisco drew activists from all stripes to begin what we know today as the gay rights movement, to when it was named the "Gay Capital of America" by *Life* magazine in 1964, and to 1977, when Harvey Milk became the first openly gay elected official in California's history.

That tradition of welcoming one and all continues today with San Francisco's myriad hotels, restaurants, and clubs. The acceptance isn't limited to the LGBTQ mecca of the Castro, where both gay and straight patrons enjoy the open, non-judgmental and accepting atmosphere, but is found throughout its many neighborhoods. Indeed, San Francisco is a beguiling charmer that can capture the heart in the blink of an eye—and we just can't stop falling in love with it.

San Francisco wears elegance as casually as a favorite cashmere cardigan. Case in point is HOTEL DRISCO, an Edwardian masterwork perched atop the tony neighborhood of Pacific Heights. A grand dame of gentility, it offers luxurious conveniences such as chauffeur services, evening wine receptions, and even a "pillow menu" to ensure the sweetest of slumbers. It's a haven for gentlemen who love a little elegant pampering. Another upscale choice is PROPER HOTEL in the Mid-Market area. A glorious flat iron, the hotel is a delicious mix of modernist, cubist, and secessionist-era design where old world glamour meets contemporary luxury. What's more, Proper offers guests unparalleled views of the City by the Bay by way of Charmaine's, a romantic rooftop lounge, and Villon, an upscale restaurant serving fabulous cocktails and a chic ambiance.

While it's true that F. Scott Fitzgerald centered his epic tale in West Egg, there's no place like THE RITZ-CARLTON for finding your inner Gatsby. The circa 1909 hotel pays homage to the city

Guests enjoy intimate dining in Gilda's Private Dining Room at the Proper Hotel.

by welcoming guests with sprawling marble foyers, sweeping views of the bay, and all the myriad indulgences The Ritz-Carlton does so well. It's also an oenophile's dream, thanks to the JCB Tasting Lounge where winemaker Jean-Charles Boisset has created an intimate, velvet-draped dream that brings together the worlds of fine wine and fashion—if you aren't already packing your smoking jacket, perhaps you should.

The INN AT THE PRESIDIO near Golden Gate Park occupies a Georgian Revival–style building that was previously known as Pershing Hall, which once served as a home away from home to dashing, bachelor officers of the U.S. Army. Today, one needn't be in the armed services to live the luxe single life at this inn, which includes beautifully appointed rooms and a dozen suites replete with fireplaces. The hotel itself is home to several dining venues including Presidio Social Club, The Commissary, and Arguello, among others, that collectively offer a treasure trove of Latin and Californian flavors set against one of the city's most romantic backdrops. Speaking of homes away from home, THE LAUREL INN is for anyone wishing to sample a San Francisco lifestyle from the comfort of their own pied-à-terre. Offering what it calls an "urban studio apartment oasis" in the posh, Pacific Heights neighborhood, a stay here comes complete with afternoon cookies, housekeeper, morning newspapers, and the scent of freshly brewed coffee. Of the hotel's accommodation, 18 rooms boast a kitchenette, allowing you to take on San Francisco like a native. What's more, Laurel Inn is dog-friendly so there's no reason to leave your best friend at home while you escape for a few days.

Styled by designer Kelly Wearstler, rooms at the Proper Hotel are a bold clash of textiles, colors, and patterns.

Much more than matcha and cronuts, San Francisco's food scene celebrates all that is wonderful in Northern California with heady wines, savory sensations, and good old-fashioned comfort food abounding.

Begin your day with breakfast at the magical TARTINE MANUFACTORY. Featuring a grab-and-go menu, the hotspot offers a mind-boggling array of freshly baked pastries, as well as lunch and dinner options alongside an ever-changing collection of wines and craft cocktails. Just how good is Tartine? For starters, its bread bakers read the weather, flour, and levain before they begin to mix the daily dough. If breakfast doesn't leave you well caffeinated, wander over to SIGHTGLASS COFFEE. With four locations plus a bi-weekly presence at the San Francisco Ferry Building farmers market, this upscale coffee roaster chooses the world's best beans, roasts them with care, and brews them with love.

For lunch, we favor ZUNI CAFÉ on Market Street. Imagine French and Italian cuisine colliding in thunderbolts of flavor and specialties that include mesquite-grilled Maryland striped bass with saffron butter sauce and a to-die-for sliced Stemple Creek Ranch beef served with grilled Piracicaba broccoli, buttermilk mashed potatoes, and black trumpet mushrooms... now you're getting it.

If you crave a laid-back, casual dinner head for the LIHOLIHO YACHT CLUB. Named after the pop-up parties chef Ravi Kapur used to throw to raise money to race Hobie catamarans in Hawaii, the Sutter Street icon serves a menu as eclectic as its customers—a mix of Hawaiian, Indian, and Chinese delights that keeps guests divinely sated. Adventurous eaters can tuck into a plate of shaved pig head or ask for the secret, off-menu spam dish, while for the more timid, there's whole Maine lobster and more traditional eastern flavors. Feel free to bring your own bottle to Liholiho, too—there's a corkage fee, but they're happy to say *welina* to the BYOB set. Another casual yet fabulous

dinner option is CALIFORNIOS. Named after the Mexican immigrants that first settled in California, it initially appeared as a pop-up in 2013 and has been filling seats ever since. The first North American restaurant serving a Mexican degustation menu to garner not one but two Michelin stars, chef Val M. Cantu charms guests with big, bold flavors spun from seasonal, locally sourced ingredients. Third on our list of "come as you are" dinner venues is FOREIGN CINEMA in the Mission neighborhood. Occupying a cavernous building, it can accommodate about 100 in the main dining room, but the main attraction is the restaurant's courtyard where another two dozen or so can be seated for a memorable meal and the film du jour, screened once the sun goes down. Foreign Cinema offers upscale dishes such as five-spice scented duck breast served with "quacklins" (see what they did there?) but the star of the show is the raw bar and caviar selection that headline the menu.

The more frenetic atmosphere at NOPA is fueled by the simple yet heady combination of seasonal food crafted with passion. The menu changes each week as local ingredients come into season, so guests can count on a culinary surprise whether they're neighborhood regulars or first-timers. The menu reads like a food lover's romance novel where Early Girl tomatoes say hello to Big Boys and warm goat cheese melts languidly.

While casual can be wonderful, what's more fun than dressing for dinner? If you're in an Anderson Cooper tie and jacket kind of mood, you'll swoon for THE BIG 4. In a wood-paneled room adorned with leather banquettes and vintage photographs, this restaurant celebrates the city's golden age. Named after Collis P. Huntington, Charles Crocker, Leland Stanford, and Mark Hopkins—the four railroad giants who collectively led San Francisco to become an industrial power-house—the restaurant is a fixture in posh Nob Hill. It offers reinvented steakhouse fare with a dash of California lightness. Lastly, celebrating the savoir-faire of your favorite Parisian bistro, we give you MONSIEUR BENJAMIN. A Francophile's delight in Hayes Valley near the opera house, ballet, and symphony hall, the restaurant serves a divine selection of small plates and hors d'oeuvres including a lobster bisque with Pernod cream. Its "plats de résistance" such as braised rabbit and de rigueur "garnitures" like haricots verts are served in a convivial atmosphere that makes you want to linger over one more glass of Côte de Brouilly.

Fresh salads made up and ready to go, at the Tartine Manufactory.

At Foreign Cinema, you can dine while watching movies.

Rainbow pedestrian crossing add a novel touch in Castro, San Francisco's first gay neighborhood.

The Stud hosts drag shows, karaoke nights, and community events—this place isn't just a hangout, it's a culture.

Arguably the most famous gay bar in San Francisco if not the West Coast, the LOOKOUT is a Castro landmark complete with balcony overlooking Market Street. A decidedly fabulous place to see and be seen, expect the best DJs and a calendar of events that includes everything from drag brunches to karaoke parties. Another option is the raucously gay and openly gourmand TRICK DOG in the Mission district. Housed in a factory with soaring ceilings and plenty of personality, its periodically changing themed menu is a fanciful celebration of craft cocktails and elevated bar bites. Everyone is welcome at this hip watering hole; you'll see men sporting beards of all shapes and sizes and women with every style of tattoo on show. If you've always had a thing for Cinderella, BAR AGRICOLE on 11th in the SoMa neighborhood will have you at hello. You see, the bar closes at midnight (11 on weekdays) so get there early before anyone loses a glass slipper. A contemporary spot in which to sip traditional cocktails crafted with

spirits created from "farmhouse distilling" processes, it also serves natural wine and food that showcases ingredients from local, biodynamic farms.

Butch meets chicly urban in the Mission district with ABV. A quintessential neighborhood bar with an extensive list of cocktails as well as a selection of beers, wines, and ciders, it's the perfect place to chat up a handsome stranger over an artisan aperitif.

With a name like THE STUD, you know precisely what you're getting. A San Francisco legend serving killer cocktails from the longest bar in SoMa, it hosts drag shows, karaoke nights, and community events—this place isn't just a hangout, it's a culture. Make sure you bring cash when you come, too— Stud Bar scoffs at plastic. Lastly, how can you not love a bar that's been hailed as "the gay Cheers"? TWIN PEAKS TAVERN, located on this historic corner of Market and Castro, offers a warm welcome along with cocktails, beers on tap, and a full wine-by-the-glass list—it's a legend worth stopping for.

Located in the Duboce Triangle area of San Francisco, menswear emporium MAAS & STACKS carries everyone from Craig Green to Visvim, Nonnative to Stone Island—it's the hip place for creating a new look or polishing your old one. Another sartorial destination worth seeking out whether you're a Levi's fan or Monitaly devotee is UNIONMADE, an upscale shop that's custom designed for the fashion-forward. Or if you're after a souvenir to remember your San Francisco sojourn by, the pure, unadulterated men's fashion found at WELCOME STRANGER seamlessly blends rugged good looks with sigh-worthy details and is 100% designed and crafted in California.

From stunning dinnerware to accessories worthy of urban legend status, HEATH CERAMICS is a celebration of handcrafted goods and a veritable Aladdin's cave for dedicated shoppers. For something more unique and distinctive, look no further than LOVED TO DEATH. San Francisco's original "oddities" boutique, this is where you can pick up a hand mirror decorated with octopus tentacles or an antique plate updated with a Frankenstein print. Finally, who doesn't love a good museum shop? PARK LIFE specializes in limited-edition artist collaborations and has joined forces with the likes of David Shrigley, Ray Geary, and Evah Fan to produce products ranging from books, zines, and prints to tees and design objects.

A newsstand at Heath Ceramics stocks a full range of periodicals, magazines, and stationery.

Fans of Heath Ceramics can join a full tour of the working factory on the 1st and 3rd Fridays of the month.

EXPLORE IT

San Francisco and the Castro are home to the GLBT HISTORICAL SOCIETY MUSEUM, internationally recognized as a leader in the field of LGBTQ public history. Pay it a visit and let your flag fly proudly. For the deliciously urbane and fans of Armistead Maupin, TOURS OF THE TALES makes the well-loved books come alive via PDF-formatted tours that you can download to your phone or print from a computer to stir your imagination in a whole new way.

Art lovers, rejoice! PRECITA EYES MURALISTS provides tours and events that use art as a self-expressive tool for positive social change. Peruse its program, browse the offerings, and revel in the knowledge that you're helping make a difference. Located in the historic Dogpatch district, MINNESOTA STREET PROJECT offers economically sustainable spaces for art galleries, artists, and related nonprofits. Inhabiting three warehouses,

it's dedicated to San Francisco's contemporary art community in the short term, while developing an internationally recognized arts destination in the long run. All galleries in the project are free to visit and open to the public. Also visit the multi-disciplinary YERBA BUENA CENTER FOR THE ARTS (YBCA) and discover a place dedicated to celebrating local, national, and international artists as well as San Francisco's diverse communities.

The Minnesota Street Project is currently home to 13 independent fine art galleries.

Put on your studded collar and head for the annual FOLSOM STREET FAIR, a BDSM and leather subculture street fair held in September. Or get ready to mingle at the CASTRO STREET FAIR. An LGBTQ festival usually held on the first Sunday in October, it was founded in the 1970s by

> Put on your studded collar and head for the annual Folsom Street Fair, a BDSM and leather subculture street fair held in September.

Harvey Milk to bring vendors and creatives together. These days, you can still buy goods from LGBTQ makers and dance to music at various stages. And while you're in a fair state of mind, don't miss STARTUP, a unique art experience where collectors and the public gather to discover the hottest talent.

Folsom Street Fair: Expect to see people dressed in everything from latex to leather with body paint and piercings.

ESCAPE IT

Explore bucolic vineyards, farmers markets, the Napa Valley Wine Train, dining, and more in NAPA, a quintessential holiday destination and Northern California's most illustrious winemaking region. At Silver Oak Winery, born in 1972 on an estate between the Silverado Trail and the town of Oakville, visitors are greeted by a display showcasing vintages nearing 50 years old in an elegant winery wrapped in limestone. Tours and tastings are available by reservation, though walk-ins are also

Wine tasting in Napa Valley. The region is particularly admired for its Cabernet Sauvignon.

> Explore bucolic vineyards, farmers markets, the Napa Valley Wine Train, dining, and more in Napa, a quintessential holiday destination.

welcome. Over in St. Helena on Zinfandel Lane (the address alone is worth the trip), you'll find the vineyards of Raymond, where guests not only tour and taste, but can also be a winemaker for a day. When the day trip ends, it will be with a bottle of the bespoke blend you've created, replete with private label. We'll cheers to that.

There are more than 400 wineries in the Napa Valley, and most of them offer great wine tastings.

IN SAN FRANCISCO, SOUND-TRACKING ESCAPE AND ABANDON

Josh Cheon

A DJ and cofounder of Dark Entries Records, Josh Cheon felt an intrinsic, mysterious connection to San Francisco on his very first visit. At the time, the New Jersey native was 25 and in the closet. "I came out to a friend and she said, 'Go to San Francisco.' I stayed in a youth hostel for a week and was immediately like, 'Woah.'" On that trip, he "met the right people, went to the right parties, heard the right music. And of course, I met a guy. It was this combination. I was back a month later with no job, no apartment, no friends—just this drive for change."

The LGBTQ utopia has a magnetic pull, and a lot of Josh's friends share the same story of how the got there. "It's an escape route, a sanctuary," he says, adding that their relocating was often based on the thought, "'I need to get out of this small town; I need to leave this repressed family.' Marginalized communities," he continues, "can come here and exist. People are moving for the same reasons, and being with so many likeminded people— it's a bubble. We're not operating like most of America or the world at large."

A biology major, Josh worked in science labs for 11 years while DJing on the side, before pursuing music full-time from 2018. "We never talked about [my sexuality] in the lab," he says. His coworkers would ask, "What are you doing this weekend?" and he'd respond, "DJing"—"not mentioning it was for 700 gay guys in harnesses." Even now, San Francisco's gay party scene continues to thrive.

"There are so many. House, techno, disco. There's still a huge circuit scene—EDM, tech house. Whatever's calling you to move. In the gay community, we need these clubs and spaces where we can dance, engage, hook up."

After some 12 years in the city, the 37-year-old's love affair with it isn't over. "It's beautiful. The weather's amazing. I enjoy the pace. I like my routine, biking everywhere. Also I have rent control. That's a huge thing, as it's unaffordable to live here." His apartment is in the Tenderloin: "always the seedy underbelly of San Francisco, and actually the original gay neighborhood, where all the bars were, the hustlers. The Pride parade came here before the Castro. It's where the Compton's Cafeteria Riot happened, before Stonewall—the first documented

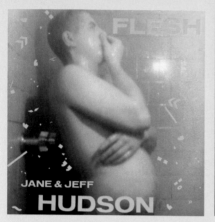

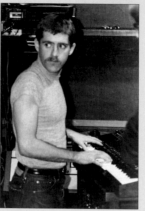

"Emancipation, freedom, cockiness, falling, picking yourself back up again."

trans riot in America." However, there is another side to this part of the city. "It has energy, but it's sadly referred to as a containment zone by police. It's where the drugs are, homelessness, tent encampments, drug abuse on the streets. It's pretty hard for people from out of town to enjoy this neighborhood. I'm still affected by it. It's difficult to come to terms with rents being so ridiculously high in a place of destitution and squalor. But I like living here. It's the least gentrified neighborhood in San Francisco."

Josh cites pioneering disco musician and composer Patrick Cowley as an example of "quintessential San Francisco." His eighties gay porn sound-

tracks have been released by Dark Entries Records and Honey Soundsystem Records in recent years, and Josh—a keen LGBTQ activist who recently staged a fundraiser for a trans suicide prevention hotline—donated the proceeds of the records to the Gay Men's Sexual Health Alliance and AIDS Housing Alliance. But Josh feels an affinity with Patrick outside of music too. It is, again, "the same story—a young, freshly out gay guy who needed to escape," he explains. "In 1971, at 21, Patrick took a bus from Buffalo, New York, and went to San Francisco with a suitcase."

I ask if Josh would like to step in a time machine to experience the San Francisco of Patrick's

heyday, with its bathhouse culture and glory hole bars. Turns out he kind of already has. "I'm transcribing Patrick's sex journal, and I'm going to publish it. He was so thorough and detailed in his day-to-day sex life. It's going to open up a lot of people's minds, and set a light on this beautiful time in San Francisco's gay history. It makes me think, 'Why haven't I written down all my tricks?!'" As Josh sums up Patrick's journey, it's clear the musician's words could easily apply to his own passage, or even to the energy of the city proper. "Emancipation, freedom, cockiness, taking chances, falling, getting your heart broken, picking yourself back up again."

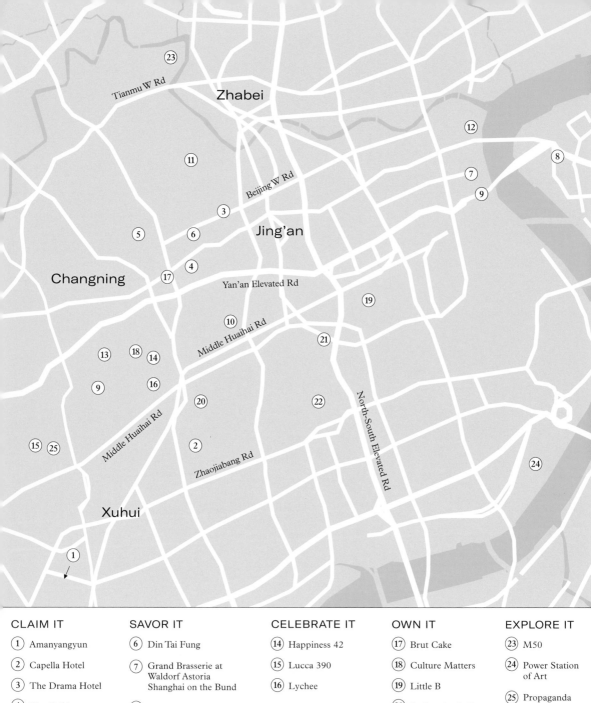

CLAIM IT

(1) Amanyangyun

(2) Capella Hotel

(3) The Drama Hotel

(4) The PuLi
Hotel and Spa

(5) URBN

SAVOR IT

(6) Din Tai Fung

(7) Grand Brasserie at
Waldorf Astoria
Shanghai on the Bund

(8) Jin Xuan in The
Ritz-Carlton, Pudong

(9) Lost Heaven

(10) Moka Bros

(11) The Commune Social

(12) Ultraviolet
by Paul Pairet

(13) Zee Tea

CELEBRATE IT

(14) Happiness 42

(15) Lucca 390

(16) Lychee

OWN IT

(17) Brut Cake

(18) Culture Matters

(19) Little B

(20) Project Aegis Co.

(21) Sinan Books

(22) Xingmu
Handicraft

EXPLORE IT

(23) M50

(24) Power Station
of Art

(25) Propaganda
Poster
Art Centre

SHANGHAI

The Far Out, Far East Temple of Indulgence

New York writer and journalist Patricia Marx was on the money when she said, "New York may be the city that never sleeps, but Shanghai doesn't even sit down." The metropolis is an intoxicating blend of ancient culture melded with futuristic attitudes. It's formal and it's a free-for-all, and it has earned its place at the top of every list devoted to wanderlust.

The ties between Shanghai and the LGBTQ community are woven into a complicated tapestry. When the world began to flood through China via the Silk Road, Shanghai's mind—as well as its ports—began to unfurl and bloom. The Tang dynasty (c. 618 through c. 907) brought with it some of the earliest examples of gay pornography, the first chronicled evidence of a male sex worker trade, and the earliest written works referencing same-sex relationships. Homosexuality was widely accepted—provided it didn't preclude marriage to and procreation with females. It was not until the reign of the Qianlong Emperor, who, despite being entirely besotted with a male member of his honor guard, helped Shanghai give way to laws prohibiting same-sex relationships outside of brothels (one must ponder what was permitted inside the brothels, but we digress).

Today, a new generation of LGBTQ activists is breaking the chains that bind China's sexuality, and while homosexual tolerance exists, gay rights do not. That said, you can rest assured that tourism to Shanghai is responsible and unerringly ethical—your presence will bring invaluable support to the gay community and much-needed economic backing to local LGBTQ businesses in a city struggling for equality.

China is nothing if not passionate about all things luxury, and its voracious appetite for indulgence is no more apparent than from the glittering surroundings of some of Shanghai's finest hotels. Case in point, the PULI HOTEL AND SPA. An urban resort that offers around-the-clock butler service, a Michelin-starred restaurant, upscale workout facilities, and a heated, infinity-edge pool (to name just a few), its biggest draw is the sheer luxury of its accommodation. From the sprawling Jing'An suite to the hotel's deluxe king rooms and everything in between, its minimalistic design meets white glove service. The hotel's club-level accommodation is made up of sumptuous havens that offer guests daily breakfast, an in-room aperitif, laundry or pressing services, high tea, and elevated bathroom amenities for which we sigh a grateful *xièxie*. Equally luxurious with an aesthetic that leans toward old-world China is CAPELLA HOTEL, where guests may choose from one, two, or three-bedroom Shikumen Villas that showcase authentic Shanghainese design melded with Parisian style. Dinner in the hotel's star-rated restaurant Le Comptoir de Pierre Gagnaire is a wonderful journey to dicover the creative world of the eponymous French kitchen legend. A day at the blissful Auriga spa is non-negotiable. Named after the constellation in which the Capella star sits, the spa offers a host of signature treatments that incorporate traditional techniques fueled by organic natural ingredients.

For a central stay, just 20-minutes' walk from Shanghai's city center, is THE DRAMA HOTEL. Offering guests an element of self-catering, the small boutique-style hotel offers rooms replete with refrigerator, electric kettle, dishwasher, and coffee

Seductive styling and low lighting are hallmarks of a stay at the Drama Hotel in Shanghai's Bund district.

maker. Despite such hands-on amenities, one needn't worry about an absence of luxury. The Drama's rooms include feather pillows, a flat screen TV, and private balcony as standard. Another boutique option is the forward-thinking URBN, where award-winning design meets sustainability. China's first carbon-neutral hotel, it features reclaimed materials and green initiatives throughout. Housed in a converted factory in Jing'An, the hotel is also just a stroll away from French Concession, Shanghai's most vibrant gay neighborhood.

Lastly, anyone who is well versed in luxury hospitality in Asia will attest that the Aman brand is second to none. In Shanghai, the AMANYANGYUN illustrates the brand's special kind of brilliance in a way you won't soon forget. Located in a seemingly enchanted camphor forest, it's made up of Ming and Qing dynasty dwellings that were rescued from the Jiangxi province and relocated brick by ancient brick. The accommodation consists of Ming Courtyard Suites and private villas, each featuring interiors crafted of wood, stone, and bamboo, and a private courtyard. At the heart of the hotel is the Nan Shu Fang cultural center. Named after the royal reading pavilion in the Forbidden City, it is a recreation of seventeenth-century scholars' studios and dedicated to art and knowledge. The hotel's entrance is also marked by an Emperor Tree, and guests are invited to gift it with water. It's a thoughtful way to nurture the past, enrich the future, and begin one of the most remarkable travel experiences one could hope for.

Guests can while away a poolside hour at PuLi Hotel's slender, mosaic-tiled infinity pool—swimming or looking out over the park.

Because you know a city break means a lot of time spent on your feet, make CULTURE MATTERS your first stop to pick up a pair of Feiyue shoes. A hundred-year-old Shanghainese brand, the sneakers are a favorite with athletes, including the 2,008 tai chi performers who all wore them for the 2008 Beijing Olympics. While we're talking wearables, don't miss PROJECT AEGIS CO., where stylish, high-end men's clothing, shoes, and accessories abound in a former villa in French Concession.

It would seem a shame to return from Shanghai without a few local crafts tucked into your carry-on, so spend some time exploring Tianzifang. Weekends bring thousands to the area's open-air cafés, bistros, and endless selection of gift shops and boutiques offering everything and anything Shanghai. XINGMU HANDICRAFT is a tiny shop chock full of exquisite, leather-bound note-books in all shapes and sizes, while inside the substantially larger SINAN BOOKS, three floors of tomes wait for you in a wonderfully historic build-ing. And don't miss the fascinating exhibit hall on its third floor, where you can peruse rare volumes, including copies of the *Communist Manifesto*.

With a gallery vibe, a futuristic feel, and a whole lot of style, LITTLE B in Shanghai's Xintiandi district is a must. Residing in a salvaged, nineteenth-century stone gatehouse, the pop-up megastar is now a permanent fixture for your shopping pleasure. Check it out for cool desk accessories, basic yet elevated home goods, and unusual gifts—and then wind up your shopping excursion with some sweet homewares at BRUT CAKE.

Sinan Books has the feel of your own private library on a truly massive scale—with each department defined by its interior design.

Discovering the benefits of TAI CHI might be the most valuable thing you can bring home from Shanghai. Originally developed for self-defense, it has evolved into a graceful form of exercise often described as "meditation in motion" and said to enhance sleep, help the immune system, improve strength, relieve both stress and joint pain, and elevate overall well-being. You'll find Tai Chi practiced every morning in many, if not all, of Shanghai's parks. Those experienced with the practice can join

in, or beginners can sign up for one of the many workshops or classes available throughout the city.

To exercise the mind as well as the body, the PROPAGANDA POSTER ART CENTRE in French Concession is an absolute gem. Exhibiting posters from the Maoist period of communist China in the basement of an apartment building on Huashan Road, it's a remarkable look into twentieth-century China. Another museum worthy of a stop is the POWER STATION OF ART, a celebration of contempo-rary works located in the former Nanshi Power Plant. Exhibitions have included "The Life and Opinions of David Shrigley," a well-respected PSA Talk Series. Another must for art lovers is a trip to 50 Moganshan Road, or M50 as it's more readily known. An art district in Shanghai reminiscent of New York's SoHo, it's home to a community of more than 100 artists with studios open to the public. Lastly, gay visitors to Shanghai will appreciate the efforts of CINEMQ, the "unrefined queer under-ground collective," which hosts screenings celebrating "filthy and gorgeous" world cinema monthly through a mix of media including short films, visuals, and music.

You won't get far in Shanghai before you see groups of people practicing Tai Chi in the open air.

Make no mistake, the Chinese love a good festival and celebrating that is SNAP!. Born in 2016, it describes itself as a "lifestyle collective" with events ranging from theme parties and community markets to fitness and networking programs, all designed for the LBGTQ community. SHANGHAI PRIDE is the city's annual LGBTQ event. Having debuted in 2009, the march has expanded to include workshops, events, and festivals from March through June. Lastly, ANGEL provides Shanghai's LGBTQ community with the biggest dance parties in China—check out its Facebook page to get hold of its latest schedule.

To find these and other events in China, as well as to use social media while in the country, be sure to download a virtual private network—or VPN— before you arrive. Internet censoring in China makes accessing social media or conducting online searches without it difficult if not impossible. Public displays of affection are frowned upon here, but at least nothing will stop you from arranging some close encounters with the locals using your favorite app.

Music, film, and art are the mainstays of the Shanghai Pride celebrations, the biggest Pride event in China.

ESCAPE IT

Escape the city by taking a day trip to HANGZHOU, the capital of China's Zhejiang province. Southwest of the ancient Grand Canal waterway, Hangzhou and its West Lake is a spectacularly beautiful area. Beloved since the ninth century, it's where you'll find islands reachable only by boat, stunning temples, pavilions, arched bridges, and countless gardens. Be sure to visit the Sunrise Terrace, Dragon Well Tea Village, and Xiaoying Island.

Tourists can take a tour of the West Lake at Hangzhou aboard a pagoda-style boat.

Along its edges, Hangzhou Lake has numerous temples and pagodas.

IN SHANGHAI, SCREENING RADICAL QUEERNESS

CINEMQ

"Like New York, but affordable, with an intense and exciting queer scene." This is how friends Matthew Barren and Will Dai describe Shanghai, the largest city in China and their current home. "The scene's fueled by youth culture and creativity," they continue. "It's an open community—one that welcomes everyone, where it isn't hard to find like-minded people."

The guys are members of CINEMQ, an underground queer collective with a focus on Chinese and East Asian queer screen culture that is comprised of people who work in creative industries, "queers, club kids, filmmakers, programmers, designers, DJs, drag lovers, and disco fiends." Some hail from Shanghai, some from elsewhere in the country, and some from around the world. In the city,

most live in the central Xuhui, Changning, and Jing'an districts, where everything the metropolis has to offer is easily accessed. "The city's brimming with luxury shopping malls, but has a great selection of independent businesses, artists, and groups," the guys enthuse. "The food culture's excellent, with any kind of cuisine you could want."

Members of the collective "met on dance floors and in dark corners, swathed in leather," say the pair. "We love faux decadence and trash aesthetics, drawing inspiration from New York City ballroom culture. Radical queerness, avant-garde cinema, and techno-fuckery feed our palette. We believe in love and confrontation."

Although same-sex sex has been legal in China since 1997, life for LGBTQs remains

challenging. Thus, it may come as a surprise to find that Shanghai is home to such vibrant queerness. "Politically, Shanghai exists to a degree in a bubble," Matthew and Will explain. "There seems to be less risk of queer venues, organizations, and activists being shut down by authorities compared to, say, Guangzhou or Beijing."

According to the pair, "one of the most significant changes for the LGBT community in the past decade is ShanghaiPRIDE," an annual film festival that celebrates diverse identities. "Nationally, it symbolizes the possibility of being out, proud, and open in your gender and sexual identity. But ever-changing regulations," they add, "particularly internet censorship, pose challenges, and stem the growth of a burgeoning queer community. The 'city clean-up' policy, which aims to

国际不再恐同恐跨日
International Day Against Homophobia & Transphobia

CINEMQ

"Like New York, but affordable, with an intense and exciting queer scene. It's an open community."

create a more harmonious city, has also seen a number of queer-friendly venues and spaces shut down. These are challenging times, but the community's bounced back from similar initiatives in the past."

Interestingly, however, the guys suggest that these days young LGBTQs feel more at home in underground bars and clubs than in LGBTQ spaces. "Queerness is very much entangled with youth culture in Shanghai, so it's highly visible," they say. "There's a fluidity within these subcultural groups that sees gender and sexuality explored and sometimes

dismantled through fashion, music, and art. The city has its share of gay and lesbian bars, but the real fire of the community comes from underground bars and clubs that aren't specifically LGBT, but which are the most accepting of diversity. Away from the nightlife scene," the friends are quick to add, "Shanghai thrives with sexuality on the fringes in the way any city does. There are saunas, cruising parks, sex workers. Perhaps the most infamous venue is the Lai Lai Dancehall, where married middle-aged men sneak away from their wives to dance with each other."

With a metropolitan population of almost 38 million, Shanghai is ever growing, ever evolving, ever exciting. "It does not stop moving," say Matthew and Will. "If you stand still too long you might disappear down the cracks of memory. The influence of its colonial past lingers heavy and sometimes controversially, and yet it embraces a sprawling internationalism with open arms. The skyline's an architectural experiment straight out of a Tarkovsky film, and one day soon enough it will disappear under the rising seas. Perhaps it moves to stay ahead of its own inherent fatalism."

Norrmalm

Ostermalm

Gamla
Stan

Södermalm

Odengatan
Birger Jarlsgatan
Sturegatan
Hornsgatan
Götgatan

CLAIM IT

1. At Six
2. Downtown Camper
   by Scandic
3. Ett Hem
4. Hotel
   Skeppsholmen
5. Lydmar Hotel

SAVOR IT

6. Johan & Nyström
7. Oaxen Krog & Slip
8. Taverna Brillo
9. Teatern
10. Tyge & Sessil
11. Urban Deli
12. Woodstockholm

CELEBRATE IT

13. Fasching
14. Folii
15. Guldbaren
    (Nobis Hotel)
16. Patricia
17. Side Track

OWN IT

18. Brandstationen
19. Grandpa
20. L:a Bruket
21. Snickarbacken 7
22. Sandqvist
23. Svenskt Tenn

EXPLORE IT

24. ABBA
    The Museum
25. Färgfabriken
26. Fotografiska
27. Spritmuseum

STOCKHOLM

A Modish Mix of Minimalist Mirth

With a winning combination of classic and contemporary charms, Stockholm's unique multi-island landscape—connected through a string of bridges—is an archaic natural wonder sprinkled with up-to-the-second design. Storied landmarks such as the Gamla Stan (Old Town) and Royal Palace evoke a fairytale feel, while the boho-cool Södermalm district, ultra-modern museums, and cutting-edge designs maintain a future-perfect synergy. Mix in a convivial café culture and ever-evolving food scene and you've found a harmonious paradise with something for everyone. Long considered one of the most progressive European countries in terms of LGBTQ rights, Sweden decriminalized same-sex relations in 1944. What's more, in 1972, it was the first country in the world to allow residents to legally change their gender after reassignment surgery. In recent years, great strides have been achieved for homosexual families, as both same-sex marriages and gay couple adoptions have been legalized. In particular, Stockholm, despite its lack of designated gay districts, actively supports the LGBTQ community through a multitude of city-wide events, clubs, bars, activities, and shops that proudly display the rainbow flag.

Built atop the one-time lodgings of King Charles XII's royal marines, HOTEL SKEPPSHOLMEN is an eco-friendly oasis—the first of its kind in Sweden—named after the tranquil tree-peppered island it rests upon. A classic façade that offers sensational waterfront views over Stockholm's landmarks hides decidedly contemporary interiors—various woods, a neutral palette for walls and furnishings, and a monochrome collection of photography that decorates public spaces. Just minutes from the Moderna Museet, each of the hotel's historically protected rooms offers a merry mix of vintage and modish design, and a choice between garden or lakeside views. Located in the tony Östermalm district, ETT HEM is a ferry ride and stroll north of the city center. Once the elegant residence of a government official, it has since been restyled as a boutique hotel. There is an earthy, home-style vibe to the bi-level interiors, which include a drawing room, library, and conservatory, with garden space on the first floor and a mishmash of antique-filled bedrooms on the second.

A tad closer to Stockholm's center, with envy-inducing waterfront views of the Royal Palace, the LYDMAR HOTEL suits style-savvy gents who prefer the pleasure of luxe surrounds. The decor—a parade of satin sofas, distressed leathers, and tan hues—screams bourgeois decadence, albeit with the carefully controlled restraint of Scandinavian design. In comparison, the rooms are small and subdued but nonetheless maintain an inviting comfort. While the posh restaurant serves French-inspired cuisine and the summer patio offers a seasonal spot to unwind with a cocktail, the true hotspot is the garden-style second-floor terrace that features live music lounges and weekend DJs.

The communal spaces at Ett Hem are spacious and homey, with luxurious furnishings and book-lined walls.

Located on the once gritty and now great Brunkebergstorg Square, DOWNTOWN CAMPER BY SCANDIC caters to the younger set, as evidenced by communal areas packed to the rafters with millennial mainstays, including a cushy hammock, urban workspaces, mood board–style typography, game rooms, and swing chairs. Yet despite its playful attributes, the overall vibe is surprisingly opulent. Rooms vary in size, from windowless nooks to suites, all while maintaining a cozy camper feel. Indulgent amenities of note include the rooftop wellness center that features yoga classes and a bird's nest-shaped sauna, an adjacent cocktail lounge, and quality rentals ranging from kayaks to bikes to outdoor clothing gear. A skip away, the ultra-mod AT SIX is a formerly uninspiring bank converted into a grand lifestyle hotel experience. Bedrooms are stark but feature luxurious extras, such as marble top desks, hardwood floors, and organic toiletries from the Swedish Lapland brand Gerd. The lobby is the central showpiece, with the dark granite and steel decor adorned with a large eye-catching marble sculpture of a man's head at the foot of the staircase. An array of dining and drinking areas feature Vietnamese-inspired menus, signature cocktail punch bowls, a cellar wine bar, and a first in Stockholm: a lounge space designed for optimum listening quality that boasts an impressive list of international DJs and music events.

The rooms and suites at Ett Hem are tastefully decorated in a neutral Nordic palette.

Stockholm's unique multi-island landscape—connected through
a string of bridges—is an archaic natural wonder.

For centuries, Swedish cuisine was centered on regionally harvested staples, including fish, game meat, potatoes, and dairy. Today, cooking trends upend tradition with influences from other national cuisines, particularly from the recipe books of culinary power players Asia and France.

Variety is the superstar diva stealing the show at TEATERN, a fancy food court that features a marvelous mix of urban bites and fine-dining master chef menus. The tempting delights at the 250-seat space include K-Märkt, where the royals' Nobel Banquet pastry chef, Daniel Roos, whips up pastries fit for queens. On the lighter side of the spectrum, The Plant-Food That Works has been called Sweden's first 100 percent eco-friendly, vegan fast food eatery. Situated in a serene space that displays handcrafted wood stools and Asian-inspired origami-shaped light fixtures, WOODSTOCKHOLM'S ambitious owners have expanded their successful furniture-making business to include an equally enterprising bistro. To keep things interesting, menus are routinely themed with wacky names, such as Scorsese's Mother's Pasta and Liz Taylor's Veggie Diet. Riding the sustainability train on a whole new track, OAXEN KROG & SLIP not only serves locally sourced products—the long-standing restaurant's furnishings are eco-friendly, the geothermal heating system is closely monitored, and waste is dutifully recycled. Nestled on the island of Djurgården, every inch of the dining process is carefully considered to ensure a purely holistic experience.

For diners who like their meals with a side of scenery, each and any of URBAN DELI's three locations would fit the bill. The multiservice establishments, which feature whimsical flourishes that overlook classic Scandinavian decor, wear many hats, oscillating between lounge, market, deli counter, restaurant, and more. At the Sveavägen location, the shop closest to the city's central train station, there's even a hip underground hotel and rooftop park. No matter what tickles your fancy, TAVERNA BRILLO has it covered. Keep it low-key at the graffiti-walled café, posh it up at the brass- and industrial-tiled restaurant, or satiate your appetite at the deli or bakery counter. And if lazy lounging makes you late to meet your fella, buy him a bouquet at the en suite flower shop.

> For centuries, Swedish cuisine was centered on regionally harvested staples, including fish, game meat, potatoes, and dairy.

Slip (pictured) is the bright, roomy bistro half of the Oaxen enterprise.

Oaxen Krog offers a ten-course tasting menu with exquisite cuisine.

Seekers of a serious cup of joe need look no further than JOHAN & NYSTRÖM. Opened in 2004 by a group of coffee-loving creatives, the brand's three award-winning locations feature craft coffee blends that have made their way directly from bean producers to stores to consumers. Beans are offered whole, ground, or espresso-style and represent top java locations around the world, including Colombia, Kenya, Guatemala, and Ethiopia. Wine lovers wishing to expand their knowledge of natural wines should sample the rotating selection at TYGE & SESSIL, a wine café that offers lesser-known varietals from around the globe. Snug yet inviting, this shabby-chic locale sells approximately 300 natural wines, with or without tasty sides, and it aims to make new wine discoveries enjoyable and easily accessible to everyone.

The art of tasting and cultivating wine is a relatively new concept on the Stockholm scene, and FOLII is one hotspot that wants to ensure its permanence. Conceptualized by a duo of crafty sommeliers, this dandy wine bar serves a selection of curated international wines paired with complementary bites. A perfect place to wet your whistle or satisfy your pre-club appetite, SIDE TRACK is the choicest gay bar for men who enjoy unwinding sans pretention. Considered the oldest gay watering hole in Stockholm, the laid-back joint offers simple Swedish cuisine on weekdays, before changing gears come Friday night, when DJs spin the hits and oldie barmen pour custom swigs.

For a different drum beat, head out to FASCHING, a live music institution open since the 1970s. Here, the specialty is jazz played with great fervor by local and international talents. For memorable moments that sizzle, the bluesy bi-level venue serves food during concerts, or if the rhythm does indeed get you, weekend DJs spin the hits of many genres, from disco to Latin to funk to soul—until the first light. Peacocks of all fancies flaunt their feathers at GULDBAREN (The Gold Bar), a swank cocktail bar in the five-star Nobis Hotel. As glitzy as the nattily attired patrons that frequent it, this nightspot's golden mirrors and dramatic lighting spotlight the bar's creative concoctions, a megamix of flavors that skirt the edge of bizarre, with fetching names like Young & Flirty and Scandal Beauty.

Let the spirit of hedonism ring out at the moored steamer ship PATRICIA, where pop, disco, and rock rule the night at the seven bar zones strewn both inside and out. A permanent fixture on the scenic Söder Mälarstrand, the best boys' festivities are held on Sundays, and the party has raged on for over two decades.

The Folii wine bar—the name is a play on the French word folie for madness.

Minimalist and clean to a fault, Stockholm design—from clothing to fine furnishings to art—has always maintained a time-stopping, effortless quality. Add to the fold a splash of unexpected color or cut of couture, and you've found the perfect marriage between classic and craft.

Representative of Sweden's stylishly spartan aesthetic, GRANDPA is a lifestyle store for all things Nordic. Casual unisex clothing and accessories are but a sample of the products on offer at its four central locations; the brand also has an interiors section that sells books, home decor, games, textiles, posters, lighting, and kitchenware. If you're planning to linger, check out the flagship store on Kungsholmen, where DJs spin the latest hits. For those who prefer to lounge, browse, and shop in one convenient location, SNICKARBACKEN 7 is a dream come true. Equal parts concept store, gallery space, and café, this venue is worth a gander. The small entrance gives way to a dimly lit coffee and cake spot that leads toward a boutique area, which offers kooky wares, books, magazines, kitchen trinkets, and even vinyl records. If antiques are your passion, scour the merchandise at BRANDSTATIONEN, a former fire station turned secondhand shop. In contrast to other stores of its kind, items here are carefully selected and are of the highest quality. Pick up a weathered leather couch, a set of polished silverware, an exceptional piece of jewelry, or, when luck strikes, a brand name luggage piece in pristine condition.

Inspired by Sweden's unspoiled natural landscape and contrasting urban spaces, the trio behind SANDQVIST creates bags and accessories for clients that favor function over fuss. As sturdy as they are stylish, all their items are made with locally sourced, recyclable materials. And speaking of sustainability, L:A BRUKET produces organic skincare sourced directly from the rugged beauty of Sweden's west coast. Packaged in no-nonsense sepia bottles with descriptive labels, their products are categorized by easy-to-follow treatments that depend on skin types and tones. Though all the merchandise is available online, the eco-company's flagship store is based in Stockholm. To add a pop of personality to any space, make a dash to SVENSKT TENN for vibrantly hued wallpapers, furniture, and other home decor tidbits, which come in both prints and solids. Established in 1924, the interior design company tends to favor textiles that take up bold floral motifs and natural scenes.

The perfect destination for hipsters, Grandpa specializes in Scandinavian clothing, home décor, and vintage furniture.

Brandstationen sells carefully selected and beautifully restored vintage pieces of exceptional quality.

World renowned for its first-rate contemporary photography exhibitions held within a mammoth space, FOTOGRAFISKA offers an annual roundup of four full-scale exhibitions and over 20 smaller presentations. Housed in a brick-faced, art nouveau–style edifice in hipster hood Södermalm, the center also includes conference rooms, a souvenir shop, galleries, and a top-floor café with a focus on seasonal dishes. In homage to Sweden's most famous musical export, ABBA THE MUSEUM offers a megawatt memorabilia experience that features authentic costumes, awards, photos, and trivia. And for diehard fans of the fab foursome, an interactive space allows visitors to try on virtual outfits as well as record and download their very own versions of the band's greatest hits.

Costumes worn by Abba at the 1974 Eurovision Song Contest—now on display at Abba The Museum.

David Shrigley's Exhibition of Giant Inflatable Swan-things at the Spiritmuseum.

The handsome facade of Färgfabriken. Built in 1889, the venue was originally a factory building.

Get your culture fix at FÄRGFABRIKEN, an art space providing a vibrant platform for thought leaders from the fields of contemporary architecture, art, social sciences, and urban development. Innovative in nature, the center's cutting-edge exhibits are often paired with seminars to encourage further off-site discussion and debate. For stimulation of a different flavor, the SPRITMUSEUM details the history and curious culture of alcohol in Sweden. Housed in an eighteenth-century naval building on the island of Djurgården, the museum offers both a permanent interactive exhibition and temporary displays, as well as a kitschy Absolut vodka art collection. Complete your visit with a vodka tasting or regional lunch in the contemporary en suite restaurant.

Founded in 1995, the focus at Färgfabriken is on art, architecture, and urban planning.

Scandinavian design takes center stage during STOCKHOLM DESIGN WEEK. Since its conception in 2002, it has established itself as the one of the most important events in the Scandinavian design calendar. Every year in February designers, architects, influencers and buyers with a penchant for the Scandinavian design aesthetic flock to the Swedish capital to discover the latest trends, expand their network and get inspired.

Revered as the most heart-pumping outdoor party space in Stockholm, TRÄDGÅRDEN delivers with a vast courtyard dance floor, a slew of bars, a burger joint, and lawn games that take place along the sidelines. Located beneath the bohemian Södermalm district's Skanstull Bridge, the venue presents guest DJs that play an eclectic mix of EDM, house, and electronica beats between the months of May and September. During the summer months, the MÄLARPAVILJONGEN restaurant and bar—backdropped by the lakeside Norr Mälarstrand and bucolic scenery—comes alive with an exclusive selection of entertainment. Aside from a dynamic lineup that includes drag shows, jazz sessions, and themed parties, since 2013 the venue has collaborated with Regnbågsfonden, a charitable organization that tirelessly champions LGBTQ rights.

Stockholm Furniture & Light Fair is the initiator behind Design Week since 2002.

ESCAPE IT

Boats leave Stockholm regularly, heading for Stora Fjäderholmen, one of four islands that make up the Fjäderholmarna archipelago.

Twenty minutes from the city's core via ferry, the FJÄDERHOLMARNA ARCHIPELAGO offers visitors a sensorial landscape of natural beauty and artistic inspiration. Day-trippers can stroll the unspoiled Baltic seaside trails or hike further inland along scattered forest footpaths. In tribute to the idyllic surrounds, summertime concerts are routinely performed at the Fjäderholmsscenen amphitheater. For creative pursuits, the diminutive island is host to a collection of museums and galleries that showcase craft artists from a bevvy of mediums, including pottery, glassblowing, jewelry making, and painting. The Allmogebåtar boat museum, which displays restored Swedish fishing boats, is among the most memorable. Take a meal break at the waterfront Fjäderholmarnas Krog seafood restaurant, or for lighter appetites, the Rökeriet serves regional deli bites. End the day with a cold beer at Fjäderholmarnas Bryggeri, where visitors are free to sample brews directly from the barrel, or for a rare tipple treat, try the Swedish single malt whisky Mackmyra.

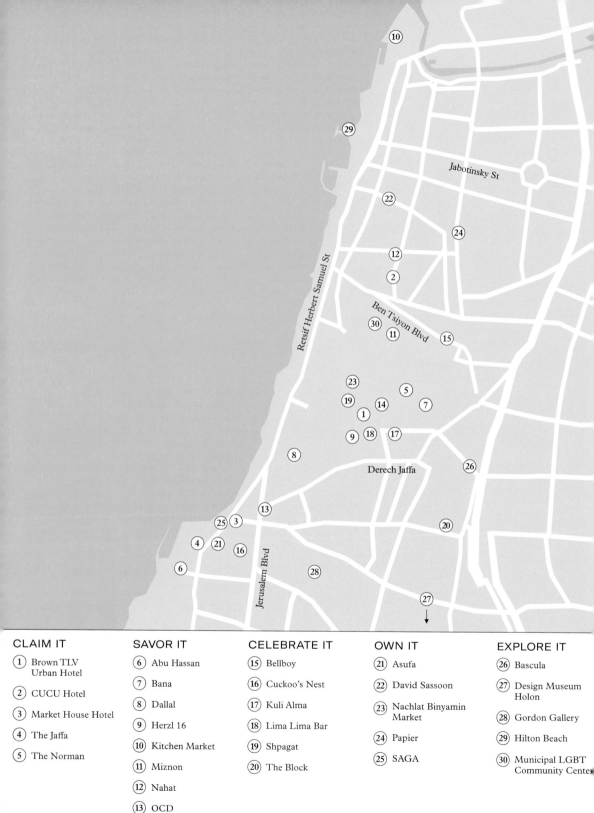

Jabotinsky St

Retsif Herbert Samuel St

Ben Tsiyon Blvd

Derech Jaffa

Jerusalem Blvd

CLAIM IT

① Brown TLV Urban Hotel
② CUCU Hotel
③ Market House Hotel
④ The Jaffa
⑤ The Norman

SAVOR IT

⑥ Abu Hassan
⑦ Bana
⑧ Dallal
⑨ Herzl 16
⑩ Kitchen Market
⑪ Miznon
⑫ Nahat
⑬ OCD
⑭ Port Said

CELEBRATE IT

⑮ Bellboy
⑯ Cuckoo's Nest
⑰ Kuli Alma
⑱ Lima Lima Bar
⑲ Shpagat
⑳ The Block

OWN IT

㉑ Asufa
㉒ David Sassoon
㉓ Nachlat Binyamin Market
㉔ Papier
㉕ SAGA

EXPLORE IT

㉖ Bascula
㉗ Design Museum Holon
㉘ Gordon Gallery
㉙ Hilton Beach
㉚ Municipal LGBT Community Center

TEL AVIV

A Mixed Mecca of Openness

It's a sacred place where cultures collide. Jews, Arabs, Christians, and atheists; artists and scientists; locals and foreigners; young and old; gay and straight—they all share this rather secular city in an otherwise very religious country. But within this diverse mixture, there is tolerance of one another, and that has created a one-of-a-kind location that is hard to duplicate. As the gay capital of the Middle East, Tel Aviv serves as a safe place for so many, which is why the urban center has landed itself on the LGBTQ travel map as one of the top destinations. In this city that doesn't sleep, perched right on the Mediterranean Sea and with almost year-round beautiful weather, you can find a massive gay population that has a sense of openness, who live for the city's thriving nightlife, and, of course, the infamous Tel Aviv Pride festival held in June every year.

While it's true the Holy Land does not have a large number of gay bars, it's equally evident that the gay communities in cities like Tel Aviv have effortlessly blended into the local scenes. So don't look for the gay neighborhood when in Tel Aviv, because chances are you'll already be standing in it. One could thus easily suggest that the city simply has no need for a designated gay neighborhood, although it does have an unofficial gay beach covered with distinct rainbow umbrellas. And despite the ongoing confrontations at the borders, tourism here is booming.

The gay-owned BROWN TLV URBAN HOTEL is a boutique accommodation option situated close to various gay nightlife venues. Stylish yet cost-conscious, it forms partnerships with local businesses to provide guests with experiences outside of the property. For example, breakfast is served at neighboring cafés that are specifically chosen by the hotel, and free access to a gym within walking distance is available. The hotel also boasts a spa suite, which offers a variety of treatments and

The Jaffa Hotel has two wings—one modern and the other set within the original 19th-century building.

Stylish yet cost-conscious, Brown TLV Urban Hotel forms partnerships with local businesses to provide guests with experiences outside of the property.

a rooftop sundeck with a panoramic view of Tel Aviv. CUCU HOTEL is the quirky new kid on the block, providing a breath of fresh air for those searching for places to stay. Playing off of their name, the hotel prides itself in being different, a place where free spirits are more than welcome. This top-quality urban hotel has everything you might need for a stay in Tel Aviv, including many opportunities to experience a sensory overload—the artwork throughout the property will continuously try to capture your attention. Located on Beit Eshel Street, next to the historic Jaffa Clock Tower and Flea Market, is the MARKET HOUSE HOTEL, which takes inspiration from the atmosphere of ancient Jaffa. Nearby are the landmark archaeological ruins of a Byzantine chapel, viewable from the glass floor in the hotel's lobby. The hotel itself offers bohemian-inspired rooms that provide a glimpse into the activity of the market below.

A former chapel now serves as a lounge and bar at the beautifully modernized Jaffa Hotel.

For an upgraded experience, THE NORMAN, which is also gay-owned, gives a nod to the glamorous days of the Roaring Twenties. Imagine barkeeps in bow ties shaking cocktails behind a mirrored bar. Decadent penthouse suites and an exceptional level of concierge service are to be expected here. But once inside the hotel, you'll see it's not all about the past. There is also a modern, clean-lined rooftop pool with views of the neighboring skyscrapers as well as a sleek sushi bar, although the hotel's signature restaurant is Alena, a flowing in- and outdoor space that offers light Mediterranean cuisine. Designed by renowned architect John Pawson in collaboration with Ramy Gill, THE JAFFA, Tel Aviv's newest luxury hotel, is a perfect example of modern meets historic. The duo transformed a nineteenth-century complex that once housed Jaffa's French Hospital into a luxury hotel while remaining true to the original heritage of the building. The Jaffa provides an unparalleled level of exclusivity and state-of-the-art luxury in the city's most fashionable neighborhood, and it is just minutes from the beach.

Guests staying at the Jaffa have access to a secluded swimming pool in a courtyard between the buildings.

It's a sacred place where cultures collide … they all share this rather secular city.

Tel Aviv's food scene is almost unrivaled, offering options influenced by North Africa, the Middle East, and the Mediterranean that are all heavy on fresh vegetables—this is why Israel has the world's highest percentage of vegans per capita. Some of the best restaurants are the ones where you can sit elbow to elbow with others while dishes circulate family-style, the progression of courses only interrupted for socializing, which is in fact a perfect description of many of Tel Aviv's best restaurants.

Every morning, pastry chef Aner Zalel bakes flaky croissants, buttery rugelach, zesty lemon tarts, and much more at DALLAL—a perfect place to start your day. The café features a sidewalk bar area and a small patio with picnic tables, in addition to a bougainvillea-covered swing just across the road, for those who prefer to enjoy their freshly baked goods right then and there. Coffee shops seem to be everywhere within city limits, but just a handful would qualify as trade specialists. NAHAT has a micro roastery, making it a mecca for Tel Aviv's bean fanatics. This cozy shop is perfect

Chefs at Kitchen Market work away at a wide range of dishes.

Informality and a lively vibe are part of the appeal at Miznon.

Well-prepared, fresh Middle Eastern dishes are on the menu at Port Said.

for conversation, remote work, or for those who simply want to pick up a blend or single origin to take home. If you're seeking out that perfect brunch spot, look no further than KITCHEN MARKET. This contemporary gourmet restaurant is located on the upper floor of the Shuk HaNamal farmers market in the Tel Aviv Port, one of the most beautiful parts of the city, offering views of the ocean on one side, while the other provides a glimpse of the vibrant colors of the bustling marketplace. Here, renowned chef Yossi Shitrit has carefully curated a menu filled with quality ingredients, most of which arrive fresh each morning, and it is sure to stimulate all of your senses.

Small plates are the main draw at HERZL 16, which is typically packed for breakfast, lunch, and dinner. The airy restaurant features fresh salads, soups, burgers, and seafood dishes—all at reasonable prices. Out back on the patio, there's an intimate bar with a small stage. Here, enjoy a meal at a communal table, where locals and tourists alike fill the seats, and drink a craft beer while taking in a performance by a local band. Vegans, or those simply wanting to experience something different, can head to BANA, one of the city's many vegan restaurants, although it's fairly easy to find plant-based food on just about any menu in town. But Bana stands out for its comfort dishes and hip scene. Or visit ABU HASSAN, one of Israel's oldest and most famous hummus restaurants, located on Dolphin Street in Jaffa. The hummus here has taken out the top spot on various lists.

There is an abundance of street food in Tel Aviv, but it's rarely made by a celebrity chef like MIZNON'S Eyal Shani. With three locations in Israel, and others in Paris and Vienna, its simple meat-in-pita concoction is proving a hit. There are also, however, vegan and fish options, and a banana pita for dessert. Chef Shani provides another option with his restaurant PORT SAID, serving dishes like eggplant with tahini and lima beans or roast beef carpaccio. Although the interior is limited in terms of space, outside, tables spill out onto the sidewalk and courtyard behind the Great Synagogue. For Middle Eastern fine dining, head to OCD. Here, the Instagram-star turned acclaimed chef Raz Rahav utilizes his detail-obsessed outlook, which has made OCD one of the best restaurants in the city. The creative dining experience is a nine-course tasting menu in which each dish is meticulously designed, employing a wild palette of colors made up of various sauce and ingredient combinations.

There's no shortage of places to go out in Tel Aviv, and no matter what scene you are looking for, the city has you covered. Start off at the CUCKOO'S NEST—part bar, part art gallery—located inside an antique shop. The art changes weekly and the cocktails are consistently amazing. In addition to exhibitions, the space hosts lectures, movie nights, and serves as a live music venue. SHPAGAT, named for the Hebrew word for the gymnastic

Since the Israeli weekend begins on Thursday, this is when the best parties take place, as the clubs can invite top international DJs without much competition.

split, essentially runs the gay nightlife scene in Tel Aviv. Here, everyone is welcome to enjoy the intimate seating that surrounds a large stage-like dance floor. Another symbol of Tel Aviv nightlife is LIMA LIMA BAR, which is known for hosting some of the city's best parties. Gay hip-hop Mondays are one of the most popular nights to visit.

However, since the Israeli weekend begins on Thursday, this is when the best parties take place, as the clubs can invite top international DJs without much competition. In south Tel Aviv,

With its low lighting, plush seating, and parquet floor, Bellboy Bar has a quirky interior design.

Customers enjoy the latest exhibition at Cuckoo's Nest. The venue also has a rooftop bar.

Whatever you order at the Bellboy Bar, you can be sure of a uniquely creative presentation.

KULI ALMA, one of the city's trendiest spots, is known for serving its trademark mojito slushies. Its two levels and labyrinth of rooms comprise a subterranean courtyard and staircase, a tiny misshapen dance floor, and even a hidden vintage clothing store. This is the kind of place where a visit will give you serious street cred with locals. Situated in the heart of the African Quarter of Tel Aviv, inside the new central bus station, THE BLOCK is a club with three main spaces, two of which forbid the use of cellphones, permitting you to fully invest in the party, which typically starts at midnight. For cocktails, try BELLBOY, which serves some of their drinks in outlandish objects. Located within a boutique hotel, its decor was carefully selected to create the feeling of being in a place completely different from Tel Aviv.

For menswear, visit DAVID SASSOON, a go-to fashion shop located near the historic Neve Tzedek area. The store's interior has a feel reminiscent of early twentieth-century Europe, and it offers everything from sportswear to a classical sartorial line for formal occasions, all of which can be described as wearable glamorous fashion. ASUFA offers design items from many young and fresh Israeli talents, making it possible to see a variety of products all in one place. The store's aesthetic represents a meeting point of industrial and interior design, and it carries many home goods that reflect that style, in addition to jewelry, stationery, and more. Spending time here will provide an insight into the creativity that runs rampant throughout the local design community. Located next to the Jaffa flea market, SAGA is another design destination, but it focuses on the future of Israeli design, furniture, and housewares. PAPIER is where style and paper meet. The stationer is the proud lovechild of Sharon Brunsher and Shiran Rockaway, whose backgrounds in fashion design resulted in this very chic paper store. Located in the heart of Tel Aviv, pay it a visit for collections of paper and lifestyle products fit for all your gift-giving and paper-loving needs.

Tel Aviv's best unkept secret might be NACHLAT BINYAMIN ARTS AND CRAFTS FAIR. Here, in one of the oldest districts within the city, adjacent to the Carmel Market, one can expect to find endless rows of creativity. The fair takes place twice a week, every Tuesday and Friday, and brings together over 200 artists who are there to sell their work. Each maker has a regular stall, so if you see something you regret not buying on Tuesday, you can always go back on Friday and hope it's still there. Each work of art is authentic and original, ranging from glass dinnerware to one-of-kind custom-made door signs.

Tel Aviv's best unkept secret might be Nachlat Binyamin Arts and Crafts Fair. Here, in one of the oldest districts within the city, one can expect to find endless rows of creativity.

Tel Aviv's flea markets are fun destinations for a wide range of bargains, from old jeans to vintage textiles and domestic wares.

With a predominantly black, white, and gray color scheme, Papier sells a range of journals, stamps, and artsy labels.

Start your search for inspiration at the MUNICIPAL LGBT COMMUNITY CENTER, established in 2008 under the premise that every person, regardless of age, race, or gender, has the right to live freely. Israel has continuously been a leader in gay rights, and the center is the country's main organizer of gay programs and activities. It's a great resource not only for locals but also for visitors. HILTON BEACH, known as the city's unofficial gay beach, is a clean sandy strip just below the Hilton Hotel in the north

To see some of Israel's major players within the country's art scene, visit Gordon Gallery.

of Tel Aviv. Here, you'll be able to meet gay locals who can potentially provide you with an insider's perspective on their city. The beach is the most liberal of all the beaches in Tel Aviv, so expect to see lots of exposed skin laying out in the sunlight.

As Tel Aviv is filled with museums and art galleries, visiting art aficionados need not worry. BASCULA is the first independent arts center in Israel

In 2016, Gordon Gallery opened a third space in Tel Aviv, focusing on contemporary art from abroad as well as Israel.

Occupying a four-story building in Ben Yehuda Street, Gordon Gallery has a reputable collection of Israeli fine art.

that promotes modern circus. Events held here range from live concerts by both local and international bands to full-on acrobatics and modern circus performances, cabaret, theater, visual arts, and variety shows. During the day, the 6,500-square-foot (600 m²) converted warehouse serves as a space for professional performers to create and rehearse their work, and is it also home to classes and workshops on contemporary circus arts.

Consistently ranked one of Israel's best museums, DESIGN MUSEUM HOLON needs to be on your list of must-sees. Just a short drive from the city, the expertly curated exhibits here display contemporary artworks. But progressive art and design are not limited to the interior, as the building's shell is composed of a masterful winding-spiral design by famed architect Ron Arad. To see some of Israel's major players within the country's art scene, visit GORDON GALLERY, with its two locations on the same block in the central city, one of which is open only by appointment. Founded in 1966, over the years it has played a major role in the emergence of Israel's contemporary art scene.

TEL AVIV PRIDE is one of the most coveted events in this part of the world, its weekend of activities drawing a massive amount of tourists to the city. It is thus recommended to book hotels, package deals, and even airfares far in advance. Typically occurring in June, the Tel Aviv Gay Pride Parade is filled with creative floats and music, and it ends with a once-in-a-lifetime beach party on the city's promenade. If pride isn't an option, FOREVER TEL AVIV, a company that has established itself as one of the leading gay circuit brands and is partially responsible for placing Tel Aviv on the map as a gay party destination, regularly hosts celebrations. The parties are usually monthly, held either at Haoman 17 or The Block—two of the city's leading nightclubs.

Beyond the parties, though, TEL AVIV ILLUS-TRATION WEEK is an incredible time for lovers of illustration to visit the city. Thousands attend each year to participate in dozens of workshops and lectures about illustration, which take place at various spots in the city, like cultural centers and sometimes even inside the homes of artists. During the 10 days and two weekends, there are also many exhibitions, meetings, pop-up shops, and more—and the good news is a lot of the activities and events are free of charge.

The Gay Pride Parade journeys through the streets of Tel Aviv, before culminating in a massive beach party.

Tel Aviv Illustration Week is an excellent showcase for up-and-coming artists as well as established illustrators.

ESCAPE IT

Tel Aviv is an incredible destination, but so is the entire country of Israel. So if you have the opportunity to explore beyond the city, take it, as there's an abundance of amazing locations that shouldn't be missed. Starting with JERUSALEM, its beautiful Old City is easily accessible from Tel Aviv through guided group or individual tours. It's also possible to make your own way there and explore on your own. Historical marvels and important landmarks in Jerusalem include King David's Tomb, the Room of the Last Supper, the Church of the Holy Sepulcher, Via Dolorosa, the Arab market, and the recently restored Roman Cardo. Wander through the Armenian and Jewish quarters, see the sacred Western Wall that has been standing for thousands of years, and then make your way to the Christian quarter. Make sure to stop by the Israel Museum, the largest cultural institution in Israel, ranked among the world's leading art and archaeology museums. Jerusalem is also home to one official gay bar, Video, which is a casual spot with a retro eighties design,

great music, and friendly staff. The bar is popular with Israelis, Palestinians, and tourists alike. It's worth making the time to go and enjoy the cocktails and drag queens in the only place where that's possible within the city.

While Tel Aviv is one of Israel's most modern cities, Jerusalem is certainly among its most ancient.

IN TEL AVIV, DESIGNING HEDONISM

Itay Blaish

"An oasis" is how creative director and graphic designer Itay Blaish describes Tel Aviv, Israel's second-largest city, after Jerusalem. "It's the gayest place on earth," he explains. "Being gay and living outside Tel Aviv can be challenging, so most gay people and the wider LGBT community concentrate here." He adds: "My straight male friends say, 'I feel like the minority.' They say, 'I'd find it easier to find a date with a guy than a girl.'"

It all started in Tel Aviv in the fifties and sixties, with activists, transgender people, and drag queens—the city has long been a place where guys can wear a dress. The community is everywhere. "In the past year it's gotten even more extreme—gay bars are closing. There's no need for the separation, a lot of people feel. I don't believe that. In my opinion, it's nice to have gay bars. But gay life is very normalized. If you want to pick up a guy, or get to know someone, you can do it in any bar. Acceptance is growing and growing."

After leaving his birthplace of Ashkelon, 35 miles (57 km) down the Israeli Mediterranean coast, and completing army service, Itay made the pilgrimage to Tel Aviv at 22, where he studied visual communications at the Shenkar College of Engineering, Design and Art. "I started freelancing during the bachelor's—connecting, communicating, initiating stuff," he says. "Then I built LaCulture, one of Israel's biggest art fairs. It's my baby. I also have my own studio for visual communications: branding, print, consulting to companies about the zeitgeist."

He's currently working as the director and designer of branding for the Maccabiah Games, or the "Jewish Olympics," the world's third-largest sporting event. But his favorite project to date was smaller in scale. "Homophile," which took place in Tel Aviv five years ago, was "an independent exhibition erected for gay culture with 25 artists presenting really amazing things."

Home is the central neighborhood of Lev Hair (literally, "the heart of the city"). Since 2013 Itay has split his time between here and Zurich, Switzerland, following an offer to run a private art collection there. "This way, I get to enjoy the best

"There's something hedonistic about Tel Aviv. Israel's a country that's in a constant state of war."

of both," he says. When I ask how Tel Aviv inspires him, his answer could not be further from the reality of the neat and tidy Swiss financial capital. "The physical architecture of Tel Aviv's built in patches—it's not a proper city by city planning standards," he says. "It's messy. Things are built next to things. You have tons of old Bauhaus, which you won't find anywhere else in the world, next to skyscrapers. From 0 to 100, everything's equal. You have stuff that's shabby, stuff that's super proper." Further contrasts emerge as I put clichéd

perceptions of Tel Aviv to Itay—namely, that beautiful gay men exist everywhere you go; that they hang out at the beach by day, party by night, and embrace gay tourists in ways their standoffish European counterparts wouldn't. "The cliché's true," he says. "There's something hedonistic about Tel Aviv. Israel's a country that's in a constant state of war. In a way, there's a nihilistic way of thinking about it: 'Tomorrow, everything might end. So if you feel like going to the beach, go to the beach.' You make the most of every day." He adds:

"There's something beautiful about this way of life," he adds. "And this from someone who's gotten used to living in Europe—especially in Switzerland, which is the opposite of Israel. A lot of Europeans would say I live on a cloud because I plan in advance but also let things happen. I don't get stressed if I don't finish something, or if I'm not planned to next year with projects." Summing up, he says, "Tel Aviv's innovative, open-minded, and free." Then, sincerely: "In my heart, and physically, I'll never leave."

Shinjuku

Taito

⑤

⑧

⑥

②

Chiyoda

①

⑰

㉑ ㉔

⑬ ⑯

③

⑱ ⑮

㉗ ⑨ ㉓ Chūō

㉒

㉙ ⑩

Shibuya ㉖

④ ⑦ ㉚

⑭ ⑪

㉘ ⑲ ㉕ ⑳

Minato

⑫

㉛

CLAIM IT

① Hoshinoya

② Hotel Ryumeikan Ochanomizu Honten

③ Park Hyatt

④ TRUNK (HOTEL)

⑤ Wired Hotel Asakusa

SAVOR IT

⑥ Kyourakutei

⑦ Sakurai

⑧ Suke6 Diner

⑨ Sushi Ya

⑩ Sushi Zanmai

⑪ Tokyo Shiba Toufuya Ukai

⑫ Yakumo Saryoō

CELEBRATE IT

⑬ AISOTOPE Lounge

⑭ Contact

⑮ Dassai Bar 23

⑯ New Sazae

⑰ Oriental Lounge

OWN IT

⑱ Akomeya

⑲ Daikanyama T-Site

⑳ Hender Scheme

㉑ Isetan

㉒ Japan Traditional Crafts Aoyama Square

㉓ Motoji

㉔ Okamalt

㉕ Okura

㉖ Ragtag

㉗ United Arrows and Sons

EXPLORE IT

㉘ Gōtokuji Temple

㉙ Kabukiza-Theater

㉚ Nezu-Museum

㉛ Saya-No-Yudokoro

TOKYO

Where Traditionalism and Modernism Merge

Tokyo is a city of contrasts quite unlike anywhere else in the world. Electrifyingly modern, with sweeping skyscrapers, flashing neon lights, and dizzying metro stops, the city also hides pockets of tranquility where traditions are alive and evident today. It's this seamless merging of ultra-modern progression with centuries-old tradition that makes Tokyo such a fascinating megacity. It is also perhaps why Japan, and Tokyo in particular, is making strides toward equality and LGBTQ rights, by many accounts leading the way in Asia. Recently, Tokyo passed a bill prohibiting discrimination on the basis of sexual orientation and gender identity. And while same-sex marriage remains illegal for now, some city districts are taking steps in the right direction, issuing certificates to grant same-sex unions the same rights as other couples. The epicenter of LGBTQ culture in Tokyo is the buzzing Shinjuku Ni-chome, home to the world's highest concentration of gay bars. Once the city's red light district, now 300 micro bars and small gay clubs lie crammed together. It's worth noting that Japanese culture tends to value group identity over personal expression, and public displays of affection are frowned upon (regardless of sexual orientation).

Even for the well-seasoned traveler, Tokyo's sheer size can make exploring this megatropolis seem like a daunting task. Luckily, there's an organization to the chaos, and the city's expansive metro system will take you just about anywhere. Whether it's dining at Michelin-starred restaurants (Tokyo has more than any other city in the world) or finding your Zen in the peaceful Buddhist and Shinto shrines, Tokyo guarantees to inspire as it keeps one foot rooted in the past while the other moves swiftly toward the future.

It doesn't get more quintessentially Japanese than a stay at a ryokan, or traditional guesthouse. Feel transported to another era the moment your kimono-clad guide greets you at HOSHINOYA. From the complimentary sake and confections in the guest lounge to the elegant flower arrangements and intricate latticework adorning the building, there's a level of attention to detail here that only the Japanese culture of perfection could obtain. Don't miss a soak in the indoor and outdoor hot spring baths, fed from water 1,500 meters beneath Tokyo's bustling surface—it's a true oasis within the frenzy of the financial district. An obvious choice for fans of *Lost in Translation* and a long-time Tokyo favorite, the five-star PARK HYATT is renowned for its unparalleled service, timeless design, and exquisite views of Mt. Fuji. It doesn't hurt either that the pulsing gay bars of Shinjuku are just minutes away. A hotel as unique as Tokyo, and in the center of the city's famed gayborhood, is the trendy TRUNK (HOTEL). A creative, 15-room concept stay showcasing upcycled materials and local artwork, it's designed to appeal to both travelers and the local community. In contrast to its on-site Japanese-Western fusion kitchen, there's a lifestyle concept store with a distinct focus on things made in Japan, along with a Japanese "soul food" bistro. Always a hub of activity, expect to meet and mingle with locals from all ways of life in any of the buzzing common areas.

The double-height entrance at Hoshinoya—a hotel that combines modern styling with traditional values.

It doesn't get more quintessentially Japanese than a stay at a ryokan.

Another hotel looking to differentiate itself from the norm, WIRED HOTEL ASAKUSA is a boutique stay with hostel options that encourages its guests to trade in typical tourist experiences for ones with more local flair. Local Asakusa artisans created the hotel's design, and the first-floor café is a popular spot for cultural and community events that seamlessly integrate the hotel into the neighborhood. Or for something a bit more intimate, encounter traditional Japanese hospitality at the HOTEL RYUMEIKAN OCHANOMIZU HONTEN. Reopened in 2014 with only nine spacious suites, this modern but traditional property has been perfecting its offering for more than a century. Start your day with a Japanese bento breakfast in bed then unwind with a special someone in your in-room *shigaraki*, or deep-soaking stone bathtub—it's refined opulence at its best.

Simple wooden furnishings and work from local artists add a contemporary Japanese vibe to the rooms of TRUNK (HOTEL).

Electrifyingly modern, with sweeping skyscrapers, flashing neon lights, and dizzying metro stops.

TOKYO SHIBA TOFUYA UKAI might be located at the base of Tokyo Tower, but as per the restaurant's mission, the grounds feel like a version of the city from centuries past. Cross through the iconic wooden gateway to enter a samurai-era merchant's house, then follow the stepping-stones past stately pine trees and an idyllic koi pond. From here, you'll be escorted to a private dining room exhibiting classic Japanese aesthetics, most notable of which are the floor-to-ceiling glass windows that gaze out at immaculately manicured gardens (it's almost impossible to believe that the grounds of this five-star dining experience were previously home to a struggling bowling alley and car park). As the restaurant's name suggests, the kaiseki tasting menus specialize in all things tofu that is made from its workshop in the Okutama mountains. For another elaborate kaiseki affair, YAKUMO SARYO innovates while still paying tribute to Japanese traditions. Each course features a unique take on fresh and local seasonal ingredients such as sea bream, wagyu beef, and daikon radish. The space itself is minimal yet elegant, the unmistakable creation of renowned designer Shinichiro Ogata, whose harmonious interior design also adorns the Andaz Tokyo and multiple Aesop stores.

The art of sushi is all about simplicity, ingenuity, and masterful execution, and in many ways is a direct reflection of Japanese culture. You'll look more like a local if you avoid overdoing it with the soy sauce and wasabi—a telltale sign that someone doesn't appreciate the quality of the fresh fish.

Suke6 Diner has a laid-back urban vibe.

For an intimate sushi experience promising direct interaction with renowned English-speaking sushi chef Takao Ishiyama, head over to the eight-person bar at SUSHI YA. Splurge on the omakase sushi set and let Ishiyama expertly craft a custom menu centered around the freshest ingredients of the day. For all-around decent sushi that won't break the bank, SUSHI ZANMAI doesn't disappoint. It might be a chain, but you're guaranteed fresh dishes at unbeatable prices at any one of its locations throughout Tokyo. Better yet, it's open 24 hours a day, 365 days a year, should you get a hankering for sushi after a night out on the town.

Tucked away in the backstreets of Kagurazaka, KYORAKUTEI takes the art of soba noodles to an entirely new level. You'll know you've arrived by the hallmark grinder that adorns the storefront window; it's not uncommon to find throngs of spectators craning to get a look at the master chef in action, too. Here buckwheat grains are carefully kneaded into fresh dough before being hand-cut into delicate noodles. The deliciously nutty juwari soba (made from 100% buckwheat) and fried tempura are must-tries. And in stark contrast to Tokyo's many formal restaurants, SUKE6 DINER is as unpretentious as it gets, proving simple, rustic food can be just as delicious as its posh counterparts. Come here for Western favorites such salmon bagels, pancakes, and fresh homemade bread, all in a hip, riverside locale.

There's no shortage of tearooms in Tokyo, but the contemporary SAKURAI is unique for its holistic environment in which customers are encouraged to use all five senses under the guidance of Shiya Sakurai himself, a tea master who dedicated 14 years to training in the art of the tea ceremony. Only top-quality leaves from around the country are used to ensure ultimate healing properties. That's not to say stronger libations are frowned upon; you'll also find tea-infused rums and vodkas. Try the five-tea tasting ceremony, or stock up on your favorite leaves to enjoy back at home.

As you look on, chef Takao Ishiyama prepares the finest sushi at Sushi Ya Ginza.

The epicenter of Tokyo's gay culture, Shinjuku Ni-chome is a gayborhood that never sleeps. By day it's a spot for coffee shops or quirky eateries, by night it's a maze of tantalizing taprooms that stay open until the early morning hours when the first metro trains run again. Amongst the hundreds of gay micro bars—most of which hold no more than 15 people—there's a stimulating spot for any interest. Historically, not all gay bars in Shinjuku Ni-chome were welcoming toward foreigners; that attitude is changing, but there are a few spots where you certainly can't go wrong. NEW SAZAE is one of the oldest gay bars in the area, first gaining prominence as a go-to dance club in the 1970s. The music and decor of the disco era live on, while glamorously flamboyant staff provide friendly service. With two spacious dance floors, AISOTOPE LOUNGE is the largest gay club in Shinjuku Ni-chome. Guaranteeing a good time any night of the week, the lounge also offers costume parties, notable DJ performances, and male-only events.

Anyone seeking a more intimate evening out will find plenty of small bars with low lighting and a gentle vibe.

> ## By night it's a maze of tantalizing taprooms that stay open until the early morning hours when the first metro trains run again.

Dim lights and candles set the tone at the Oriental Lounge, with stunning views over the city at dusk.

Outside Shinjuku Ni-chome, ORIENTAL LOUNGE is an obvious choice. Located on the 38th floor of the Mandarin Oriental hotel, here you can sip superbly crafted cocktails while taking in the spectacular city views. We recommend doing a Carrie Bradshaw and ordering one of their exquisite cosmopolitans or stopping by in the afternoon for their famous high tea, which boasts fabulous finger sandwiches and scrumptious scones. Continue your taste-testing at the DASSAI BAR 23. Famed both in Japan and abroad, cozy up at the bar for a flight of its premium Dassai sake line, including bubbly and the exclusive Dassai Beyond.

One of the hottest clubs in Tokyo, CONTACT is a go-to for discerning music lovers, especially those with a fondness for electronic and techno. Located in a basement in the always-pulsating Shibuya neighborhood, this fashionable club has a noticeably European flair. Alcohol and cameras aren't allowed inside the main studio, which is reserved for dancing, maintaining a true "what happens on the dance floor, stays on the dance floor" vibe. Be sure to pre-register online to access the venue.

Shibuya is known for its neon signage—flanking the world's busiest pedestrian crossing.

Whether it's designer labels or the latest in street fashion, Tokyo knows how to deliver a one-of-a-kind shopping experience. Bargain hunters and collectors alike won't want to miss the array of high-quality secondhand designer pieces available at RAGTAG. The latest three-story Harajuku branch on trendy Cat Street is impossible to miss, and with a hundred-odd items being added to the collection daily, it's worth stopping in a second and third time.

Speaking of designer pieces, no one does leather footwear quite like Japanese brand HENDER SCHEME. An auto parts factory turned flagship shop, it's a haven for unique yet stylish footwear and accessories. Another made-in-Japan fashion experience, OKURA boasts an in-house clothing brand that specializes in traditional craftsmanship. Following ancient Japanese methods, most pieces are dyed in indigo following the practice of aizome. For something even more traditionally Japanese, MOTOJI creates stunning, modern kimonos from premium silk, and also specializes in robes for men.

Synonymous with the city of Tokyo are the many vending machines one encounters on the city's streets.

Craft items from artisans and artists across the whole of Japan are available at the Japan Traditional Crafts Aoyama Square.

The archetypal Japanese craft item: a cast-iron teapot, or *tetsubin*, used for boiling and pouring hot water when making tea.

Japan knows how to do department stores, and ISETAN is probably the trendiest of them all. There's an entire building dedicated to menswear alone, along with a noteworthy made-to-measure section. Keep an eye out for a seasonal trunk show to top off the bespoke shopping experience. Gents who know style also know UNITED ARROWS & SONS. The brainchild of creative director Motofumi Kogi (AKA Poggy), the shop's classically cool take on menswear is as iconic as ever.

Short of traveling the length and breadth of the country in search of the best arts and crafts, a meander around the JAPAN TRADITIONAL CRAFTS AOYAMA SQUARE is as good as it gets. The Japanese government runs the show here, so you're guaranteed authentic pieces at exceptional prices. From the washi (handmade paper) to ceramics to wood-carvings to expert exhibitions, it's a far cry from the typical kitschy tourist shop. Meanwhile, foodies and amateur chefs alike will drool over AKOMEYA, a rice-themed lifestyle shop. Alongside Japan's essential meal component, expect tableware, traditional rice cookers, and other kitchen staples.

Revered writer, magazine editor, and gay pioneer To Ogura is better known in many drag queen circles as Margarette, and his book café, OKAMALT, is a fascinating shop dedicated specifically to LGBTQ literature. Explore some 600 titles as you mingle with snacks and drinks in this Tokyo institution. Then, continue your literary exploration at the mammoth DAIKANYAMA T-SITE, a conglomerate of books, albums, movies, and stationery housed in an award-winning "library in the woods." Don't skip the upstairs Anjin Library & Lounge, where you can skim through 30,000-plus vintage magazines while sipping on coffee or cocktails.

More than your average museum, the NEZU MUSEUM is a haven of well-groomed Japanese gardens, cutting-edge architecture, and an exquisite collection of more than 7,000 Japanese and East Asian works of art. Renovated by renowned architect Kengo Kuma, the Nezu demands at least a few hours to fully do it justice; better yet, make a day of it with a picnic lunch in the gardens. To appreciate the legendary birthplace of the beckoning cat, or maneki-neko, visit the GOTOKUJI TEMPLE and view hundreds of waving feline figurines on display, each ranging from 3 to 30 centimeters tall. Don't leave without checking out the nearby streets dotted with cat-themed artwork. Less unusual but equally interesting is the KABUKIZA THEATRE, famed for its highly stylized kabuki dance-dramas that are shown nearly every day. A traditional Japanese art form, it features elaborate costumes, makeup and wigs, and is still performed exclusively by men.

To unwind after a day of shopping and sightseeing, a visit to a traditional onsen will revive the mind, body, and spirit. There's a smattering of these natural hot spring facilities throughout Tokyo, but SAYA-NO-YUDOKORO is worth seeking out. Well equipped with a variety of bath types, including open-air, hydro-massage, and lie-down baths, what makes this onsen unique is the free-flowing hot springs that feed the baths— a rarity even in Japan. Those inclined to relaxing through the arts will love an ikebana workshop exploring the Japanese art of flower arranging. Sogetsu-certified instructor MIKA OTANI offers one of the best in a century-old ryokan, where she teaches the fundamentals of ikebana before leading students through their own arrangement.

A visit to a traditional onsen will revive the mind, body, and spirit.

Away from the bustle of the city center, there's plenty exploring to be done in Tokyo's suburbs.

Get your glam on at Tokyo's one-of-a-kind irregular gay dance party, GLAMOROUS TOKYO, which is held throughout the city every few months. From go-go dancers to drag queen performances, it's an epic event in a welcoming environment open to all sexual preferences. Desire something with a little more dazzle? A costume party for the fashion-forward at one of Tokyo's hottest gay dance clubs, FANCY HIM, is an opportunity to let loose and dress fancy even if it's not Halloween.

Rainbow Pride, Japan's largest annual LGBTQ celebration, features numerous events and activities across Tokyo.

> **Get your glam on at Tokyo's one-of-a-kind irregular gay dance party, Glamorous Tokyo. From go-go dancers to drag queen performances, it's an epic event in a welcoming environment open to all sexual preferences.**

Celebrate Pride in Tokyo at its annual RAINBOW PRIDE PARADE every May, with some 60 events over the week culminating in a three-kilometer march around the Harajuku and Shibuya districts. Expect performances, floats, and an all-around good time with Japanese and foreigners from different walks of life coming together to support LGBTQ rights.

Yoyogi Park plays a central role in the Gay Pride festivities, hosting as many as 60 events in all.

ESCAPE IT

With a day trip to KAMAKURA, it's possible to soak up the seaside without straying far from the neon lights. Start the morning catching waves at the city's popular Yuigahama beach and still be back downtown in time for sightseeing in the afternoon. Just south of Tokyo, Kamakura was once the political center of medieval Japan, and is still home to dozens of Buddhist and Shinto shrines. Most notice-ably, the Kotoku-in Temple houses the Great Buddha, a 13-meter-high bronze statue cast in 1252 that has remained standing despite the notorious fifteenth-century tsunami that largely devastated the area. What's more, avid hikers will be pleased by the various mountain trails that wind past cave tombs and scenic landscapes, far removed yet easily accessible from Tokyo's urban jungle.

The Great Buddha of Kamakura. This bronze statue is one of the country's most famous icons.

IN TOKYO, SCULPTING REBELLION AND NON-CONFORMITY

Akira the Hustler

Proudly political, deeply personal, and sometimes eye-poppingly sexual, the work of artist Akira the Hustler often exudes a rebellious spirit. This is especially true of his beautiful Red String "Lovers" sculpture from 2012, which features two soul mates connected by a piece of thread, their erect penises touching.

Characteristic rebelliousness melds Akira to Tokyo, his home city and the largest in Japan. "I was born in Tokyo and moved to Germany when I was two years old because of my father's business," he explains. "I went back to Japan aged eight and stayed in Kyoto and Kobe until I graduated from university. People who live in western parts of Japan don't like Tokyo—but I had a kind of rebellious spirit, so I went back. It was my attempt to do something interesting in Tokyo: a city hated city by some."

The city is Japan's LGBTQ capital, and Akira has a theory as to why this might have come

about: "I heard that, as people in Tokyo do not show much interest in their neighbors' affairs, the sexual minority could live relatively freely in the past," he says. However, the road to sexual equality of course remains long and challenging—for example, LGBTQs in Japan, like in the entirety of Asia, excluding Taiwan, are yet to secure marriage equality.

Akira's description of his community's response to recent disparaging claims from public officials—that childless LGBTQ couples are "unproductive" and therefore a waste of taxpayer money—sounds like the prelude to a political re-energization. "Lots of people, including those from the sexual minorities, expressed their anger and protested," he says. "Despite the long and continuous efforts of discussions and lobbying, I was deeply touched because—at last!—people started to express their anger in the public space.

And it was different from a parade or festival. I suppose the expression of that anger was the real coming out for the LGBTI community."

But his relationship with the 9.7-million-person-strong city remains a conflicted one. While he cites Popotame—"a bookstore selling mainly radical East Asian artists' books and artworks," located in his local, and very cultural, ward of Toshima—as an example of somewhere he loves to visit, there's plenty about it he dislikes. He describes the city's essence as one of "pessimism, abandonment, irresponsibility," and he predicts a decline after the 2020 Olympics that he hopes will further inspire his creativity.

"What Tokyo gives me is a hopeless gaze, sarcasm, and a small light that generates and burns in me," he says. "I feel the anger and impatience against this city can become my energy to live."

"What Tokyo gives me is a hopeless gaze, sarcasm, and a small light that burns in me."

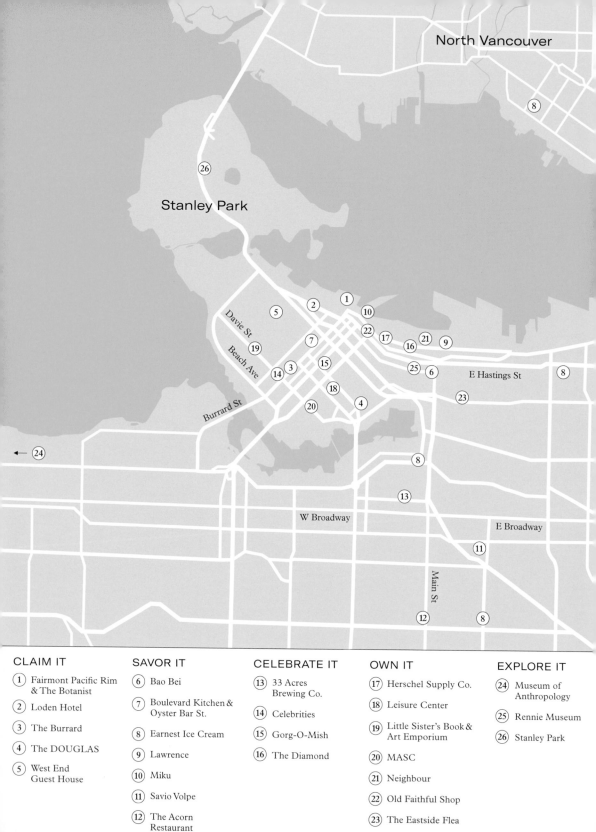

North Vancouver

Stanley Park

Davie St

Beach Ave

Burrard St

E Hastings St

W Broadway

E Broadway

Main St

CLAIM IT

1. Fairmont Pacific Rim & The Botanist
2. Loden Hotel
3. The Burrard
4. The DOUGLAS
5. West End Guest House

SAVOR IT

6. Bao Bei
7. Boulevard Kitchen & Oyster Bar St.
8. Earnest Ice Cream
9. Lawrence
10. Miku
11. Savio Volpe
12. The Acorn Restaurant

CELEBRATE IT

13. 33 Acres Brewing Co.
14. Celebrities
15. Gorg-O-Mish
16. The Diamond

OWN IT

17. Herschel Supply Co.
18. Leisure Center
19. Little Sister's Book & Art Emporium
20. MASC
21. Neighbour
22. Old Faithful Shop
23. The Eastside Flea

EXPLORE IT

24. Museum of Anthropology
25. Rennie Museum
26. Stanley Park

VANCOUVER

A Pacific Urban Paradise

When the morning mist clears, the sun hits the glass skyscrapers of the Vancouver skyline making the city sparkle like a kaleidoscope. The glare is softened only by the shadow of the North Shore Mountains that dwarf the city and lull its active residents for morning trail runs through ancient forests. Then the city begins to buzz as the tankers come into Canada's biggest port and its diverse communities begin their days preparing the kitchens of the country's best food spots and opening the gallery doors of an effervescent art scene. As Canada's most sought-after city many dream of making Vancouver home and its international tourism flourishes year round. The majestic scenery that includes urban forest, mountains, and stunning coastlines, supports an outdoorsy, sporty lifestyle. During the summer, the beaches are packed, with English Bay Beach playing host to Vancouver's gay community. During the winter months, world-class skiing is found in nearby Whistler, which also hosts a pride event during the snowy months. In Vancouver itself, Davie Village, the city's gayborhood, was the first place in Canada to have a permanent rainbow crosswalk installed in 2013; although, with the liberal, free-thinking attitude most Vancouverites share, LGBTQ residents and visitors can rest assured that they will feel welcome throughout the entire city.

With captivating views of the water and mountains, the stylish rooms and unique suites at the FAIRMONT PACIFIC RIM integrate naturally inspired materials and state-of-the-art technology. Sophisticated and contemporary, the luxury property also boasts Botanist, which offers one of the city's best dining atmospheres with a lounge, outdoor terrace, craft bar, and extravagant dining space. From the pastry chef's bread, the sommelier's extensive list, and the chef's local ingredients, everything is top-notch. For something a little more vintage, look no further than the Heritage Registered WEST END GUEST HOUSE, built in 1906. The interior furnishings are reminiscent of an era gone by, yet are accented with modern amenities making a stay here a lot more up to date. The gallery in the hall is worth exploring as it displays photos of old Vancouver, helping bring the inn to life.

> **Sophisticated and contemporary, the luxury property also boasts Botanist, which offers one of the city's best dining atmosphere. From the pastry chef's bread, the sommelier's extensive list, and the chef's local ingredients, everything is top-notch.**

A balanced mixture of history and future, nature and city, THE DOUGLAS presents attentively appointed rooms and suites, all designed with the modern traveler in mind. The hotel is located within Parq Vancouver, a world-class casino resort featuring an elevated roof park that sits six stories high in the middle of the city. For a boutique option, LODEN HOTEL prides itself on its personalized service. Its timber and copper exterior and earthy interior shades draw their inspiration from the natural surroundings of coastal British Columbia and complement its central yet quiet setting within the city. For anyone looking for an affordable but really cool place to stay, THE BURRARD is your best bet. A converted Vancouver motor hotel from 1956, its bright and airy rooms come with a strong sense of design and all the extras you come to expect from a luxury hotel, like Nespresso units and free Wi-Fi.

Rooms at the Douglas Hotel feature elegant contemporary furnishings and a subtle color palette.

A courtyard oasis at the Burrard provides the perfect spot for outdoor lounging and ping pong.

The majestic scenery that includes urban forest, mountains, and stunning coastlines, supports an outdoorsy, sporty lifestyle.

As a city that prides itself on its diverse immigrant cultures, Vancouver brings world cuisine to Canada's West Coast. In a place where 40% of Metro Vancouver residents have some sort of Eastern heritage, top-notch Asian venues dominate the city, from Filipino delights to authentic Indian and Chinese staples.

Catch-of-the-day menus are no stranger to Vancouver, and with the city's thriving Asian influence, finding amazing sushi isn't hard to do. MIKU may be one of its most popular sushi restaurants and specializes in Aburi (flame-seared) cuisine. An extensive sake list keeps guests warm as they look out of the wall-to-wall windows toward the harbor. For traditional seafood fare, take advantage of the fresh, local specialties at BOULEVARD KITCHEN & OYSTER BAR. Seasonal tasting menus are creative and ever changing, but regulars stick to their favorite seafood tower, which can be ordered for two or four.

Catch-of-the-day menus are no stranger to Vancouver.

International flavors can be found at SAVIO VOLPE, an Italian-style osteria that uses fresh ingredients gathered from the nearby lakes, oceans, farms, and fields. Pasta is handmade fresh every day while proteins are prepared over the wood-fired grill and rotisserie. Of course, there's an extensive list of Italian wines to perfectly pair with each course, too. For classic French fare with a Québécois twist, head to ST LAWRENCE. Its rustic menu is inspired by memories of food from chef J.C. Poirier's childhood and reimagined for today's palate.

Over in Chinatown, BAO BEI cultivates an intimate dining experience by serving small sharing plates from a menu that puts a modern spin on flavors from Taiwan, Shanghai, and the Sichuan province. The restaurant is also known for its distinctive list of libations. Meanwhile, vegetarians in Vancouver will find thoughtfully presented, delicious, and filling meals at THE ACORN RESTAURANT at the top of Main Street. Who could say no to smoked caramelized parsnip and potato paté followed by beer-battered halloumi? As for dessert, EARNEST ICE CREAM only works in small batches, which allows it to experiment with foraged ingredients such as fresh spruce bud and elderflower as well as offering classics including milk chocolate and salted caramel. It also packs pints in returnable and reusable glass jars as part of its zero-waste policy.

In the dining room at Botanist a pastel palette provides the perfect backdrop for the wealth of foliage.

The St Lawrence restaurant has a homey vibe, with simple wooden furniture and walls painted a lovely royal blue.

If you're looking to meet people and get to know the locals, 33 ACRES BREWING CO. is the place to be. An inclusive space, the idea of a community sharing drink, food, conversation, space, and ideas is the vision behind the brewery. Its menu, which so eloquently describes the incredible list of rotating beers, is a thing of joy. For something a bit more

> When it's time for dancing, Celebrities, a Vancouver icon since the 1980s, is your best bet. The club is outfitted with the latest in sound and visual light shows.

intimate, THE DIAMOND is an unassuming Gastown cocktail lounge and a cool, laid-back place to meet with friends and imbibe updated versions of classic concoctions. The vintage room is unpretentious and inviting, and the music is never turned up to an overpowering level, allowing guests to interact with one another.

33 Acres of Ocean—just one of numerous beers available from the 33 Acres Brewing Company.

Expect a packed dancefloor at Gorg-o-mish, Vancouver's top spot in the underground techno scene.

Dark and swanky, the Keefer Bar serves cocktails made with homemade tinctures and Asian-inspired snacks.

When it's time for dancing, CELEBRITIES, a Vancouver icon since the 1980s, is your best bet. Growing and evolving along with the community, the club is outfitted with the latest in sound and visual light shows and even has two VIP table-service sections for those needing some exclusivity in their lives. Any late night revelers need only make their way to GORG-O-MISH, Downtown Vancouver's first legal after-hours spot, established in 2003. The club runs every Friday and Saturday through to the early hours of the morning and plays mainly house and techno.

Domestic wares at the Old Faithful Shop include woven laundry baskets, canvas totes, and old-style citrus juicers.

For more unique finds, NEIGHBOUR is a men's shop that carries a selection of clothing, footwear, accessories, and homewares that are carefully selected before finding their place on the sales floor. Or to find one-of-a-kind vintage collectibles and handmade goodies, head to EASTSIDE FLEA. Here, local food trucks will fuel you while you hunt as live vinyl-playing DJs help set the mood. Finally, for those looking to get everything under one roof, there's the two-level, 22,000-square-foot (2,000 sq m) LEISURE CENTER lifestyle emporium, built on the bones of a former envelope factory in a 1930s art deco building in Yaletown. Expect to find luxury fashion, art, music, books, homewares, cosmetics, and even refreshments in a space filled with L-shaped aluminum panels by architect Casper Mueller Kneer in a move that gives the space the appearance of a futuristic souk.

The Old Faithful shop prides itself on offering goods of the finest quality, displayed with minimalist style.

LITTLE SISTER'S BOOK & ART EMPORIUM is a legendary queer retail store that's existed in Davie Village since the 1980s. It stocks a selection of books, greetings cards, clothes, and novelty items and is one of the last of its kind that can be found in gay villages, so it's worth a visit even if you just support them by buying a lapel pin. Alternatively, pretend you're in the pages of *Dwell* magazine at OLD FAITHFUL SHOP in Downtown. Billed as a modern day general store, its shelves are stocked with quality housewares by brands such as Hay, Skagerak, and David Mellor, alongside books and scents. Most customers spend hours daydreaming and plotting ways to ship the store's incredible goods to their own home.

When it comes to larger, well-known Canadian brands, start off by treating your skin at MASC, a brand that's been tending to men's grooming since 2007. With an incredible product selection and outstanding customer service, a visit can be beneficial whether you're on top of your skincare routine or need some guidance. Another Vancouver staple is HERSCHEL SUPPLY CO., founded in 2009 by the Cormack brothers. A design-driven accessories brand that can be found in stores all over the world, its Gastown flagship is slightly overwhelming in size but also oddly exhilarating as every one of its products is at your fingertips.

"Look good, feel great" is the motto at MASC, the best Vancouver has to offer in male grooming.

History buffs can spend a couple of hours taking THE REALLY GAY HISTORY TOUR that takes in Davie Street, one of North America's most vibrant gay villages. Vancouver Pride draws in tens of thousands of people each year and the city even has openly gay politicians and monuments dedicated to gay activists, but it wasn't always this way and this entertaining walking tour provides the opportunity to learn about the city's gay past.

Once you've mastered Vancouver's gay history, make your way to the RENNIE MUSEUM, one of the largest assemblages of contemporary art in Canada. The space has evolved during its existence to include and focus on works related to identity, social commentary, injustice, appropriation, the nature of painting, photography, and film. The gallery features both emerging and international artists, and while the collection is based in Vancouver, it's typically spread across the globe on loan to other institutions. THE MUSEUM OF ANTHROPOLOGY is another incredible option and traces Vancouver's long native history, which stretches back more than 8,000 years. Visitors are greeted by a stand of totems by the modern industrial entrance, while inside works and cultures of the First Nations are spotlighted and complemented by rare artifacts from a plethora of other civilizations.

Topping the list of places to spend a morning or afternoon is STANLEY PARK, Vancouver's largest and most beloved urban park. A green oasis in the middle of the city, it consists of 400 hectares of natural West Coast rainforest where visitors can enjoy the views of water, mountains, sky, and majestic trees along the park's famous seawall. It's also home to Canada's largest aquarium, as well as kilometers of trails, beaches, cultural and historical landmarks, and great places to eat.

Discover Vancouver's diverse history, from the Really Gay History Tour (above left) to the Museum of Anthropology (right).

Explore Vancouver's waterfront activities (above) or take a trip on the Grouse Mountain skyride (opposite).

The QUEER ARTS FESTIVAL is an annual showcase of queer arts, culture, and history. It features a curated visual arts show, a community art show, and three weeks of cutting-edge performances and workshops from all artistic disciplines, all while celebrating the creative expressions of queer visual and performing artists.

> For next-level wine lovers, the Vancouver International Wine Festival is one of the biggest and oldest wine events in the world.

For food and wine enthusiasts, the DINE OUT FESTIVAL is a 17-day schedule of unique culinary experiences that includes guided dining adventures, brunch crawls, cocktail master classes, global guest-chef collaboration dinners, British Columbia Vintners Quality Alliance wine and craft beer tastings, and street food markets. And for next-level wine lovers, the VANCOUVER INTERNATIONAL WINE FESTIVAL is one of the biggest and oldest wine events in the world. Besides seminars, vintage tastings, and winery dinners, the focus of the festival is the Tasting Room, where the public can choose from approximately 750 wines at four International Festival Tastings.

In summer, visitors to Vancouver can join locals chilling out on one of the city's many beaches.

ESCAPE IT

Vancouver's NORTH SHORE isn't just a spectacular backdrop for the scenic city; it's also teeming with life, both wild and urban. For watersports enthusiasts, the coves and islands on the coastline make for perfect paddling trips in addition to some of the best diving in the world. The North Shore is also blessed with vibrant Coast Mountain rainforest, making the trails here a mecca for all levels of hikers and pedal bikers. Once you've explored the outdoors, take some time to stroll the North Shore's community shopping districts—Deep Cove, Lonsdale, Lower Lonsdale, Edgemont Village, Ambleside, Dundarave, Caulfield, and Horseshoe Bay—all of which are plentiful with shops, galleries, and eateries. Few places in the world offer guests the opportunity to spend the morning skiing or boarding and then an afternoon enjoying a stroll near the waterfront.

The Capilano Suspension Bridge crosses the Capilano River in the District of North Vancouver.

Leopoldstadt

Innere Stadt

Taborstrasse

Burgring

Stubenring

Burggasse

Rennstrasse

CLAIM IT

(1) Daniel
(2) Hotel am Brillantengrund
(3) magdas HOTEL
(4) Sans Souci
(5) The Guesthouse

SAVOR IT

(6) Gasthaus Woracziczky
(7) Market
(8) Motto
(9) Palmenhaus
(10) Spelunke
(11) Steirereck
(12) ULRICH

CELEBRATE IT

(13) Café Savoy
(14) krypt.
(15) Onyx Bar
(16) phil
(17) Volksgarten

OWN IT

(18) Löwenherz
(19) Mühlbauer
(20) Naschmarkt
(21) Saint Charles Apotheke
(22) strictly HERRMANN
(23) WienerBlut

EXPLORE IT

(24) Donauinsel
(25) Grinzing
(26) mumok
(27) Musikverein
(28) WestLicht

VIENNA

Where Tradition and Modern Values Meet

Paris has got Le Marais, New York's got Chelsea, and Barcelona's got "Gaixample," but Vienna doesn't limit itself to one gay area. Here, you can feel free and accepted throughout the city with even the occasional side-eye becoming scarce. No matter whom or how you love, Vienna welcomes gay visitors from all over the world. You can walk hand in hand with your partner on Kärntner Straße, embrace each other on the hill of Schönbrunn's Gloriette while listening to a midsummer night's concert, or share a kiss on top of Kahlenberg, overlooking this magnificent city. Even though Vienna is cool with all facets of love, your primary goal probably isn't making out at every corner in town. Having been a cultural and political hub for centuries, the list of things to do in and around the city is endless. Arts, culture, cuisine, architecture, and nightlife are only the beginning of what makes the former capital of the Habsburg Empire worth visiting. Homosexuality is nothing new to Vienna's people. Born in the mid-nineteenth century and brother to Austrian Emperor Franz Joseph I, Archduke Ludwig Viktor was publicly known to be gay and a regular guest of the Centralbad (which today is known as the Kaiserbründl), Vienna's most famous and arguably one of the world's most beautiful gay bathhouses.

Vienna is renowned for its cultural and artistic assets, so why not stay at a hotel that is somewhat of a gallery itself? At the edge of Neubau, one of Vienna's most vibrant districts, you'll find the SANS SOUCI, one of the city's newest and finest luxury hotels. Decorated with the owner's impressive art collection, including Roy Lichtensteins and Steve Kaufmans, handpicked antiques, and exclusive modern furniture, it has a sense of luxurious opulence, but also succeeds in creating a casual and laid-back atmosphere. Whether in the morning or after a long day exploring, you can also swim laps in the hotel's indoor sports pool or enjoy the vast spa area. Of the same high standard, but even more centrally located next to key tourist attractions such as the State Opera and the Albertina Museum, you can find THE GUESTHOUSE. British designer Sir Terence Conran left nothing to chance when creating the interior and has conjured up an ambiance of coziness that allows people to unfold in the most relaxing way imaginable. Straight-lined with a touch of extravagance, the hotel strikes a balance between making you feel at home and bringing some of Vienna's traditions to its guests.

In case you're looking for less opulent lodgings, HOTEL DANIEL is just the place. A self-professed smart luxury hotel, it could be the little sister of a grand, five-star big brother. While no less comfortable or enjoyable, the Daniel emphasizes flexibility and fair prices that the modern urban traveler will appreciate. The design concept is simply elegant, and rooms are available in a broad range of categories, even with some technically not being rooms–it even offers a trailer. For an alternative that is stylish and contributes to the integration of people with migration backgrounds, consider a stay at MAGDAS HOTEL. The place is run as a social business that aims to give people who left their homes in countries affected by crisis a fresh start. The idea is not to exclude people from society just because they don't speak the language, appreciating instead the diversity of its staff and the richness of cultures. Apart from the added social value, Magdas provides all the amenities and services you would expect from a boutique hotel. The interior design was thoroughly thought through and boasts a mixture of antiques, as well as re- and upcycled items.

Our previous statement that Vienna does not have a specific gay area might only partly be true. The 7th district is one of the hippest, most open-minded and artistic areas in the city

Guests can while away an hour or so in the intimate, plant-filled courtyard of Hotel am Brillantengrund.

Light, bright, and simply furnished, rooms at The Guesthouse have an "at home" ambience.

and therefore attracts its fair share of gay visitors. HOTEL AM BRILLANTENGRUND is located right in the heart of this neighborhood, which is home to independent designers, art galleries, and hundreds of restaurants, coffee shops, and bars. The hotel itself is arguably one of the most homey and relaxed places to stay in town. The interior includes a fine selection of furniture from the late nineteenth century and takes you back in time without really pinpointing a specific era.

Arts, culture, cuisine, architecture, and nightlife are only the beginning of what makes Vienna worth visiting.

Due to the country's position in the heart of Europe, Vienna's cuisine is influenced by a host of different regions and cultural circles such as Hungary and Bohemia. WORACZICZKY GASTHAUS offers wonderful, typically Austrian dishes made with regional produce that lends the food an even more distinct Viennese touch. The setting within an old tavern that has retained its paneled walls and small séparées guarantees an unforgettable evening. Then there's MOTTO, an institution both within and without Vienna's LGBTQ scene, which has been attracting gays, musicians, and creatives to its tables since the 1980s. Its menu offers both Austrian and international classics, and its unique interior always provides plenty of food for thought. The green velvet banquettes, distressed walls, and black marble details all work perfectly together, creating an atmosphere that harks back to a 1960s dinner club.

Step up your culinary game at STEIRERECK. With four Gault&Milaut toques and two Michelin stars under its belt, this top foodie spot continually experiments with the aromas and flavors of Austria to create mesmerizing dishes. Nearby, and one of the hottest tickets in town, SPELUNKE serves up dishes with a focus on fish and seafood throughout the day. From the cocktails, poured by award-winning mixologists, to the works by famous graffiti artists, this place will help you up the Instagram ante. In case a craving for Asian food takes hold, make your way to MARKET. Situated next to the Naschmarkt and surrounded by various gay bars and small clubs, this restaurant serves fabulous Asian-fusion food. If the weather permits, the little tables out front are the perfect spot to enjoy a coffee and watch the handsome locals pass by.

After a long night out on the town, what other option could there be but food? If you happen to miss your hotel's breakfast window, don't worry and head to the picturesque St. Ulrichs-Platz to find a café and restaurant of the same name. Being Vienna's number-one brunch destination, ULRICH has all you need to fend off that looming hangover. Another worthy contender is PALMENHAUS, which owes its name to its setting within an old imperial greenhouse designed in the art nouveau style. Whether you want breakfast, brunch, dinner or just a drink, this place will cater to your every whim whatever the time of day. Its location next to the Albertina Museum and Imperial Palace also makes it the perfect place for a break when exploring central Vienna.

Centrally located in Vienna's Stadtpark, the über-modern exterior of Steirereck stands out.

Customers dine amid tropical plants in the striking Jugendstil steel-and-glass Palmenhaus.

Motto serves up modern interpretations of bistro classics, such as goose, red cabbage, and dumplings.

Vienna's nightlife might be a bit smaller than that of other major European cities, but it's big enough for you to have a blast. Start your night out with a drink at KRYPT. Mostly known to insiders, this watering hole invites guests to sip exquisite cocktails in its high-ceilinged basement complete with bare brick walls and black marble herringbone floor. Another excellent cocktail venue is ONYX BAR on the sixth floor of the arty Haas House overlooking Stephansplatz. On weekends, a DJ plays everything from smooth jazz to funky house.

If you're aiming for a less ceremonial venue, we have two recommendations. A café by day and bar by night, CAFÉ SAVOY is probably Vienna's oldest gay coffee house. The traditional interior with its endless mirrors sits in contrast to the cafe's mindset, which is anything but antiquated. Meanwhile, PHIL on Gumpendorferstraße sits close to various restaurants and gay bars, and is as cozy as can be. In addition to sampling the hipster-worthy drinks and snacks, you can peruse books, records, and decorative items in the bar's integrated little shop.

For those who fancy a bit of clubbing after a couple of cocktails and feel like dressing up and stepping out among Vienna's bold and beautiful, head to local party institution VOLKSGARTEN. Alternatively, ask a local; a lot of the city's gay nightlife consists of parties taking place in rotating locations.

Enjoy the glitz of the Café Savoy at night, when the huge mirrors reflect the sparkle of the antique chandelier.

The urbane, luxurious Onyx bar attracts a classy clientele—dress smartly if you intend to join them.

An impressive 30ft (7m) black marble bar takes center stage at krypt, offset with a huge mural of foliage on the wall.

Whether you want to buy souvenirs for your loved ones or add the latest trends to your wardrobe, Vienna has some serious contenders in the retail therapy department. Having a stroll through the enormous open-air market area of NASCHMARKT with its delis and delicatessens is a must. In addition to the regular market, the parking lot next door turns into a flea market every Saturday. If you take the time to look through all the antiques, paintings, and curiosities, you're sure to spot some unique little treasures.

> ## Whether buying souvenirs for your loved ones or adding the latest trends to your wardrobe, Vienna has some serious contenders in the retail therapy department.

Upgrading your wardrobe is child's play at STRICTLY HERRMANN, a concept store that has devoted itself to making men happy by curating a stellar selection of menswear and watches, as well as a beautiful collection of electronic gadgets, stationery, and fragrances. What else does a modern dandy need? A hat, perhaps? MÜHLBAUER is a well-established, artisanal maker that has been turning out headgear of the finest quality since 1903. Feted by Viennese and international fashionistas alike, each of its hats is unique.

At the St Charles Apothecary, the interior is lined with vintage wooden cabinets and tincture bottle-laden shelves.

Mühlbauer's felt hats are steamed, formed, and dried in an oven (pictured) before finishing.

Everyone can buy perfume at the duty-free, but if you want to bring home a spectacular scent to remind you of Vienna, you should get a flacon from WIENERBLUT. This house uses formulas and compositions from nineteenth-century Austrian practice, bringing back some of the opulence of imperial times. Gents with a penchant for advanced grooming will also appreciate SAINT CHARLES APOTHECARY. This local purveyor specializes in natural treatments and homeopathy, based on traditional European medicine. For further enhancements that are more about brains than beauty, stop by LÖWENHERZ, which sells LGBTQ literature alongside international bestsellers.

Wall-to-wall headgear on display at the Vienna outlet of traditional hatmaker Mühlbauer.

Even if you're not a fan of classical music, not visiting a concert in Vienna is like not seeing the Eiffel Tower in Paris. One of the city's most famous orchestras, the Vienna Philharmonic resides at the MUSIKVEREIN, a concert hall world famous for its unmatched acoustics. As well as classical music, Vienna has numerous museums and art galleries, showcasing everything from contemporary to classical works. One such museum worth visiting for both its exhibitions and its architecture is MUMOK. Focusing on the modern, it hosts shows from internationally acclaimed artists and isn't afraid to be controversial and push boundaries. A stone's throw from mumok you'll find WESTLICHT, a museum and exhibition space dedicated to photography that hosts interesting exhibitions such as the World Press Photo or by big names such as Annie Leibovitz.

Green spaces can be hard to come by in big cities, but not Vienna. At the fringe of the 19th district, GRINZING unfolds between vineyards and woods. Stroll among the wineries, climb to the top of Vienna's backyard mountains, and finish your trip with a visit to one of the area's numerous taverns—or *heurigen* as the Viennese call them—serving excellent local wines and specialties. One of the most popular recreational areas in Vienna, DONAUINSEL is ideal for leaving the city hustle behind. The island stretches more than 21 kilometers and invites visitors to bike, skate, run, swim, or stretch out on the grass and relax. Here, you can also find clothing-optional spots, appreciated not only by the gay community but by all of Vienna's naturists.

mumok owns 10,000 works of modern and contemporary art, including several from the Vienna Actionism movement.

An intimate exhibition focuses on the queer-lustrous and passionate universe of New York duo Fischerspooner.

The weekend-long LIFE BALL, Europe's largest charity event in the fight against HIV and AIDS, takes place every year in Vienna. Highlights include the grand opening show with international acts and artistic performances, and a final fashion show by some of the most renowned couture labels. Crazier, gayer, and more homegrown is the VIENNA

> ## The Vienna Boylesque Festival opens its doors every year around May. Drag artists, burlesque dancers, and more perform during two days, inviting the audience to rethink and overcome stereotypes and old-fashioned social norms.

CITY TUNTATHLON. Here, drag queens compete in three disciplines—purse throwing, sprinting in heels, and synchronized ironing—in the hope of bagging the coveted broken-heel trophy. More artistic but not less draggy, the VIENNA BOYLESQUE FESTIVAL BY JACQUES PATRIAQUE opens its doors every year around May. Drag artists, burlesque dancers, and more perform during two days, inviting the audience to rethink and overcome stereotypes and old-fashioned social norms.

About forty artists perform at the Boylesque Festival, which takes place at Vienna's Stadtsaal.

ESCAPE IT

Even though the list of things to do in Vienna is endless, you should consider a day trip to the WACHAU VALLEY. Situated along the river Danube, it stretches out between the towns of Krems and Melk, and is listed as a UNESCO World Heritage Site. Besides its picturesque appearance, the valley is renowned for its apricots and wines, which are served in a generous number of local taverns alongside typical Austrian cuisine. With the Danube connecting Vienna to the Wachau Valley, the most spectacular way to get there is by boat. At the end of your trip, you should not skip a visit to the Melk Abbey, one of the largest baroque convents in Europe. Also a UNESCO site, the abbey's architecture in combination with its location on an outcrop overlooking its surroundings never fails to impress.

The impressive Melk Abbey enjoys a high vantage point on a rocky outcrop above the Danube River.

IN VIENNA, WRITING OF ELEGANCE, "NEVER-MINDEDNESS"

Christopher Wurmdobler

Author Christopher Wurmdobler hails from Germany but has lived in the Austrian capital of Vienna for most of his adult life. "I met a Viennese guy in Berlin who happened to become my boyfriend for the following 22 years," he says of his initial connection to the city. However, what greeted him on his first-ever visit in 1989 was categorically not the city that would inspire his first novel, *Solo*, which, as Christopher explains, is about a "group of queer friends living their bohemian bourgeois lifestyle; essentially an homage to Vienna, the city I love most."

"There was still this 'Iron Curtain' atmosphere," Christopher recalls of the Vienna of old. "Everything was gray and cold. There seemed to be only old people out on the streets. Vienna literally was the end of the Western world. But after the fall of the Soviet Bloc, the city changed rather

quickly into something fresh and new, and left its dullness behind."

Christopher began writing for Austrian newspapers and magazines while studying theater in Giessen, Germany, where he commuted to from Vienna—and today he is still active as an actor and performance artist. Then, upon making Vienna his full-time home in the nineties, he began a near 20-year tenure as an editor at the weekly newspaper *Falter*, writing about urban issues and the arts. "I also wrote nonfiction books on Vienna, such as on coffeehouses, or *kaffeehäuser*, and became sort of an expert for everything Vienna-related," he says.

What is his favorite coffee-house in town? "Café Eiles, one of the biggest in Vienna—you can say you are a regular when the waiter knows how you want your coffee. It has a mixed crowd: politicians, artists, students, old and

young people." Besides visiting the café, one of Christopher's favorite activities is to "browse the farmers market" in his home neighborhood of Yppenplatz, Ottakring, on Saturday mornings, before enjoying a "second breakfast with friends. Frida, An Do, or Café C. I. are my favorites here."

When asked about his first work of fiction, the writer explains that it came about almost by chance. "My current publishers asked me to write a novel. So in fact, it wasn't my own idea at all! But I still loved doing it. Writing fiction sure is great fun." In *Solo*, Christopher channels both personal experience and the spirit of his home city. "People have told me it feels specifically Viennese," he says. "In my opinion, that's a big compliment. The owner of the gay bookstore Löwenherz said it is actually the first queer novel exclusively set in Vienna. Of course it

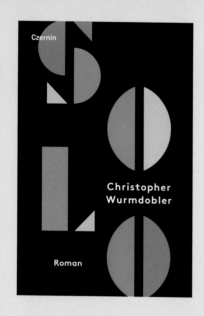

"Its elegance, its casualness, the culture scene, the nature in and around the city."

was influenced by the city a lot. However, I tried to avoid the big, familiar places and touristic sites. I wanted to describe my experience of Vienna."

The book also offers a glimpse into Christopher's personal and professional "queer bubble," a "close network" within an LGBTQ community he calls "moderately sized." He adds, "I'm very lucky to be surrounded by so many wonderful people within the community making books, art, theater, and—hopefully—political

statements as well." Christopher says that the pending introduction of marriage equality in Austria is the biggest political change for gay people of the last 10 years—albeit "not a political decision, but a ruling by the Constitutional Court, or Verfassungsgerichtshof, forcing Austrian politics to follow along."

The city continues to inspire Christopher's work every day. "I see people on public transport, in cafés, at the supermarket," he says. "A few days later I find

myself describing a character inspired by the people I have observed." He remains as enamored with the city as ever, and has no plans to leave. "I love its easygoing atmosphere," he says. "Its trademark *Wurschtigkeit*, or 'nevermindness,' its elegance, its casualness, the arts and culture scene, the nature in and around the city, and the fact that it's quite open-minded. The rest of Austria does not compare in many of these regards. For me, it's like there's a sort of a layer of beauty on everything here."

AMSTERDAM

Mood images: Alana Dimou (pp. 9, 14 bottom);
Nicole Franzen (pp. 10 top, 12, 18/19)

Profile Ferry van der Nat (pp. 20–23), photos: Ferry van der Nat

Claim it (p. 8)
art'otel, artotels.com,
Prins Hendrikkade 33, 1012 TM Amsterdam
Conservatorium Hotel, conservatoriumhotel.com,
Van Baerlestraat 27, 1071 AN Amsterdam,
photo: Today's Brew and Amit Geron (top and middle)
Hotel TwentySeven, hoteltwentyseven.com,
Dam 27, 1012 JS Amsterdam,
photo: Courtesy of Hotel TwentySeven (bottom)
Mr. Jordaan, mrjordaan.nl,
Bloemgracht 102, 1015 TN Amsterdam
The Dylan, dylanamsterdam.com,
Keizersgracht 384, 1016 GB Amsterdam
QO Amsterdam, qo-amsterdam.com,
Amstelvlietstraat 4, 1096 GG Amsterdam

Savor it (p. 10)
Anna, restaurantanna.nl,
Warmoesstraat 111, 1012 JA Amsterdam
Cafe George, cafegeorge.nl,
Leidsegracht 84, 1016 CR Amsterdam,
De Kas, restaurantdekas.nl,
Kamerlingh Onneslaan 3, 1097 DE Amsterdam,
Envy, envy.nl,
Prinsengracht 381, 1016 HL Amsterdam
George Marina, cafegeorge.nl/george-marina,
Spaklerweg 10 A, 1096 AC Amsterdam
photo: Courtesy of Cafe George (bottom)
Georgette, cafegeorgette.nl,
Pieter Cornelisz Hooftstraat 87A, 1071 BP Amsterdam
Georgio's, cafegeorge.nl/georgios,
Stadhouderskade 7, 1054 ES Amsterdam
Izakaya, izakaya-restaurant.com,
Albert Cuypstraat 2–6, 1072 CT Amsterdam
Kaagman & Kortekaas, kaagmanenkortekaas.nl,
Sint Nicolaasstraat 43, 1012 NJ Amsterdam

Celebrate it (p. 11)
Baut, restaurantbaut.amsterdam,
Spaarndammerstraat 460, 1013 SZ Amsterdam,
photos: Dishtales
Cafe 't Mandje, cafetmandje.business.site,
Zeedijk 63, 1012 AS Amsterdam
Club NL, clubnl.nl,
Nieuwezijds Voorburgwal 169, 1012 RK Amsterdam
De Hallen, dehallen-amsterdam.nl,
Hannie Dankbaarpassage 47, 1053 RT Amsterdam
De Trut, trutfonds.nl,
Bilderdijkstraat 165-E, 1053 KP Amsterdam
Door 74, door-74.com,
Reguliersdwarsstraat 74, 1017 BN Amsterdam

Own it (p. 13)
Boerejongens Coffeeshop, boerejongens.com,
Utrechtsestraat 21, 1017 VH Amsterdam;
Bonairestraat 78, 1058 XL Amsterdam;
Baarsjesweg 239, 1058 AA Amsterdam
Concrete Matter, concrete-matter.com,
Gasthuismolensteeg 12, 1016 AN Amsterdam
Hester van Eeghen, hestervaneeghen.com,
Nieuwe Spiegelstraat 32, 1017 DG Amsterdam
matter .of material, matterofmaterial.com,
Kerkstraat 163, 1017 GG Amsterdam
Misc, misc-store.com,
De Clercqstraat 130, 1052 NP Amsterdam
X BANK, xbank.amsterdam, Spuistraat 172, 1012 VT
Amsterdam, photos: Michiel van Oosten

Explore it (p. 14)
A'dam Toren, adamtoren.nl,
Overhoeksplein 1, 1031 KS Amsterdam
Amsterdam City Archives, amsterdam.nl/stadsarchief,
Vijzelstraat 32, 1017 HK Amsterdam
EYE Filmmuseum, eyefilm.nl,
IJpromenade 1, 1031 KT Amsterdam,
photo: Courtesy of EYE Filmmuseum (top)
Foam, foam.org,
Keizersgracht 609, 1017 DS Amsterdam
The Pulitzer, pulitzeramsterdam.com,
Prinsengracht 323, 1016 GZ Amsterdam,
photo: Courtesy of Pulitzer (middle)

Join it (p. 15)
**International Documentary Film
Festival Amsterdam (IDFA),** idfa.nl
Amsterdam Dance Event, amsterdam-dance-event.nl,
photo: Courtesy of Amsterdam Dance Event (bottom)
Cello Biennale, cellobiennale.nl
Milkshake, milkshakefestival.com,
photos: Alina Krasieva for Milkshake Festival
(pp. 15 top, 16, 17 bottom)
Spellbound, spellbound-amsterdam.nl
Canal Pride, amsterdamgaypride.nl/canal_parade

Escape it (p. 17)
Bloemendaal, photo: iStock by Getty Images/Julia700702 (top)

BERLIN

Mood images: Michael Schulz/@Berlinstagram
(pp. 27, 30, 33, 34)

Profile Jurassica Parka (pp. 36–39),
photos: © Jurassica Parka + Jaycap Photography (p. 36);
Jurassica Parka © Guido Woller (p. 38);
Jurassica Parka 2 © Maximilian König (p. 39)

Claim it (p. 26)
25hours Hotel Bikini, 25hours-hotels.com,
Budapester Str. 40, 10787 Berlin
Ackselhaus, ackselhaus.de,
Belforter Str. 21, 10405 Berlin
Hotel Oderberger, hotel-oderberger.berlin,
Oderberger Str. 57, 10435 Berlin
Hotel Zoo, hotelzoo.de,
Kurfürstendamm 25, 10719 Berlin,
photo: Courtesy of Hotel Zoo Berlin (bottom)
Soho House Berlin, sohohouseberlin.com,
Torstraße 1, 10119 Berlin,
photo: Courtesy of Soho House (top)

Savor it (p. 28)
Benedict, benedict-breakfast.de,
Uhlandstraße 49, 10719 Berlin
CODA, coda-berlin.de,
Friedelstraße 47, 12047 Berlin
Lucky Leek, lucky-leek.com,
Kollwitzstraße 54, 10405 Berlin
Markthalle Neun, markthalleneun.de,
Eisenbahnstraße 42/43, 10997 Berlin,
photo: Shantanu Starick (bottom)
Mogg, moggmogg.com,
Auguststraße 11–13, 10117 Berlin
ORA, ora-berlin.de,
Oranienpl. 14, 10999 Berlin
Pauly Saal, paulysaal.com,
Auguststraße 11–13, 10117 Berlin,
photo: Robert Rieger for FvF Productions (top)

BRUSSELS

Brussels Food Truck Festival, brusselsfoodtruckfestival.com
Bruxelles les Bains, bruxelleslesbains.be
BXLBeerFest, bxlbeerfest.com

Escape it (p. 49)
Ghent, photo: iStock by Getty Images/Flavio Vallenari (bottom)

CHICAGO

Mood images: Sandy Noto (pp. 57, 58, 60 bottom, 61, 62, 64 bottom); Courtesy of Lollapalooza (p. 65)

Profile Mikael Burke (pp. 66–69) photos: Mikael Burke

Claim it (p. 56)
Chicago Athletic Association, chicagoathletichotel.com, 12 S Michigan Ave, Chicago, IL 60603
FieldHouse Jones, fieldhousejones.com, 312 W Chestnut St, Chicago, IL 60610
The Publishing House, publishinghousebnb.com, 108 N May St, Chicago, IL 60607, photo: Joshua Haines
The Robey, therobey.com, 2018 W North Ave, Chicago, IL 60647
Viceroy, viceroyhotelsandresorts.com, 1118 N State St, Chicago, IL 60610

Savor it (p. 59)
Entente, ententechicago.com, 3056 N Lincoln Ave, Chicago, IL 60657
Lost Larson, lostlarson.com, 5318 N Clark St, Chicago, IL 60640, photos: Courtesy of Lost Larson
Passerotto, passerottochicago.com, 5420 N Clark St, Chicago, IL 60640
Roister, roisterrestaurant.com, 951 W Fulton Market, Chicago, IL 60607
Southport Grocery and Café, southportgrocery.com, 3552 N Southport Ave, Chicago, IL 60657
Vincent, vincentchicago.com, 1475 W Balmoral Ave, Chicago, IL 60640

Celebrate it (p. 60)
Devereaux, devereauxchicago.com, 1112 N State Street, Chicago, IL 60610, photo: Devereaux/Anthony Tahlier (top)
Disco, discochicago.com, 111 W Hubbard St, Chicago, IL 60654
Elixir Lakeview, elixirandersonville.com, 1509 W Balmoral Ave, Chicago, IL 60640
RM Champagne Salon, rmchampagnesalon.com, 116 N Green St, Chicago, IL 60607
Sidetrack, sidetrackchicago.com, 3349 N Halsted St, Chicago, IL 60657
The Second City, secondcity.com, 1616 N Wells St, Chicago, IL 60614, photo: Courtesy of The Second City (middle)

Own it (p. 63)
Asrai Garden, asraigarden.com, 1935 W North Ave, Chicago, IL 60622
Blind Barber, blindbarber.com, 948 W Fulton Market, Chicago, IL 60607
Rotofugi, rotofugi.com, 2780 N Lincoln Ave, Chicago, IL 60614
Stock Mfg. Co., stockmfg.co, 2136 W Fulton St unit j, Chicago, IL 60612, photos: Courtesy of Stock Mfg (top + middle)
Volumes Bookcafe, volumesbooks.com, 1474 N Milwaukee Ave, Chicago, IL 60622

Explore it (p. 63)
Auditorium Theatre, auditoriumtheatre.org, 50 E W Ida B. Wells Dr, Chicago, IL 60605, photo: John Boehm/Courtesy of the Auditorium Theater (bottom)
Center on Halsted, centeronhalsted.org, 3656 N Halsted St, Chicago, IL 60613
Museum Of Contemporary Art, mcachicago.org, 220 E Chicago Ave, Chicago, IL 60611

Join it (p. 64)
Chicago Blues Festival, chicagobluesfestival.us
Lollapalooza, lollapalooza.com, photos: Courtesy of Lollapalooza (64 top, 65)
Northalsted Market Days, northalsted.com/marketdays

Escape it (p. 64)
Oak Park, visitoakpark.com, photo: iStock by Getty Images/littleny (middle)

LISBON

Mood images: Kevin Faingnaert (pp. 73, 79 top, 82/83); Virginie Garnier (pp. 74, 77, 78)

Claim it (p. 72)
Lisboa Pessoa, pessoa.luxhotels.pt, R. da Oliveira ao Carmo 8, 1200–309 Lisbon
The Independente Suites & Terrace, theindependente.pt, R. de São Pedro de Alcântara 83, 1250–238 Lisbon
The Late Birds Lisbon, thelatebirdslisbon.com, Tv. André Valente 21, 1200–024 Lisbon
The Lumiares, thelumiares.com, R. do Diário de Notícias 142, 1200–146 Lisbon
Valverde Hotel, valverdehotel.com, Avenida da Liberdade, 164, 1250–146 Lisbon, photo: Courtesy of Valverde Hotel

Savor it (p. 75)
Bairro do Avillez, bairrodoavillez.pt, R. Nova da Trindade 18, 1200–303 Lisbon
Clube de Jornalistas, restauranteclubedejornalistas.com, R. Trinas 129, 1200–860 Lisbon
Hello, Kristof, hellokristof.com, R. do Poço dos Negros 103, 1200–350 Lisbon
Manteigaria, facebook.com/manteigaria.oficial, Rua do Loreto 2, 1200–108 Lisbon
Prado, pradorestaurante.com, Tv. Pedras Negras 2, 1100–404 Lisbon, photo: Courtesy of Prado Restaurante (top)
SEA ME—peixaria moderna, peixariamoderna.com, Rua do Loreto 21, 1200–169 Lisbon
Tapisco, tapisco.pt, R. Dom Pedro V 80, 1250–096 Lisbon
Time Out Market, cm-Lisbon.pt, Av. 24 de Julho s/n, 1200–481 Lisbon, photo: Courtesy of Time Out Market Lisboa (bottom)

Celebrate it (p. 76)
Adega Machado, adegamachado.pt, Rua do Norte, nº 91, 1200–284 Lisbon
A Severa, asevera.com, 51, R. das Gáveas, 1200–206 Lisbon
Pensão Amor, pensaoamor.pt, R. do Alecrim 19, 1200–292 Lisbo, photos: Teresa Lopes da Silva
Purex, facebook.com/purexclub, 1200 241, R. das Salgadeiras 28, 1200–169 Lisbon
Red Frog, facebook.com/redfrogspeakeasy, R. do Salitre 5A, 1250–196 Lisbon
Tasca Do Chico, facebook.com/atasca.dochico, R. do Diário de Notícias 39, 1200–141 Lisbon

LONDON

LOS ANGELES

Mood images: Ingrid Hofstra (pp. 109, 112 bottom right, 114 bottom, 115); Nana Hagel (pp. 105, 106, 112 bottom left); Ludwig Favre (p. 110)

Profile Michael Lannan (pp. 116–119)
photo: Roman Udalov (p. 116);
Michael Lannan (pp. 118,119)

Claim it (p. 104)
Hotel Covell, hotelcovell.com,
4626 Hollywood Blvd, Los Angeles, CA 90027,
photos: Courtesy of Hotel Covell
Kimpton La Peer Hotel, lapeerhotel.com,
627 N La Peer Dr, West Hollywood, CA 90069
Petit Ermitage, petitermitage.com,
8822 Cynthia St, West Hollywood, CA 90069
The Ambrose, ambrosehotel.com,
1255 20th St, Santa Monica, CA 90404
The NoMad Hotel, thenomadhotel.com,
649 S Olive St, Los Angeles, CA 90014

Savor it (p. 107)
A.O.C., aocwinebar.com,
8700 W 3rd St, Los Angeles, CA 90048
Alfred, alfred.la,
8428 Melrose Pl, Los Angeles, CA 90069
Bavel, baveldtla.com,
500 Mateo St, Los Angeles, CA 90013,
photos: Dylan + Jeni
Cafe Gratitude, cafegratitude.com,
639 N Larchmont Blvd, Los Angeles, CA 90004
Craig's, craigs.la,
8826 Melrose Ave, West Hollywood, CA 90069
Norah, norahrestaurant.com,
8279 Santa Monica Blvd, West Hollywood, CA 90046
République, republiquela.com,
624 South La Brea Ave, Los Angeles, CA 90036
Sawyer, sawyerlosangeles.com,
3709 Sunset Blvd, Los Angeles, CA 90026

Celebrate it (p. 108)
Akbar, akbarsilverlake.com,
4356 Sunset Blvd, Los Angeles, CA 90029,
photo: Courtesy of Akbar (bottom)
E.P.&L.P., eplosangeles.com,
603 N La Cienega Blvd, West Hollywood, CA 90069,
photos: Courtesy of E.P.&L.P (top and middle)
Moonlight Rollerway, moonlightrollerway.com,
5110 San Fernando Rd, Glendale, CA 91204
Precinct, precinctdtla.com,
357 S Broadway, Los Angeles, CA 90013
The Chapel at The Abbey,
shop.theabbeyweho.com,
692 N Robertson Blvd, West Hollywood, CA 90069

Own it (p. 111)
Cactus Store, hotcactus.la,
1505 1/2 Echo Park Ave, Los Angeles, CA 90026,
photo: Courtesy of Cactus Store (bottom)
Carlton Drew, carltondrew.com,
8024 W 3rd St, Los Angeles, CA 90048
County Ltd., countyltd.com,
1837 Hyperion Ave, Los Angeles, CA 90027
Garrett Leight California Optical,
garrettleight.com,
165 South La Brea Ave, Los Angeles, CA 90036,
photo: Courtesy of Garrett Leight California Optical (top)
Melrose Place Farmers Market, rawinspiration.org,
8400 Melrose Ave, Los Angeles, CA 90069
The Elder Statesman, elder-statesman.com,
607 Huntley Dr, West Hollywood, CA 90069

Explore it (p. 112)
Griffith Park, laparks.org,
4730 Crystal Springs Dr, Los Angeles, CA 90027
Marciano Art Foundation, marcianoartfoundation.org,
4357 Wilshire Blvd, Los Angeles, CA 90010
Phoenix Effect, phoenixeffectla.com,
7264 Melrose Ave, Los Angeles, CA 90046
Tom of Finland Foundation, tomoffinlandfoundation.org,
1421 Laveta Terrace, Los Angeles, CA 90026
Will Rogers State Beach, beaches.lacounty.gov/will-rogers-beach,
17000 Pacific Coast Hwy, Pacific Palisades, CA 90272

Join it (p. 113)
Hollywood Bowl Concerts, hollywoodbowl.com
Outfest, outfest.org
Queer Biennial, queerbiennial.org,
photos: Ruben Esparanza/Queer Biennale
West Hollywood Halloween Carnaval,
visitwesthollywood.com/halloween-carnaval

Escape it (p. 114)
Palm Springs,
photo: iStock by Getty Images/constantgardener (top)

MADRID

Mood images: Alana Dimou (pp. 123, 130, 131 bottom);
Courtesy of Madrid Pride 132/133

Claim it (p. 122)
7 Islas Hotel, 7islashotel.com,
Calle de Valverde, 14, 28004 Madrid
Axel Hotel Madrid, axelhotels.com,
Calle de Atocha, 49, 28012 Madrid,
photos: Courtesy of Alex Hotel Madrid
Only You, onlyyouhotels.com,
Calle del Barquillo, 21, 28004 Madrid
Urso Hotel & Spa, hotelurso.com,
Calle de Mejía Lequerica, 8, 28004 Madrid
Vincci The Mint, vinccithemint.com,
Calle Gran Vía, 10, 28013 Madrid

Savor it (p. 124)
Angelita, madrid-angelita.es, Calle Reina, 4, 28004 Madrid
CEBO, cebomadrid.com,
Carrera de S. Jerónimo, 34, 28014 Madrid
Celso y Manolo, celsoymanolo.es,
Calle Libertad, 1, 28004 Madrid
Federal Café, federalcafe.es,
Plaza del Conde de Barajas, 3, 28005 Madrid;
Plaza de las Comendadoras, 9, 28015 Madrid
Honest Greens, honestgreens.com,
Calle de Hortaleza, 100, 28004 Madrid;
Velázquez, 123, 28006 Madrid;
Paseo de la Castellana, 89, 28046 Madrid
La Duquesita, laduquesita.es,
Calle de Fernando VI, 2, 28004 Madrid
Mercado de San Miguel, mercadodesanmiguel.es,
Plaza de San Miguel, 28005 Madrid,
photos: Courtesy of Mercado de San Miguel

Celebrate it (p. 125)
Cha Chá The Club, xceed.me, Calle de Alcalá, 20, 28014 Madrid
Hemingway, casasuecia.es,
Calle del Marqués de Casa Riera, 4, 28014 Madrid
Macera TallerBar, maceradrinks.com,
Calle de San Mateo, 21, 28004 Madrid
Marta, Cariño!, Calle de Luchana, 38, 28010 Madrid
Medias Puri, mediaspuri.com, Plaza de Tirso de Molina, 1,
28012 Madrid, photo: Courtesy of Medias Puri (bottom)

Sala Equis, salaequis.es,
Calle del Duque de Alba, 4, 28012 Madrid,
photo: Lucia Marcano (top)

Own it (p. 127)
El Moderno, elmoderno.es,
Corredera Baja de San Pablo, 19, 28004 Madrid
García Madrid, garciamadrid.com,
Corredera Baja de San Pablo, 28, 28004 Madrid;
Calle del, Calle Conde de Aranda, 6, 28001 Madrid
Mercado de Motores, mercadodemotores.es,
Museo del Ferrocarril, Paseo de las Delicias, 61, 28045 Madrid,
photo: Josetxu Miguel (top)
Oliver & Co., oliverandcoperfumes.com,
Calle de la Palma, 58, 28015 Madrid
Orquídea Drácula, orquideadracula.com,
Calle Amaniel 20, local 10, 28015 Madrid
Xoan Viqueira, xoanviqueira.com,
Calle Gravina 22 Local 5, 28004 Madrid,
photos: Courtesy of Xoan Viqueira store (126, 127 bottom)

Explore it (p. 128)
Caixa Forum, caixaforum.es,
Paseo del Prado, 36, 28014 Madrid
La Casa Encendida, lacasaencendida.es,
Ronda de Valencia, 2, 28012 Madrid
Matadero Madrid, mataderomadrid.org,
Paseo de la Chopera, 10, 28045 Madrid,
photos: Courtesy of Matadero Madrid
Museo Sorolla, culturaydeporte.gob.es/msorolla,
Paseo del General Martínez Campos, 37, 28010 Madrid

Join it (p. 129)
ARCOmadrid, arco.ifema.es,
photo: Alejandro Cayetano/Arco Madrid (bottom)
LesGaiCineMad, lesgaicinemad.com
Madrid Pride, madridorgullo.com,
photo: Courtesy of Madrid Pride (top)
Noches del Botánico, nochesdelbotanico.com

Escape it (p. 131)
Ribera del Duero,
photo: iStock by Getty Images/Sima_ha (top)

MEXICO CITY

Mood images: Nicole Franzen (pp. 137, 140, 143, 144)

Claim it (p. 136)
Casa Prim, casaprim.mx,
Calle Gral. Prim 72, Juárez, 06600 Mexico City
El Patio 77, elpatio77.com,
Joaquin Garcia Icazbalceta 77, San Rafael, 06470 Mexico City,
photos: Courtesy of El Patio 77 (top + middle)
Hotel Villa Condesa, villacondesa.com.mx,
Colima 428, Roma Nte., 06700 Mexico City
La Valise, lavalise.com,
Tonalá 53, Roma Nte., 06700 Mexico City
Nima Local House, nimalocalhousehotel.com,
Colima 236, Roma Nte., 06700 Mexico City,
photo: Courtesy of Nima Local House (bottom)

Savor it (p. 138)
Amaya, amayamexico.com,
Calle Gral. Prim 95, Juárez, 06600 Mexico City
Contramar, contramar.com.mx,
Calle de Durango 202, Roma Nte., 06700 Cuauhtémoc
Eno, eno.com.mx,
Petrarca 258, Polanco, Polanco V Secc, 11560 Mexico City,
photos: Maureen M. Evans and Claudio Castro

Forte, Calle Querétaro 116, Roma Nte., 06700 Mexico City
Lorea, lorea.mx,
Sinaloa 141, Roma Nte., 06700 Mexico City
Milán 44, milan44.mx,
Calle Milan 44, Juárez, 06600 Colonia Juárez
Panadería Rosetta, rosetta.com.mx,
Colima 179, Roma Nte., 06700 Mexico City
Por Siempre Vegana, facebook.com/porsiemprevegataqueria,
Manzanillo, Roma Norte, Roma Nte., 06760 Cuauhtémoc
Pujol, pujol.com.mx,
Tennyson 133, Polanco, Polanco IV Secc, 11550 Mexico City

Celebrate it (p. 139)
Baltra Bar, baltra.bar,
Iztaccihuatl 36D, Condesa, Hipódromo, 06100 Mexico City
Guilt, envytheclub.com/guilt,
Anatole France 120, Polanco III Sección,
Polanco III Secc, 11550 Mexico City
Jules Basement, julesbasement.com,
Calle Julio Verne 93, Polanco, Polanco IV Secc,
11560 Mexico City
La Botica, labotica.com.mx,
Alfonso Reyes 120, Hipódromo Condesa, 06170 Mexico City
Saint, Campos Eliseos 290, Polanco,
Polanco IV Secc, 11550 Mexico City
Teatro Bar El Vicio, elvicio.com.mx,
Calle Madrid 13, Del Carmen, 04100 Mexico City

Own it (p. 141)
Bi Yuu, biyuu.mx,
Avenida Prado Norte 235, Lomas-Virreyes,
Lomas de Chapultepec V Secc, 11000 Mexico City
El Bazaar Sábado, bazaarsabado.com,
Plaza San Jacinto 11, San Ángel TNT,
San Ángel, 01000 Mexico City
Onora, onoracasa.com,
Lope de Vega 330, Polanco, Polanco V Secc, 11560 Mexico City
Stendhal Store, stendhalstore.com,
Av. 360, loc. 9H, Av. Pdte. Masaryk 360, Polanco,
Polanco III Secc, 11550 Mexico City,
photo: Courtesy of Stendhal Store (top)
The Pack, Av. Veracruz 111, Condesa, 06140 Mexico City
Voces en Tinta, vocesentinta.com,
Calle de Niza 23, Juárez, 06600 Mexico City
Xinú, xinu.mx,
Alejandro Dumas 161, Polanco, Polanco IV Secc, 11560 Mexico
City, photo: Courtesy of Xinú Perfumes (bottom)

Explore it (p. 142)
ArtSpace, artspacemexico.com,
Art gallery, Campeche 281, Hipódromo,
06100 Mexico City,
photo: Courtesy of ArtSpace México
Casa Luis Barragán, casaluisbarragan.org,
Gral. Francisco Ramírez 12–14, Ampliación Daniel Garza,
Amp Daniel Garza, 11840 Mexico City
Museo Dolores Olmedo, museodoloresolmedo.org.mx,
Av Mexico 5843, La Noria, 16030 Mexico City
Museo Memoria y Tolerancia, myt.org.mx,
Av. Juárez 8, Colonia Centro, Centro, 06010 Cuauhtémoc
Museo Nacional de Antropología, mna.inah.gob.mx,
Av. Paseo de la Reforma s/n, Polanco,
Bosque de Chapultepec I Secc, 11560 Mexico City

Join it (p. 145)
Mexico City Gay Pride,
facebook.com/MarchaLGBTCDMX
Salon ACME, salonacme.com,
photo: Alum Gálvez (top and middle)
Queer Room, facebook.com/queerroommx,
photo: Courtesy of Queer Room (p. 139)

Escape it (p. 145)
Teotihuacán, photo: iStock by Getty Images/benedek (bottom)

NEW YORK CITY

Mood images: Ingrid Hofstra (pp. 149, 150, 155, 156, 157 bottom, 158/159)

Claim it (p. 148)
1 Hotel Brooklyn Bridge, 1hotels.com,
60 Furman St, Brooklyn, NY 11201
Franklin Guesthouse, franklinguesthouse.com,
214 Franklin St, Brooklyn, NY 11222
Pod 39, thepodhotel.com,
145 E 39th St, New York, NY 10016,
photo: Courtesy of Pod 39
Pod BK, thepodhotel.com,
247 Metropolitan Ave, Brooklyn, NY 11211
PUBLIC Hotel, publichotels.com,
215 Chrystie St, New York, NY 10002
The Bowery Hotel, theboweryhotel.com,
335 Bowery, New York, NY 10003

Savor it (p. 151)
American Cut Steakhouse, americancutsteakhouse.com,
363 Greenwich St, New York, NY 10013
Avant Garden, avantgardennyc.com,
188 Havemeyer St, Brooklyn, NY 11211
Big Gay Ice Cream, biggayicecream.com,
125 E 7th St, New York, NY 10009;
61 Grove St, New York, NY 10014;
207 Front St, New York, NY 10038
Frankel's Delicatessen, frankelsdelicatessen.com,
631 Manhattan Ave, Brooklyn, NY 11222
Gotham West Market, gothamwestmarket.com,
600 11th Ave, New York, NY 10036
Hunan Slurp, hunanslurp.com,
112 1st Avenue, New York, NY 10009,
photo: Courtesy of Hunan Slurp (top)
Legacy Records, legacyrecordsnyc.com,
517 W 38th St, New York, NY 10018,
photo: Douglas Friedman (bottom)
MeMe's Diner, memesdiner.com,
657 Washington Ave, Brooklyn, NY 11238
Pietro NoLita, pietronolita.com,
174 Elizabeth St, New York, NY 10012

Celebrate it (p. 153)
Attaboy, attaboy.us,
134 Eldridge St, New York, NY 10002
Baby's All Right, babysallright.com,
146 Broadway, Brooklyn, NY 11211
Club Cumming, clubcummingnyc.com,
505 E 6th St, New York, NY 10009
Industry Bar, industry-bar.com,
355 W 52nd St, New York, NY 10019
Sleep No More, mckittrickhotel.com,
530 W 27th St, New York, NY 10001,
photo: DrielyS for The McKittrick Hotel (bottom)
Stonewall Inn, thestonewallinnnyc.com,
53 Christopher St, New York, NY 10014,
photos: iStock by Getty Images/OlegAlbinsky (top);
iStock by Getty Images/PeskyMonkey (middle)

Own it (p. 153)
Bureau of General Services—Queer Division,
bgsqd.com,
208 W 13th St #210, New York, NY 10011
Coming Soon, comingsoonnewyork.com,
37 Orchard St, New York, NY 10002
De Vera, deveraobjects.com,
1 Crosby St, New York, NY 10013
Front General Store, frontgeneralstore.com,
143 Front St, Brooklyn, NY 11201
MAST Chocolate, mastchocolate.com,
111 N 3rd St, Brooklyn, NY 11249,
photo: Dean Kaufman (top)

STORY, thisisstory.com,
144 10th Ave, New York, NY 10011

Explore it (p. 153)
Dia Art Foundation, diaart.org,
535 W 22nd St, New York, NY 10011
Leslie-Lohman Museum, leslielohman.org,
26 Wooster St, New York, NY 10013,
photo: Tom Stoelker (bottom)
NYC LGBT Historic Sites Project, nyclgbtsites.org
The High Line, thehighline.org,
High Line, New York, NY 10001

Join it (p. 154)
Billy Joel residency @ Madison Square Garden,
billyjoel.com
NY Art Book Fair, nyartbookfair.com
NYC Pride, nycpride.org,
photos: Kena Betancur/Getty Images (middle);
Volkan Furuncu/Anadolu Agency/Getty Images (bottom)
The Latex Ball, facebook.com/TheLatexBall,
photo: Dustin Moore (top)

Escape it (p. 157)
The Hamptons, photo: iStock by Getty Images/littleny (top)

PARIS

Mood images: Nicole Franzen (p. 163, 164,168),
Ingrid Hofstra (p. 171)

Claim it (p. 162)
Bourg Tibourg, bourgtibourg.com,
19 Rue du Bourg Tibourg, 75004 Paris,
photo: Courtesy of Bourg Tibourg Hotel (bottom)
Hôtel Grand Amour, hotelamourparis.fr,
18 Rue de la Fidélité, 75010 Paris
Hotel Monte Cristo, hotelmontecristoparis.com,
20–22 Rue Pascal, 75005 Paris
Le Meurice, dorchestercollection.com,
228 Rue de Rivoli, 75001 Paris
Le Roch Hôtel & Spa, leroch-hotel.com,
28 Rue Saint-Roch, 75001 Paris,
photos: Francis Amiand (top + middle)

Savor it (p. 165)
Café de la Nouvelle Mairie,
19 Rue des Fossés Saint-Jacques, 75005 Paris
Café Pouchkine, cafe-pouchkine.fr,
Paris-8E-Arrondissement, 16 Place de la Madeleine,
75008 Paris
Carbón, carbonparis.com,
14 Rue Charlot, 75003 Paris
Chez Georges, facebook.com/chezgeorges1965,
1 Rue du Mail, 75002 Paris
La Tour d'Argent, tourdargent.com,
17 Quai de la Tournelle, 75005 Paris
Le Temps des Cerises, letempsdescerises-restaurant.fr,
31 Rue de la Cerisaie, 75004 Paris
Pharamond, pharamond.fr,
24 Rue de la Grande Truanderie, 75001 Paris,
photo: Courtesy of Pharamond
Septime, septime-charonne.fr,
80 Rue de Charonne, 75011 Paris

Celebrate it (p. 166)
Au Passage, restaurant-aupassage.fr,
1bis Passage Saint-Sébastien, 75011 Paris
Le Dokhan's, hotelledokhansparis.com,
117 Rue Lauriston, 75116 Paris

Les Souffleurs, facebook.com/lessouffleursofficiel,
7 Rue de la Verrerie, 75004 Paris
Le Syndicat, syndicatcocktailclub.com,
51 Rue du Faubourg Saint-Denis, 75010 Paris,
photo: Courtesy of Le Syndicat
Maxim's, maxims-de-paris.com,
3 Rue Royale, 75008 Paris

Own it (p. 167)
Anatomica, anatomica.fr,
14 Rue du Bourg Tibourg, 75004 Paris
Astier de Villatte, astierdevillatte.com,
173 Rue Saint Honoré, 75001 Paris
Buly 1803, buly1803.com,
6 Rue Bonaparte, 75006 Paris,
photo: Ramdane Touhami&Victoire de Taillac (top)
Deyrolle, deyrolle.com,
46 Rue du Bac, 75007 Paris
Etat Libre d'Orange, etatlibredorange.com,
69 Rue des Archives, 75003 Paris
La Compagnie des Hommes,
48 Rue des Archives, 75004 Paris
Leclaireur, leclaireur.com,
10 Rue Boissy d'Anglas, 75008 Paris;
40 Rue de Sévigné, 75003 Paris;
10 Rue Hérold, 75001 Paris,
photos: Courtesy of Leclaireur (middle + bottom)

Explore it (p. 169)
Astronomy Tower of the Sorbonne,
17 Rue de la Sorbonne, 75005 Paris
Coulée verte René-Dumont,
Coulée verte René-Dumont, 75012 Paris
Fondation Louis Vuitton, fondationlouisvuitton.fr,
8 Avenue du Mahatma Gandhi, 75116 Paris,
photo: Andrew Holbrooke/Corbis/Getty Images (bottom)
Grande Mosquée de Paris, mosqueedeparis.net,
2bis Place du Puits de l'Ermite, 75005 Paris
Jardin de Plantes, jardindesplantesdeparis.fr,
57 Rue Cuvier, 75005 Paris
Musée de la Chasse et de la Nature, chassenature.org,
62 Rue des Archives, 75003 Paris,
photos: Courtesy of Musée de la Chasse et de la Nature
(top + middle)
Muséum national d'Histoire naturelle,
mnhn.fr,
57 Rue Cuvier, 75005 Paris

Join it (p. 170)
Cité de la Musique, citedelamusique.fr,
photos: Courtesy of Cité de la Musique (top + middle)
FIAC, fiac.com
Paris Photo, parisphoto.com
VendrediX/MercrediX, vendredix.fr

Escape it (p. 170)
Reims, photo: iStock by Getty Images/
southtownboy (bottom)

PORTLAND

Mood images: iStock by Getty Images/GarysFRP (p.175);
iStock by Getty Images/simonkr (p.178);
Carly Diaz (p. 181), iStock by Getty Images/Joel Carillet (p.182)

Claim it (p. 174)
Ace Hotel, acehotel.com,
1022 SW Stark St, Portland, OR 97205
Caravan—The Tiny House Hotel, tinyhousehotel.com,
5009 NE 11th Ave, Portland, OR 97211

Hotel Eastlund, hoteleastlund.com,
1021 NE Grand Ave, Portland, OR 97232
Jupiter NEXT, jupiterhotel.com,
900 E Burnside St, Portland, OR 97214,
photos: Chris Dibble
Sentinel, sentinelhotel.com,
614 SW 11th Ave, Portland, OR 97205

Savor it (p. 176)
Ava Gene's, avagenes.com,
3377 SE Division St, Portland, OR 97202
Canteen, canteenpdx.com,
2816 SE Stark St, Portland, OR 97214
Coava Coffee Roasters, coavacoffee.com,
1015 SE Main St, Portland, OR 97214
Han Oak, hanoakpdx.com,
511 NE 24th Ave, Portland, OR 97232
Hat Yai, hatyaipdx.com,
1605 NE Killingsworth St, Portland, OR 97211
Kachka, kachkapdx.com,
960 SE 11th Ave, Portland, OR 97214,
photo: Carly Diaz (bottom)
Langbaan, langbaanpdx.com,
6 SE 28th Ave, Portland, OR 97214
Nomad.PDX, nomadpdx.com,
575 NE 24th Ave, Portland, OR 97232,
photo: Jordan Fox/Rabbit Hole Photo (top)
Tasty n Sons, tastynsons.com,
3808 N Williams Ave C, Portland, OR 97227,
photo: Courtesy of Tasty n Sons (middle)
Tusk, tuskpdx.com,
2448 E Burnside St, Portland, OR 97214

Celebrate it (p. 177)
Coopers Hall, coopershall.com,
404 SE 6th Ave, Portland, OR 97214
Crush, crushbar.com,
1400 SE Morrison St, Portland, OR 97214
Departure, departureportland.com,
525 SW Morrison St, Portland, OR 97204
Dig A Pony, digaponyportland.com,
736 SE Grand Ave, Portland, OR 97214
Expatriate, expatriatepdx.com,
5424 NE 30th Ave, Portland, OR 97211
Multnomah Whiskey Library, mwlpdx.com,
1124 SW Alder St, Portland, OR 97205,
photo: Dina Avila
Stag PDX, facebook.com/stagpdx,
317 NW Broadway, Portland, OR 97209

Own it (p. 179)
Ampersand Gallery & Fine Books,
ampersandgallerypdx.com,
2916 NE Alberta St, Portland, OR 97211
Beam & Anchor, beamandanchor.com,
2710 N Interstate Ave, Portland, OR 97227
Machus, machusonline.com,
542 E Burnside St, Portland, OR 97214
Monograph Bookwerks, monographbookwerks.com,
5005 NE 27th Ave, Portland, OR 97211
Serra, shopserra.com,
220 SW 1st Ave, Portland, OR 97204,
photos: Courtesy of Serra
Union Way, facebook.com/UnionWayPDX,
1022 W Burnside St, Portland, OR 97209

Explore it (p. 180)
Disjecta, disjecta.org,
8371 N Interstate Ave, Portland, OR 97217
Forest Park, forestparkconservancy.org/forest-park,
Portland, OR 97231
Lumber Room, lumberroom.com,
419 NW 9th Ave, Portland, OR 97209
Mississippi Studios, mississippistudios.com,
3939 N Mississippi Ave, Portland, OR 97227

Revolution Hall, revolutionhall.com,
1300 SE Stark St #110, Portland, OR 97214
Washington Park, explorewashingtonpark.org,
4033 Southwest Canyon Road, Portland, OR 97221,
photo: Courtesy of Portland Japanese Garden

Join it (p. 183)
Ballroom culture, facebook.com/pdxball
Peacock in the Park, peacockinthepark.org
Red Dress Party, reddresspdx.org,
photo: Courtesy of Red Dress PDX (top)
Qdoc, qdocfilmfest.org

Escape it (p. 183)
Columbia River Gorge,
photo: iStock by Getty Images/alptraum (bottom)

ROME

Mood images: Nicole Franzen (pp. 187, 193);
iStock by Getty Images/Calin Stan (p. 190)

Claim it (p. 186)
Elizabeth Unique Hotel, ehrome.com,
Via delle Colonnette 35, 00186 Rome,
photo: Courtesy of Design Hotel AG (bottom)
G-Rough, g-rough.it,
Piazza di Pasquino 69, 00186 Rome,
photo: Courtesy of Design Hotel AG (top)
Horti 14, horti14.com,
Via di S. Francesco di Sales 14, 00165 Rome
The Shire, theshirehotel.com,
Via Vittorio Veneto 146, 00187 Rome
Villa Spalletti Trivelli, villaspalletti.it,
Via Piacenza 4, 00184 Rome

Savor it (p. 188)
Come il Latte, comeillatte.it,
Via Silvio Spaventa 24/26, 00187 Rome
Coromandel, coromandel.it,
Via di Monte Giordano 60/61, 00186 Rome
Faro, farorome.com,
Via Piave 55, 00187 Rome
Glass Hostaria, glasshostaria.it,
Vicolo de' Cinque 58, 00153 Rome,
photos: Courtesy of Glass Hostaria
Lanificio Cucina, lanificio.com,
Via di Pietralata 159A, 00158 Rome
Mercato Testaccio, mercatoditestaccio.it,
Via Beniamino Franklin, 00118 Rome
Panificio Bonci, bonci.it,
Via Trionfale 36, 00195 Rome
Roscioli, roscioli.com,
Via dei Giubbonari 21/22, 00186 Rome

Celebrate it (p. 189)
Amigdala, facebook.com/amigdalaparty
Goa Club, goaclub.com,
Via Giuseppe Libetta 13, 00154 Rome,
photo: Courtesy of Goa Club
Jerry Thomas Speakeasy,
thejerrythomasproject.it,
Vicolo Cellini 30, 00186 Rome
Muccassassina, muccassassina.com,
Via di Portonaccio 212, 00159 Rome
Salotto42, salotto42.it,
Piazza di Pietra 42, 00186 Rome

Own it (p. 191)
Bocache & Salvucci, bocachesalvucci.com,

Via Francesco Crispi 115A, 00187 Rome,
photos: Courtesy of Bocache & Salvucci (top + middle)
Cartoleria Pantheon, pantheon-roma.it,
Via della Maddalena 41, 00186 Rome;
Piazza Navona 42, 00186 Rome
Chez Dede, chezdede.com,
Via di Monserrato 35, 00186 Rome
Mercato Vintage Ecosolidale,
facebook.com/MercatoVintageEcosolidale,
Via del Porto Fluviale 2, 00154 Rome
Tartufi & Friends, tartufiandfriends.it,
Via Borgognona 4/E, 00187 Rome,
photos: Courtesy of Tartufi & Friends (bottom)

Explore it (p. 192)
All Saints' Anglican Church, allsaintsrome.org,
Via del Babuino 153, 00187 Rome
MACRO, museomacro.it,
Via Nizza 138, 00198 Rome
Palazzo Massimo alle Terme,
archeoroma.beniculturali.it,
Largo di Villa Peretti 2, 00185 Rome
Sacripante Gallery,
facebook.com/sacripantegallery,
Via Panisperna 59, 00184 Rome,
photo: Courtesy of Sacripante Gallery
Sant'Agnese in Agone, santagneseinagone.org,
Via di Santa Maria dell'Anima 30/A, 00186 Rome
Untold History Tour/Untold History Vatican Tour,
untoldhistorytour.com

Join it (p. 195)
Gay Village, gayvillage.it
G I A M, facebook.com/GIAMRoma
Roma Pride, romapride.it,
photos: Jacopo Landi/NurPhoto via Getty Images (p. 194);
Stefano Montesi—Corbis/Getty Images (p. 195 middle left + top);
NurPhoto/NurPhoto via Getty Images (p. 195 middle right)

Escape it (p. 195)
Sperlonga,
photo: iStock by Getty Images/MatthiasRabbione (bottom)

SAN FRANCISCO

Mood images: Nana Hagel (p.199);
iStock by Getty Images/bluejayphoto (p.200);
iStock by Getty Images/xavierarnau (p.201);
iStock by Getty Images/heyengel (p. 203);
iStock by Getty Images/ibsky (p.204);
iStock by Getty Images/diegograndi (pp. 208/209)

Profile Josh Cheon (pp. 210–213) photos: Josh Cheon

Claim it (p. 198)
Hotel Drisco, hoteldrisco.com,
2901 Pacific Ave, San Francisco, CA 94115
Inn at the Presidio, presidiolodging.com,
42 Moraga Ave, San Francisco, CA 94129
Proper Hotel, properhotel.com,
1100 Market St, San Francisco, CA 94102,
photos: Proper Hospitality
The Laurel Inn, jdvhotels.com,
444 Presidio Ave, San Francisco, CA 94115
The Ritz-Carlton, ritzcarlton.com,
600 Stockton St, San Francisco, CA 94108

Savor it (p. 201)
Californios, californiossf.com,
3115 22nd St, San Francisco, CA 94110

Foreign Cinema, foreigncinema.com,
2534 Mission St, San Francisco, CA 94110,
photo: Courtesy of Foreign Cinema restaurant (bottom right)
Liholiho Yacht Club, liholihoyachtclub.com,
871 Sutter St, San Francisco, CA 94109
Monsieur Benjamin, monsieurbenjamin.com,
451 Gough St, San Francisco, CA 94102
Nopa, nopasf.com,
560 Divisadero St, San Francisco, CA 94117
Sightglass Coffee, sightglasscoffee.com,
270 7th St, San Francisco, CA 94103;
301 Divisadero St, San Francisco, CA 94117;
3014 20th St, San Francisco, CA 94110;
SFMOMA, 151 3rd St, San Francisco, CA 94103
Tartine Manufactory, tartinebakery.com,
595 Alabama St, San Francisco, CA 94110,
photo: Courtesy of Tartine Manufactory (bottom left)
The Big 4, big4restaurant.com,
1075 California St, San Francisco, CA 94108
Zuni Café, zunicafe.com,
1658 Market St, San Francisco, CA 94102

Celebrate it (p. 202)
ABV, abvsf.com, 3174 16th St, San Francisco, CA 94103
Bar Agricole, baragricole.com,
355 11th St, San Francisco, CA 94103
Lookout, lookoutsf.com,
3600 16th St, San Francisco, CA 94114
The Stud, studsf.com,
399 9th St, San Francisco, CA 94103
Trick Dog, trickdogbar.com,
3010 20th St, San Francisco, CA 94110
Twin Peaks Tavern, twinpeakstavern.com,
401 Castro St, San Francisco, CA 94114

Own it (p. 205)
Heath Ceramics, heathceramics.com,
2900 18th St, San Francisco, CA 94110,
photos: Mariko Reed and Eszter Matheson (top + middle)
Loved To Death, lovedtodeath.com,
1681 Haight St, San Francisco, CA 94117
Maas & Stacks, maasandstacks.com,
2128 Market St, San Francisco, CA 94114
Park Life, parklifestore.com,
220 Clement St, San Francisco, CA 94118
Unionmade, unionmadegoods.com,
493 Sanchez St, San Francisco, CA 94114
Welcome Stranger, welcomestranger.com,
460 Gough St, San Francisco, CA 94102

Explore it (p. 205)
GLBT Historical Society Museum,
glbthistory.org,
4127 18th St, San Francisco, CA 94114
Minnesota Street Project,
minnesotastreetproject.com,
1275 Minnesota St, San Francisco, CA 94107,
photo: Phil Bond Photography.
Courtesy of Minnesota Street Project (bottom)
Precita Eyes Muralists, precitaeyes.org,
2981 24th St, San Francisco, CA 94110
Tours of the Tales, toursofthetales.com
Yerba Buena Center for the Arts, ybca.org,
701 Mission St, San Francisco, CA 94103

Join it (p. 206)
Castro Street Fair, castrostreetfair.org
Folsom Street Fair,
folsomstreetevents.org/folsom-street-fair,
photos: Gooch (206 top, 207)
stARTup Fair, startupartfair.com

Escape it (p. 206)
Napa, photo: iStock by Getty Images/wilpumt (middle),
iStock by Getty Images/YinYang (bottom)

SHANGHAI

Mood images: iStock by Getty Images/pidjoe (p.217);
Simone Anne (pp. 220, 223, 224/225)

Profile CINEMQ (pp. 226–229)
photos: Alejandro Scott (pp.226, 229 bottom);
Tingting Shi (p. 229 top)

Claim it (p. 216)
Amanyangyun, aman.com,
6161 Yuanjiang Rd, Minhang Qu, 201111
Capella Hotel, capellahotels.com,
480 West Jianguo Road, Xuhui District, Shanghai Shi, 200031
The Drama Hotel,
1013 Bei Jing Xi Lu, Jingan Qu, Shanghai Shi, 200085,
photo: Courtesy of The Drama Hotel (top)
The PuLi Hotel and Spa, thepuli.com,
1 Changde Rd, JingAnSi, Jingan Qu, Shanghai Shi, 200040,
photo: Courtesy of The PuLi Hotel and Spa (bottom)
URBN, urbnhotels.com,
183 Jiaozhou Rd, Jingan Qu, Shanghai Shi, 200040

Savor it (p. 218)
Din Tai Fung, dintaifung.com.cn,
JingAn Distinguish NanJing West Road 1376,
ShangHai ShangCheng 1 Floor a104, 200085
Grand Brasserie at Waldorf Astoria
Shanghai on the Bund,
waldorfastoriashanghai.com,
2 Zhongshan East 1st Rd, WaiTan, Huangpu Qu,
Shanghai Shi, 200002
Jin Xuan in The Ritz-Carlton, Pudong,
marriott.com.cn,
8 Century Ave, LuJiaZui, Pudong Xinqu, 200085,
photo: Courtesy of Jin Xuan in The Ritz-Carlton (bottom)
Lost Heaven, lostheaven.com.cn,
38 Gaoyou Rd, Xuhui Qu, Shanghai Shi, 200085;
17 Yan'an E Rd, WaiTan, Huangpu Qu, 200002
Moka Bros, mokabros.com,
108 Xiang Yang Bei Lu, HuaiHai Lu XiDuan,
Xuhui Qu, Shanghai Shi, 200085,
photo: Courtesy of MOKA Bros (top)
The Commune Social, communesocial.com,
511 Jiangning Rd, Jingan Qu, Shanghai Shi, 200085,
photo: Marius Ionita/Kollektiv Creative Hub
for Commune Social (middle)
Ultraviolet by Paul Pairet, uvbypp.cc,
Waitan, Huangpu, Shanghai, 200002
Zee Tea, 74 Tong Ren Lu, Jingan Qu,
Shanghai Shi, 200040

Celebrate it (p. 219)
French Concession,
Puxi Central, Huangpu District, Shanghai Shi, 200000
Happiness 42,
Xing Fu Lu, 42, Changning Qu, Shanghai Shi, 200085
Lucca 390, lucca.cc, 390 Panyu Rd, Changning Qu, Shanghai Shi, 200085
Lychee, 49 Fu Xing Xi Lu, Xuhui Qu, Shanghai Shi, 200085,
photos: Courtesy of Lychee

Own it (p. 221)
Brut Cake, brutcake.com,
232 Anfu Rd, Xuhui Qu, Shanghai Shi, 200085
Culture Matters, 206 Wu Lu Mu Qi Zhong Lu, Xuhui Qu,
Shanghai Shi, 200085
Little B, 123 Xing Ye Lu, XinTianDi, Huangpu Qu,
Shanghai Shi, 200085
Project Aegis Co., projectaegis.com,
1–3 Taojiang Rd, Xuhui Qu, Shanghai Shi, 200085
Sinan Books, 517 Fu Xing Zhong Lu, Huangpu Qu,
Shanghai Shi, 200085, photo: Courtesy of Sinan Books (top)
Xingmu Handicraft, 258–260 Tai Kang Lu, Huangpu Qu,
DaPuQiao, Shanghai Shi

STOCKHOLM

TEL AVIV

Okura, hrm.co.jp,
20–11 Sarugakucho, Shibuya-ku, Tokyo
Ragtag, ragtag.jp,
6–14–2 Jingumae, Shibuya-ku, Tokyo
United Arrows and Sons, store.united-arrows.co.jp,
B1–1F, 3–28–1 Jingumae, Shibuya-ku, Tokyo

Explore it (p. 268)
Gotokuji Temple, city.setagaya.lg.jp,
2–24–7 Gotokuji, Setagaya-ku, Tokyo
Kabukiza Theatre, kabuki-za.co.jp,
4–12–15 Ginza, Chuo-ku, Tokyo
Mika Otani, atelier-soka.com,
5–17–16 Kinuta, Setagaya-ku, Tokyo
Nezu Museum, nezu-muse.or.jp,
6–5–1 Minamiaoyama, Minato-ku, Tokyo
Saya-No-Yudokoro, sayanoyudokoro.co.jp,
3–41–1 Maenocho, Itabashi-ku, Tokyo

Join it (p. 269)
fancyHIM, facebook.com/fancyhimtokyo
Glamourous Tokyo, twitter.com/glamoroustokyo
Tokyo Rainbow Pride, tokyorainbowpride.com,
photo: Alessandro Di Ciommo/NurPhoto via Getty Images (top),
Courtesy of Tokyo Rainbow Pride (middle)

Escape it (p. 269)
Kamakura, photo: iStock by Getty Images/Mustang_79 (bottom)

VANCOUVER

Mood images: Kamil Bialous (pp. 279, 281 bottom left,
282, 284 bottom, 285, 286, 287 top, 288/289)

Claim it (p. 278)
Fairmont Pacific Rim, fairmont.com,
1038 Canada Pl, Vancouver, BC V6C 0B9
Loden, theloden.com,
1177 Melville St, Vancouver, BC V6E 0A3
The Burrard, theburrard.com,
1100 Burrard St, Vancouver, BC V6Z 1Y7,
photo: Martin Tessler (bottom)
the DOUGLAS, thedouglasvancouver.com,
45 Smithe St, Vancouver, BC V6B 0R3,
photo: Courtesy of the DOUGLAS (top)
West End Guest House, westendguesthouse.com,
1362 Haro St, Vancouver, BC V6E 1G2

Savor it (p. 280)
Bao Bei, bao-bei.ca,
163 Keefer St, Vancouver, BC V6A 1X4
Boulevard Kitchen & Oyster Bar, boulevardvancouver.ca,
845 Burrard St, Vancouver, BC V6Z 2K6
Earnest Ice Cream, earnesticecream.com,
3992 Fraser St, Vancouver, BC V5V 4E4;
1829 Quebec St, Vancouver, BC V5T 2Z3;
1485 Frances St, Vancouver, BC V5L 1Z1;
127 W 1st St, North Vancouver, BC V7M 1B1
Miku, mikurestaurant.com,
200 Granville St #70, Vancouver, BC V6C 1S4
Savio Volpe, saviovolpe.com,
615 Kingsway, Vancouver, BC V5T 3K5
St Lawrence, stlawrencerestaurant.com,
269 Powell St, Vancouver, BC V6A 1G3,
photo: Courtesy of St Lawrence (bottom)
The Acorn Restaurant, theacornrestaurant.ca,
3995 Main St, Vancouver, BC V5V 3P3
The Botanist, botanistrestaurant.com,
1038 Canada Place, Vancouver, BC V6C 0B9,
photo: Ema Peter (top)

Celebrate it (p. 281)
33 Acres Brewing Co.,
33acresbrewing.com,
15 W 8th Ave, Vancouver, BC V5Y 1M8,
photo: Courtesy of 33 Acres Brewing Co. (top)
Celebrities, celebritiesnightclub.com,
1022 Davie St, Vancouver, BC V6E 1M3
Gorg-O-Mish, gorgomish.com,
695 Smithe St, Vancouver, BC V6B 2C9,
photo: Sam Steele Photography (middle right)
The Diamond, di6mond.com,
6 Powell St, Vancouver, BC V6A 1E9

Own it (p. 283)
Eastside Flea, eastsideflea.com,
550 Malkin Ave, Vancouver, BC V6A 3X2
Herschel Supply Co., herschel.ca,
347 Water St, Vancouver, BC V6B 1B8
Leisure Center, leisure-center.com,
950 Homer St, Vancouver, BC V6B 2W7
Little Sister's Book & Art Emporium,
littlesisters.ca,
1238 Davie St, Vancouver, BC V6E 1N3
MASC, shopmasc.com,
433 Davie St, Vancouver, BC V6B 2G2,
photo: Courtesy of MASC (bottom)
Neighbour, shopneighbour.com,
12 Water St #125, Vancouver, BC V6B 1A5
Old Faithful Shop, oldfaithfulshop.com,
320 W Cordova St, Vancouver, BC V6B 1E8,
photo: Courtesy of Old Faithful Shop (top + middle)

Explore it (p. 284)
Museum of Anthropology, moa.ubc.ca,
6393 NW Marine Dr, Vancouver, BC V6T 1Z2,
photo: Cory Dawson/Courtesy of Museum of
Anthropology at UBC (top right)
Rennie Museum, renniemuseum.org,
51 E Pender St, Vancouver, BC V6A 1S9
Stanley Park, vancouver.ca,
Vancouver, BC V6G 1Z4
The Really Gay History Tour,
forbiddenvancouver.ca/really-gay-history-tour,
photo: Courtesy of The Really Gay History Tour (top left)

Join it (p. 287)
Dine Out Festival, dineoutvancouver.com
Queer Arts Festival, queerartsfestival.com
Vancouver International Wine Festival,
vanwinefest.ca

Escape it (p. 287)
North Shore, vancouversnorthshore.com,
photo: Courtesy of Capilano Suspension Bridge Park (bottom)

VIENNA

Mood images: iStock by Getty Images/manfredxy (p.293)

Profile Christopher Wurmdobler (pp. 302–305)
photos: Gregor Hofbauer (p. 302); Manfred Langer (p. 305)

Claim it (p. 292)
Hotel am Brillantengrund, brillantengrund.com,
Bandgasse 4, 1070 Vienna,
photo: Courtesy of Hotel am Brillantengrund (top)
Hotel Daniel, hoteldaniel.com,
Landstraßer Gürtel 5, 1030 Vienna
Magdas Hotel, magdas-hotel.at,
Laufbergergasse 12, 1020 Vienna